Letters from a
North Carolina Unionist

Letters from a North Carolina Unionist

JOHN A. HEDRICK TO BENJAMIN S. HEDRICK

1862-1865

Edited by

Judkin Browning
and
Michael Thomas Smith

Division of Archives and History
North Carolina Department of Cultural Resources
Raleigh
2001

Contents

Illustrations

Following Page 175

Foreword

Few collections of the letters of civilians in the Union-occupied South during the Civil War have been published. Michael Smith and Judkin Browning have partly remedied this neglect with their edition of the letters of John A. Hedrick, a well-educated North Carolinian. Hedrick's letters were to his famous brother Benjamin S. Hedrick, who, having been driven from the state after announcing his support for the antislavery Republican Party, lived in Washington where he worked in a government office. John Hedrick, though a strong Unionist, did not share the intense antislavery fervor of his older brother.

Most of Hedrick's letters were written from his vantage point at Beaufort, North Carolina, where he was a U.S. collector of revenue. Hedrick commented on almost all aspects of life in eastern North Carolina—economic conditions, political affairs, including Lincoln's failed effort to establish a Union civil government there, racial and social relationships, military activities, and the frightening yellow fever epidemic of 1864. Despite his moderate antislavery views, Hedrick was able to relate easily with his neighbors, who did not possess the strong devotion to the Confederate cause found among North Carolinians of the interior.

A small, sleepy port before the Federal occupation, Beaufort became an important base for Federal blockading vessels and for troops assaulting Fort Fisher and Confederate areas along the Atlantic coast. One of the most valuable aspects of the Hedrick letters is the description of the relationship of Union troops and other Federal personnel to the citizens of the area. Hedrick made frequent references to the two North Carolina white Union regiments in Beaufort, whom Confederates derisively called "buffaloes," and also to black Federal troops. Both whites and blacks from the eastern no-man's-land flocked to Beaufort where they could find relative security—and in the case of blacks, freedom.

Both Michael Smith and Judkin Browning are graduates of the M.A. program at North Carolina State University (Smith in history and Browning in public history). Smith is a Ph.D. student at Pennsylvania State University and Browning at the University of Georgia. Both have published important articles in the *North Carolina Historical Review*. Their well-written introduction to Hedrick's letters provides the reader with a splendid historical context for the published collection.

William C. Harris
North Carolina State University

Acknowledgments

The two of us originally undertook this work about two years ago. Judkin, upon first encountering John Hedrick's Civil War letters while conducting research into Unionist activity in eastern North Carolina, casually thought that they would be an ideal documentary editing project. After further serious reflection, he realized that he knew just the collaborator to approach—his friend Mike, then about a year into his ongoing research on Benjamin Hedrick, John's brother. So one Saturday afternoon in September 1998, Judkin, while killing time at his job at a local historic site, called Mike and proposed the project, whereupon Mike eagerly agreed to get involved. Although we did not then fully appreciate the labor this project would entail, we are grateful for what we have learned about the process, and for all the generous assistance that has been provided to us along the way, much of which can never be repaid.

Judkin would first like to thank his family for their continuous support of his graduate work. His younger brother, Jeremy, who always paid for meals when Judkin "forgot" his wallet, deserves special mention. Judkin also wishes to thank his extended family—Elaine, Troy, Christy, Gene, Valda, Mike, Granny, Roger, Jenny, Brande, Carrie, Jaye, and Caitlin (some of the latter of whom are too young to understand what the heck this book is even about) for never doubting that he would one day become a scholar, and for providing a wonderful family atmosphere and home-cooked meals whenever he returned home. Judkin also regrets that his mother, Joann, and his father, Jason, were not able to live to see the first academic fruits of their oldest boy, but he wishes to dedicate this volume to them. Finally, Judkin would be remiss if he did not specially thank Greta for her constant love and support in all things, fortunately not just those related to John Hedrick.

Mike gratefully acknowledges his colossal indebtedness to his father, Harry R. Smith, and his mother, Sue Johnson, for their untiringly patient and generous love and support. His sisters, Kathy and Sarah, should know how much their encouragement has meant to him, and how much they are always in his thoughts. To Jane, who has learned much more about John Hedrick and Beaufort, North Carolina, than she could possibly have expected or desired during the course of this project, Mike owes a special debt for her always-enthusiastic confidence that it would one day come to a successful end. He hopes to repay her love, kindness, and support with a lifetime of devotion.

We would like to express our deep gratitude to Professors William C. Harris and John David Smith at North Carolina State University for their guidance and friendship. Several libraries and archives have given indispensable assistance. We would particularly like to thank the staffs of the Special Collections Department at Duke University Library; the North Carolina Collection and the Southern Historical Collection at the University of North Carolina at Chapel Hill; the North Carolina Division of Archives and History; Brown Library in Washington, North Carolina; and D. H. Hill Library at North Carolina State University.

Our editor, Lang Baradell, provided astonishingly thorough and skillful help, and substantially improved the final result. We would also like to thank Anne Miller of the *North Carolina Historical Review* for her assistance and Lisa D. Bailey for proofreading the manuscript. Finally, we wish to extend a special personal thanks to Joe A. Mobley, head of the Historical Publications Section of the Division of Archives and History. Without his unexpectedly warm encouragement and unflagging support, this project could not have been completed and would, in fact, not have been attempted.

Introduction

The letters John A. Hedrick wrote to his brother Benjamin from 1862 to 1865 offer an unusual perspective of events and conditions in Union-occupied eastern North Carolina. While many soldiers stationed in the state for limited periods of time have left diaries and letters, Hedrick, as the U.S. Treasury Department collector for the port of Beaufort, remained in the region throughout the Federal occupation and could comment on a broader range of events. During this period, John wrote his brother devotedly, averaging more than a letter a week. His letters are one of the longest unbroken chains of civilian correspondence to emerge from Union-held North Carolina. Hedrick's letter are also extraordinary because they were written by a Southern Unionist, a group that has left little written material. The letters not only offer lucid descriptions of everyday life in Beaufort, and occasionally New Bern, but also present commentary on political, social, military, cultural, and economic events. As historians delve into the long-neglected social and cultural history of the Civil War era, these letters should prove to be of significant value.

John A. Hedrick was born in August 1837, in Davidson County, North Carolina. He was the sixth of the seven children of John Leonard Hedrick and Elizabeth Sherwood Hedrick. John A. Hedrick's mother died before his fifth birthday, leaving his father, a brickmason by trade, to raise and support three boys and four girls on his own. After his wife's death, John Leonard Hedrick gave up laying bricks and turned to farming in order to eliminate the extended travel required to ply his trade. He did not remarry until the 1850s, when the older children were beginning to leave the nest.[1]

John Leonard Hedrick purchased slaves after taking up farming in the 1840s and remained a slave owner until 1865, when he negotiated a deal with his former slaves to continue to work for him in exchange for a share of the crop.[2] His first wife, however, came from a family of dissenters on the slavery issue. Her father and brother opposed the "peculiar institution" on moral and economic grounds, and she probably shared their views, although none of her writings survive. The Hedrick children understandably held varying opinions on slavery. Benjamin, the oldest, who had been schooled at home by his mother before attending the University of North Carolina and Harvard's Lawrence Scientific School, held the strongest antislavery views. Adam, Elizabeth, Mary, Sarah, and Martha, none of whom ever lived or studied outside of North Carolina, leaned more toward their father's proslavery stance. John, more than any of the other children, was torn between these conflicting viewpoints.[3]

In October 1856, John, then attending Catawba College and preparing to enter the University of North Carolina, was unexpectedly forced to re-evaluate his ambiguous position. His brother Benjamin, who was at the time a professor in Chapel Hill, became the target of bitter public criticism after newspapers reported that he supported the antislavery Republican presidential candidate, John C. Frémont. After being dismissed by the university's board of trustees and harassed by a mob in Salisbury, Benjamin left the state to seek employment elsewhere. While he would make a few brief visits to his native state, Benjamin would live north of the Mason-Dixon line for the remainder of his life.[4]

These events affected John Hedrick's future. He abandoned plans to attend school in Chapel Hill, where his brother had been mistreated and where John himself might also be abused. Instead he entered nearby Davidson College and pondered his future. John wanted to know Benjamin's plans so that he could determine his own: "Since things turned out as they have I will not know what to do except you do. . . . Write immediately."[5] Hoping to make their sudden relocation seem "less like exile," Benjamin and his wife, Mary Ellen, wanted John to come and live with them once Benjamin had found a job and they had settled down.[6] In 1857, Benjamin and Mary Ellen moved to New York City, where Benjamin was hired first as a chemist and then as a clerk in the mayor's office.[7] John did not immediately join them, however. He attended Davidson College for three years before transferring to New York's Cooper Institute in the fall of 1859, around the time that Benjamin joined the school's faculty.[8] John seemed reluctant to leave his family in North Carolina and tie his fortunes to those of his antislavery brother, who remained widely unpopular in his home state. John, however, overcame this reluctance and did not look back.

A few weeks after John graduated from Cooper Institute in early 1861, North Carolina seceded from the Union.[9] Benjamin and John evidently did not hesitate to remain in the North, away from their father and most of the family, and cast their lots with the United States government. For Benjamin this decision was not surprising. He had been rejected and humiliated in his home state and had subsequently developed close ties with the Republican Party in the North. John's choice, however, seems less obvious, but whatever his motivations, he, like his brother, was now a dissenter. During the ensuing Civil War, they would emerge as two of the state's most prominent Unionists. (Their brother Adam also considered himself a Unionist, though he was drafted into the Confederate army.)[10]

John's letters contain few indications that he held strong opinions on slavery or Southern rights, one way or the other. Benjamin was a zealous abolitionist, even before the September 1862 Emancipation Proclamation. John's letters, however, give no hint that he viewed the issue with similar deep concern.[11] John's support for the Union, therefore, may have stemmed more from practical than ideological factors.

By the time North Carolina left the Union, Benjamin was in the nation's capital hoping to find lucrative jobs under the incoming Lincoln administration for himself and John, and he seemed to have every prospect for success. Benjamin informed his wife that "the best men"— prominent Republicans like Senators Henry Wilson and Charles Sumner, Postmaster General Montgomery Blair, and Secretary of the Treasury Salmon P. Chase—had promised him that he would "be provided for."[12] In April 1861, these promises were fulfilled, and Benjamin became an examiner in the U.S. Patent Office, where he would work for the remaining twenty-five years of his life.[13] John, however, had to wait longer for his ship to come in. In late May, Benjamin conceded, "I have been unable to do little about getting a place for John."[14]

By July, Benjamin and Mary Ellen both privately expressed concern over the still-unemployed John. Mary Ellen imagined that he was "completely disheartened," and added, "I do not give him credit for great perseverance in such things, though I don't doubt he has it in other directions."[15] Benjamin observed that John seemed "to take it quietly about his disappointments," and complained to his wife that John did "not do as much as he ought himself. I cannot get him to go around and become acquainted with the men."[16] Younger, less accomplished, and less brilliant than his brother, John was evidently daunted by the prospect of having to impress Republican leaders in Washington with his qualifications and personality. Benjamin had by no means found this process easy either, at one point complaining to his patron Salmon P. Chase of "the wear and tear of self respect which it seems to be necessary to undergo here among the applicants for office."[17] Benjamin nevertheless emerged during the war years as a leading spokesman for North Carolina Unionists, forwarding petitions to the administration and playing a key role in the dispensation of Treasury Department patronage.[18]

In December 1861, Benjamin finally found a government position for his younger brother—collector for the Treasury Department at Fort Hatteras, North Carolina, which had recently fallen to Union forces under Benjamin F. Butler. Unfortunately, John did not like the job. Soon after arriving to assume his duties, he wrote unhappily to Benjamin, "I hope I may be relieved from my duty as early as possible." Not only were there no customs to collect in the blockaded port, but, according to John, this Outer Banks site was "the most desolate place" he had ever seen.[19] After having spent the previous year and a half in New York and Washington, John must have found the change of scenery extreme. He did not stay in Hatteras long, however. A few days after arriving, he returned to New York, where he remained until he was offered another government job.[20]

In May 1862, John left New York to become collector at Beaufort, North Carolina, a position that would prove to be more agreeable. Even a Union officer from Massachusetts who held North Carolina and its inhabitants in low regard said that Beaufort was "the pleasantest place to me in [occupied] North Carolina." It was, he said, "the only place where you can enjoy a prospect extending more than half a mile."[21] Despite John Hedrick's improved circumstances, his heavy work load, carried out at times amid wartime chaos, would ensure that his stay in this once quiet coastal town would be far from idyllic.

While traveling from New York to Beaufort, Hedrick stopped in an unseasonably cold New Bern on June 9, 1862. He found that in the town "[q]uite a number of squares [had either] been burnt down by the taking of the city or by the Rebels as they left."[22] New Bern, which had been organized as a major army depot, was full of activity, however. Largely "occupied by soldiers and negroes," New Bern enjoyed a sudden influx of currency and teemed with sutlers, who followed the soldiers with their wares. In addition, "perhaps fifty or sixty" schooners were in the harbor. Hedrick learned that the provost marshal had banned the sale of liquor to residents and soldiers, and that several houses had "military protections" on them, though Hedrick did not know the reason.[23] Hedrick had moved from a relatively tranquil sector to a hub of activity. New Bern had been occupied for less than three months, and Confederates were nearby. New Bern and Beaufort would serve as staging areas for Union expeditions and as recruiting centers for Federal troops.

Hedrick finally arrived in Beaufort on June 12, 1862.[24] He would not leave the port town, except for brief trips to New Bern, for the remainder of the war. As he became familiar with the town, Hedrick noted differences between Beaufort and New Bern to his brother. "The town is about a third as large as New Bern," John wrote, yet there were "four times as many white folks here as there."[25] John immediately set up his office and began his duties in this town of about fifteen hundred residents, while continuing to write his brother regularly.[26]

Beaufort had fallen into Union hands on March 25, 1862. Two companies of the Fourth Rhode Island Infantry from Ambrose E. Burnside's army entered the town early in the morning while most of the inhabitants were asleep. Fort Macon, which defended Beaufort Inlet, fell a month later. The residents remaining in the region—that is, those who had neither joined the Confederate army nor fled westward with their slaves—were not thought to be deeply committed to the Southern cause. One Virginia secessionist complained in 1861 of "the apathy, or apparent indifference of the people . . . to the war that is right at their door. . . . Nothing would wake them up but the sound of the last trumpet."[27] Like John Hedrick, most Beaufort residents cared more about making a living than about ideology. Occupying Union forces and Federal agents were, for the most part, welcomed, if not with open arms, at least with civility and resignation. A New York correspondent noted in July 1862 that Beaufort's citizens "are becoming every day more and more well disposed toward our officers and men. They treat them with great respect and a high degree of cordiality."[28] Although some of this friendliness may have been deceptive, John Hedrick's good relations with the local citizens suggest that they were not deeply hostile to the Union cause.

Hedrick's job required that he stay abreast of commercial affairs. As a result, he was well informed on economic conditions in eastern North Carolina, and his letters detail economic fluctuations in the region. When he arrived in Beaufort, Hedrick found that "eatables were very dear," though the price of food was within reason—"forty cents for a pair of chickens the size of partridges."[29] Rampant inflation, however, eventually forced the provost marshal to set food prices. In September 1863, Hedrick found that the price for the same size chickens had been fixed at sixty-three cents for a pair.[30]

Hedrick observed commercial traffic at Beaufort and other ports in the region. He apparently took pride in his work and meticulously detailed his activities to his elder brother. His letters reveal the importance of Beaufort as a port, as well as the scale of business activity in occupied North Carolina. In his first quarter as a collector, Hedrick received only $417.47 in import duties, fees, and hospital payments.[31] Trade was soon thriving, however. By April 1863, Hedrick had collected $1,899.58 from the same fees for the first quarter of the year.[32] Salt, molasses, and sugar from the West Indies were in demand along the coast, and they constituted a large portion of the imports. John updated his brother on the level of activity in the port, noting, for example, that trade slackened when military operations were in preparation or under way.

The difficulty in controlling trade between the lines, which was technically illegal unless specifically authorized by the Treasury Department, is a recurring theme in John Hedrick's correspondence. John did not note, however, that he had landed in the midst of an investigation by agents of the department's military commander, Benjamin F. Butler, when he issued permits to local merchants who subsequently traded with the enemy. The department's judge advocate, challenging Hedrick's relative independence as a representative of the executive branch, argued that "the license given to Agents of the Treasury Department to give permits to trade in any quarter of the Department needs some restrictions or surveillance on the part of the military authorities."[33] John narrowly escaped censure, while a local merchant to whom he had issued a permit was imprisoned for several months.[34]

In addition to providing information on economic conditions, Hedrick's letters also reveal much about the political machinations in eastern North Carolina, particularly in 1862 and early 1863. The occupied area of the state was a volatile political battleground at that time. President Lincoln sought to establish a loyal government in North Carolina to facilitate the readmission of the state to the Union. According to Lincoln's plan of reconstruction, when 10 percent of a state's prewar voting population took an oath of allegiance to the Union, the state was to be readmitted and representatives would be elected to Congress. Lincoln appointed Edward Stanly, a Craven County native and former Whig, as military governor of North Carolina on May 20, 1862. The president gave Stanly the seemingly impossible mission of reestablishing Federal authority in the state and regaining the loyalty of its white citizens.[35]

Hedrick, who had frequent contact with Stanly, respected the combative, conservative governor and even accepted Stanly's offer to serve as his private secretary.[36] Soon thereafter, however, Stanly resigned, thus eliminating Hedrick's job opportunity. Stanly, under Lincoln's orders, called for elections in the First and Second Congressional Districts to select representatives to the U.S. Congress. Hedrick detested one of the candidates, Charles Henry Foster. A native of Maine, Foster moved to North Carolina before the war and edited a Murfreesboro newspaper.[37] Foster unsuccessfully employed devious means to win the election. John and Benjamin shared an obsessive antipathy for the "humbug Foster," and John kept his brother informed of Foster's activities. "[Foster] will use all the means that rascality can devise," lamented John. "I shall do all that I can to defeat him."[38]

John Hedrick was so intent on denying Foster the election that he considered running against him. "I do not wish to run for Congress if I can get a good man to run against Foster," John declared in a September 1862 letter to his brother, "but if no one else will oppose him, I guess I must."[39] John Hedrick ultimately championed Jennings Pigott, a respected acquaintance of both John and Benjamin, and Governor Stanly's choice for the post.[40] John's letters throughout the fall of 1862 and January 1863 document the turbulent, vitriolic race between Pigott and Foster. Pigott won the election, but because Congress refused to uphold the result, he never took his seat.

John Hedrick frequently commented on the movement of Union troops in the area and the recruitment of locals into the U.S. Army. At times he questioned the commitment of the white citizens to the Union cause. "The people here are so so," he wrote. "They profess to be Union, but are not fighting Union men."[41] Hedrick did not take up arms either, though he did express interest in volunteering in a District of Columbia or Virginia regiment, if he could be appointed as a first or second lieutenant. Such a situation never developed, however.[42] When describing the local men in the First and Second North Carolina Union Regiments, soldiers who were known as "buffaloes," he did state that they made "a better appearance than the Yankee Soldiers."[43] Volunteers for these Union regiments hailed almost entirely from the occupied counties and enlisted in towns such as Beaufort, New Bern, Plymouth, and Washington.[44]

Hedrick often referred to these soldiers, commenting on their appearance, the methods used to induce their enlistment, and their family situations. Hedrick reported the use of force to persuade locals to join the Union regiments in a November 29, 1863, letter to his brother. "The way, the deserters and refugees are treated," he said, "is to put them in prison until they are willing to volunteer in the Union army."[45] Though he was not sure how long they remained in prison, he did know that "they always let them out when they [did] volunteer."[46] Peer pressure also encouraged enlistment. As Hedrick reported, "When a refugee comes in . . . [a]ll the Buffaloes get after him, and before he knows what he is about he has joined the regiment."[47] Hedrick offers perhaps more details on the "buffaloes" than any other contemporary source.

Hedrick also commented on the controversial policy of enlisting African American soldiers. While as a loyal Republican, John generally opposed slavery, he was not sympathetic to blacks. He revealed his prejudices when he admitted: "I don't like to see the negro regiments sent to this state. We have too many negroes here now. I would much rather see a hundred negroes sent from than one into the State."[48] After seeing African American troops in uniform, John's only praise for their appearance was, "[T]hey don't look as dangerous and bloodthirsty as might be expected."[49] Most Beaufort whites, according to John, held even harsher views. "They wish to get rid of slavery and negroes," he wrote, "and if they can not dispose of the latter any other way, they wish to kill them."[50] John's strong streak of racism, shared by most white North Carolinians at the time, probably helped him to maintain friendly relations with his neighbors during and after the war. Though the enlistment of black troops displeased many whites, Beaufort continued to serve as a recruiting station for African American soldiers throughout the war.

Like many of the war's noncombatants, John Hedrick was intensely interested in military activities. Federal forces launched several expeditions from Beaufort and New Bern into the Confederate hinterland between 1862 and 1865. Hedrick noted the formation of each and recorded their varying results. He first mentioned the launching of an expedition on August 17, 1862. Four days later he reported to his brother that the troops had traveled to Swansboro and had "found nobody, destroyed some salt works, killed some hogs and stole a lot of chickens, ducks and geese."[51] He would offer similar frank assessments of subsequent missions. In fact, John developed a rather sardonic wit when it came to reporting local military activities. For example, in late November 1863, when Gen. John G. Foster canceled an expedition, Hedrick commented wryly, "[T]he chickens and geese may be thankful that Gen. Foster did not get a chance to make his expedition."[52]

Confederate threats in the Beaufort region interested Hedrick for obvious reasons. He noted actions at Plymouth and Washington in 1863 and 1864. When Confederates under George Pickett threatened New Bern and Beaufort in February 1864, John provided his brother with a lucid portrait of the chaotic scene. "We have just past through one of the greatest panics that has happened during the war,"[53] he declared. John told Benjamin of Union soldiers in Beaufort scrambling to barricade streets, their intoxicated commander, and the general air of fear and excitement that prevailed in the town. The commandant, according to John, "was expecting the Rebs in town every minute, and so remained in my office till that night so that I might be on hand should the enemy make an attack." John dryly noted, "Morning came and brought no rebs."[54] John was unimpressed with the army's reaction in Beaufort and dubbed the redoubt, made of plank and cordwood fence and hastily constructed in the street, "Fort Folly."[55] Though there were a handful of scares, no fighting occurred in Beaufort during Hedrick's residency.

Finally, John Hedrick witnessed and commented on various social and cultural aspects of life in Beaufort during the war. He frequently recorded accounts of African American activities, such as the Independence Day celebration among black residents described in a letter of July 5, 1863. The "negro picnic" held on Shackleford Banks involved about four hundred people. Hedrick wrote that there was "singing, speaking, promenading and cheering for the Union cause and officers, and groaning for the Confederates."[56] Hedrick observed the presence of representatives from three northern benevolent societies and a fight between two men at the end of the festivities, which almost everyone, including John, gathered around to watch and cheer.[57]

Hedrick often wrote of his own personal interaction with Beaufort citizens, especially with his host family, the Norcums. The Norcums owned slaves, and John often debated Mrs. Norcum good-naturedly on the issue of slavery. He enjoyed the company of the Norcums and became close to the family, sharing their joys and sorrows. John wrote his brother of the death of the Norcums' eight-month-old baby on June 21, 1863: "Mrs. Norcum's youngest child, little Laura, died last night after an illness of about three weeks."[58] John was noticeably more distraught over the death of the Norcums' vivacious fifteen-year-old daughter, Alice. John's distress is evident in his uncharacteristically terse letter of December 3, 1864: "Alice Norcum died to-day at 11:15 A.M. of Diphtheria. Rest all well. Mail closes immediately."[59] John typically wrote lengthy letters, even if the mail was about to leave, but on this occasion he apparently could not find the inspiration to write anything more.

Disease was a common enemy for all, civilian and military alike. A yellow fever epidemic struck Beaufort and New Bern in the summer and fall of 1864. John first mentioned the threat of the disease casually on June 3, 1864, after several refugees had been reported ill in New Bern. "There are rumors of yellow fever in the place," he wrote, "but I think there is none here."[60] As late as September 19, John reported to Benjamin's wife, Mary Ellen Hedrick, that the disease had not yet spread to Beaufort. He acknowledged that "[t]here is a very bad fever raging in Newbern," but declared, "I am confident it is not Yellow fever."[61] The disease soon spread, however, and ran rampant through both coastal communities during the autumn. On October 8, John stated that there were "between 80 & 100 cases of sickness in this place."[62] For several weeks, John, who never contracted the deadly virus, kept a list of those who had succumbed to the disease. Finally, on November 25, he could write that "[t]he Yellow Fever has entirely ceased at this place,"[63] but not before it caused about one thousand fatalities in New Bern and Beaufort. The yellow fever epidemic of 1864 caused more casualties in the Beaufort region than any military confrontation in the area during the war.[64]

After 1865, John's path, which had paralleled Benjamin's during the war, began to diverge. While Benjamin advocated legal and voting rights for African Americans and worked to bring the Republican Party to North Carolina, John's interest in politics declined. In September 1868, he responded indifferently to his inquisitive brother: "I can not tell much how politics are going here [in Beaufort]."[65] Nor was he enthusiastic about cooperating with African Americans to strengthen the Republican Party in the South. He complained in 1868 about the need "to carry the eternal nigger."[66]

Although Benjamin tried to secure the more remunerative collectorship in Wilmington for John, arguing that his brother had "served . . . I believe with entire satisfaction to the [Treasury] Department," no such promotion was forthcoming.[67] The Hedrick brothers' break in 1868 with the dominant faction in North Carolina's Republican Party, led by William W. Holden, reduced the likelihood that John would keep his job. The incoming Grant administration replaced him in Beaufort, and he moved back home to the western Piedmont.[68]

While Benjamin worked for the Patent Office in Washington, D.C., until his death in 1886, John became a merchant and farmer, accumulating substantial property in Rowan and Davidson Counties.[69] In 1875, he married Maggie M. Cox, who was fourteen years his junior and with whom he would have five children.[70] In an indication of the esteem with which he was held locally, John Hedrick was elected to the state legislature as a Republican in 1890, a year in which the Democrats nearly swept Davidson County.[71] During his lone term in the state house of representatives, Hedrick supported such uncontroversial measures as a bill to keep dogs from running loose and another to prevent minors from buying cigarettes. He, along with most of his fellow Republicans, unsuccessfully opposed the nomination of Zebulon B. Vance to another term in the U.S. Senate.[72] If his fellow citizens resented his adherence to the Republican Party, John Hedrick's decency, moderation, and disinclination to challenge the status quo evidently won them over. Upon his death in 1907, a local newspaper praised John Hedrick as "one of the most prominent and highly respected citizens of this county . . . a man of sterling worth and the strictest integrity. He was one of those men who do more than the world is aware of, to help those around him and to assist in building up his community."[73]

Although he remained in touch with his Beaufort friends during his later years, John was seemingly content to put his Civil War experiences behind him.[74] Considering the death, turmoil, intrigue, and chaos he witnessed in occupied eastern North Carolina between 1862 and 1865, it is no wonder that he chose to spend the remainder of his life elsewhere.

---

[1] Benjamin S. Hedrick to Benjamin Sherwood, July 1851, Benjamin Sherwood Hedrick Papers, Special Collections Department, Duke University Library, Durham; Sixth and Seventh Censuses of the United States, 1840 and 1850: Davidson County, North Carolina, Population Schedules, National Archives, Washington, D.C. (microfilm, Genealogical Services, State Library of North Carolina, Raleigh); Eighth Census of the United States, 1860: Rowan County, North Carolina, Population Schedule, National Archives, Washington, D.C. (microfilm, Genealogical Services, State Library of North Carolina, Raleigh).

[2] John A. Hedrick to Benjamin S. Hedrick, July 10, 1865, Hedrick Papers, Duke Special Collections.

[3] On the antislavery views of John's older brother, see Michael Thomas Smith, " 'A Traitor and a Scoundrel': Benjamin S. Hedrick and the Making of a Dissenter in the Old South," *North Carolina Historical Review* 76 (July 1999): 316-336.

[4] Benjamin Hedrick's dismissal is discussed in Monty Woodall Cox, "Freedom During the Frémont Campaign: The Fate of One North Carolina Republican in 1856," *North Carolina Historical Review* 45 (October 1968): 357-383. Some of the relevant primary sources are published in J. G. de Roulhac Hamilton, "Benjamin Sherwood Hedrick," *James Sprunt Historical Publications* 10 (1910): 1-42.

[5] John A. Hedrick to Benjamin S. Hedrick, October 28, 1856, Benjamin Sherwood Hedrick Papers, Southern Historical Collection, University of North Carolina Library, Chapel Hill.

[6] Benjamin S. Hedrick to Mary Ellen Hedrick, November 5, 1856, Hedrick Papers, Southern Historical Collection.

[7] Charles Phillips to Benjamin S. Hedrick, July 1, 1857, and Benjamin S. Hedrick to Thompson Bird, July 10, 1858, Hedrick Papers, Duke Special Collections.

[8] John A. Hedrick to Benjamin S. Hedrick, June 26, 1858, and W. C. Kerr to Benjamin S. Hedrick, September 30, 1859, Hedrick Papers, Duke Special Collections.

[9] John A. Hedrick to Benjamin S. Hedrick, March 10, 1861, Hedrick Papers, Southern Historical Collection.

[10] John A. Hedrick to Benjamin S. Hedrick, September 2, 1865, and Adam S. Hedrick to Benjamin S. Hedrick, June 24, 1865, Hedrick Papers, Duke Special Collections.

[11] Benjamin S. Hedrick to Horace Greeley, September 15, 1861, Hedrick Papers, Duke Special Collections; Benjamin S. Hedrick to Abraham Lincoln, September 23, 1862, Abraham Lincoln Papers, Library of Congress, Washington, D.C. (microfilm, D. H. Hill Library, North Carolina State University, Raleigh).

[12] Benjamin S. Hedrick to Mary Ellen Hedrick, March 1, 1861, Hedrick Papers, Duke Special Collections.

[13] Benjamin S. Hedrick to Salmon P. Chase, February 9, 1861, and Benjamin S. Hedrick to Mary Ellen Hedrick, April 11, 1861, Hedrick Papers, Duke Special Collections.

[14] Benjamin S. Hedrick to Mary Ellen Hedrick, May 25, 1861, Hedrick Papers, Duke Special Collections.

[15] Mary Ellen Hedrick to Benjamin S. Hedrick, July 17, 1861, Hedrick Papers, Duke Special Collections.

[16] Benjamin S. Hedrick to Mary Ellen Hedrick, July 19, 1861, Hedrick Papers, Duke Special Collections.

[17] Benjamin S. Hedrick to Salmon P. Chase, March 13, 1861, Hedrick Papers, Southern Historical Collection. On the difficulties faced by Southern Unionists in gaining appointments from the Lincoln administration, see also Carl N. Degler, *The Other South: Southern Dissenters in the Nineteenth Century* (New York: Harper and Row, 1974), 70-71.

[18] Benjamin S. Hedrick to Salmon P. Chase, September 14, 1861; Benjamin S. Hedrick to Abraham Lincoln, September 30, 1863; John Graham Tull to Benjamin S. Hedrick, March 18, 1864, all in Abraham Lincoln Papers.

[19] John A. Hedrick to Benjamin S. Hedrick, December 16, 1861, Hedrick Papers, Southern Historical Collection.

[20] Salmon P. Chase to John A. Hedrick, May 27, 1862, Salmon P. Chase Papers, Library of Congress, Washington, D.C. (microfilm, Pennsylvania State University Library, State College).

[21] Rowland M. Hall to Caroline M. Hall, February 13, 1863, Julia Ward Stickley Papers, Private Collections, State Archives, Division of Archives and History, Raleigh.

[22] John A. Hedrick to Benjamin S. Hedrick, June 10, 1862, Hedrick Papers, Duke Special Collections.

[23] John A. Hedrick to Benjamin S. Hedrick, June 10, 1862, Hedrick Papers, Duke Special Collections.

[24] John A. Hedrick to Benjamin S. Hedrick, June 14, 1862, Hedrick Papers, Southern Historical Collection.

[25] John A. Hedrick to Benjamin S. Hedrick, June 14, 1862, Hedrick Papers, Southern Historical Collection.

[26] John A. Hedrick to Benjamin S. Hedrick, July 29, 1862, Hedrick Papers, Southern Historical Collection.

[27] *Charleston Mercury*, September 12, 1861.

[28] *New York Herald*, July 27, 1862.

[29] John A. Hedrick to Benjamin S. Hedrick, June 14, 1862, Hedrick Papers, Southern Historical Collection.

[30] John A. Hedrick to Benjamin S. Hedrick, September 6, 1863, Hedrick Papers, Southern Historical Collection.

[31] John A. Hedrick to Benjamin S. Hedrick, October 16, 1862, Hedrick Papers, Duke Special Collections.

[32] John A. Hedrick to Benjamin S. Hedrick, April 5, 1863, Hedrick Papers, Southern Historical Collection.

[33] *Private and Official Correspondence of Gen. Benjamin F. Butler During the Period of the Civil War*, 5 vols. (Norwood, Mass.: Plimpton Press, 1917), 4:27.

[34] Isaiah Respess to Mary Respess, December 10, 1863, Mary F. Credle Papers, Southern Historical Collection, University of North Carolina Library, Chapel Hill.

[35] On wartime reconstruction in North Carolina, see William C. Harris, *With Charity for All: Lincoln and the Restoration of the Union* (Lexington: University Press of Kentucky, 1997), 58-71.

[36] John A. Hedrick to Benjamin S. Hedrick, December 31, 1862, Hedrick Papers, Southern Historical Collection.

[37] *Dictionary of North Carolina Biography*, s.v. "Foster, Charles."

[38] John A. Hedrick to Benjamin S. Hedrick, September 4, 1862, Hedrick Papers, Southern Historical Collection.

[39] John A. Hedrick to Benjamin S. Hedrick, September 4, 1862, Hedrick Papers, Southern Historical Collection.

[40] John A. Hedrick to Benjamin S. Hedrick, September 4, 7, 1862, Hedrick Papers, Southern Historical Collection.

[41] John A. Hedrick to Benjamin S. Hedrick, July 27, 1862, Hedrick Papers, Southern Historical Collection.

[42] John A. Hedrick to Benjamin S. Hedrick, August 11, 1862, Hedrick Papers, Southern Historical Collection.

[43] John A. Hedrick to Benjamin S. Hedrick, October 13, 1862, Hedrick Papers, Duke Special Collections.

[44] For a more detailed analysis of the buffaloes, see Judkin Jay Browning, " 'Little Souled Mercenaries'? The Buffaloes of Eastern North Carolina during the Civil War," *North Carolina Historical Review* 77 (July 2000): 337-363.

[45] John A. Hedrick to Benjamin S. Hedrick, November 29, 1863, Hedrick Papers, Duke Special Collections.

[46] John A. Hedrick to Benjamin S. Hedrick, March 13, 1864, Hedrick Papers, Duke Special Collections.

[47] John A. Hedrick to Benjamin S. Hedrick, March 13, 1864, Hedrick Papers, Duke Special Collections.

[48] John A. Hedrick to Benjamin S. Hedrick, July 20, 1863, Hedrick Papers, Duke Special Collections.

[49] John A. Hedrick to Benjamin S. Hedrick, June 19, 1863, Hedrick Papers, Southern Historical Collection.

[50] John A. Hedrick to Benjamin S. Hedrick, May 3, 1863, Hedrick Papers, Southern Historical Collection.

[51] John A. Hedrick to Benjamin S. Hedrick, August 21, 1862, Hedrick Papers, Southern Historical Collection.

[52] John A. Hedrick to Benjamin S. Hedrick, November 29, 1863, Hedrick Papers, Duke Special Collections.

[53] John A. Hedrick to Benjamin S. Hedrick, February 6, 1864, Hedrick Papers, Duke Special Collections.

[54] John A. Hedrick to Benjamin S. Hedrick, February 6, 1864, Hedrick Papers, Duke Special Collections.

[55] John A. Hedrick to Benjamin S. Hedrick, February 6, 1864, Hedrick Papers, Duke Special Collections.

[56] John A. Hedrick to Benjamin S. Hedrick, July 5, 1863, Hedrick Papers, Duke Special Collections.

[57] John A. Hedrick to Benjamin S. Hedrick, July 5, 1863, Hedrick Papers, Duke Special Collections.

[58] John A. Hedrick to Benjamin S. Hedrick, June 21, 1863, Hedrick Papers, Southern Historical Collection.

[59] John A. Hedrick to Benjamin S. Hedrick, December 3, 1864, Hedrick Papers, Duke Special Collections.

[60] John A. Hedrick to Benjamin S. Hedrick, June 3, 1864, Hedrick Papers, Duke Special Collections.

[61] John A. Hedrick to Mary Ellen Hedrick, September 19, 1864, Hedrick Papers, Duke Special Collections.

[62] John A. Hedrick to Benjamin S. Hedrick, October 8, 1864, Hedrick Papers, Duke Special Collections.

[63] John A. Hedrick to Benjamin S. Hedrick, November 25, 1864, Hedrick Papers, Duke Special Collections.

[64] See Thomas J. Farnham and Francis P. King, " 'The March of the Destroyer': The New Bern Yellow Fever Epidemic of 1864," *North Carolina Historical Review* 73 (October 1996): 435-483.

[65] John A. Hedrick to Benjamin S. Hedrick, September 11, 1868, Hedrick Papers, Duke Special Collections.

[66] John A. Hedrick to Benjamin S. Hedrick, March 2, 1868, Hedrick Papers, Duke Special Collections; John A. Hedrick to Benjamin S. Hedrick, June 21, July 31, 1876, Hedrick Papers, Southern Historical Collection.

[67] Benjamin S. Hedrick to Jonathan Worth, June 20, 1866, *The Correspondence of Jonathan Worth*, ed. J. G. de Roulhac Hamilton, vol. 1 (Raleigh: Edwards and Broughton, 1909), 639.

[68] John A. Hedrick to Benjamin S. Hedrick, April 16, 22, 1869, Hedrick Papers, Duke Special Collections; John A. Hedrick to Benjamin S. Hedrick, May 24, 1869, Hedrick Papers, Southern Historical Collection.

[69] John A. Hedrick to Benjamin S. Hedrick, March 23, 1875, Hedrick Papers, Southern Historical Collection; Estate of John A. Hedrick, 1907, Rowan County Estates Records, State Archives, Division of Archives and History, Raleigh.

[70] Mary Ellen Hedrick to Benjamin S. Hedrick, August 24, 1875, Hedrick Papers, Southern Historical Collection; Tenth and Twelfth Censuses of the United States, 1880 and 1900: Rowan County, North Carolina, Population Schedules, National Archives, Washington, D.C. (microfilm, Genealogical Services, State Library of North Carolina, Raleigh).

[71] *News and Observer* (Raleigh), November 9, 1890; John L. Cheney, ed., *North Carolina Government: 1585-1974, A Narrative and Statistical History* (Raleigh: North Carolina Department of the Secretary of State, 1975), 469.

[72] *Journal of the House of Representatives of the General Assembly of the State of North Carolina at its Session of 1891* (Raleigh: Edwards and Broughton, 1891), 97, 273-274, 99.

[73] *Carolina Watchman* (Salisbury), June 12, 1907.

[74] John A. Hedrick to Benjamin S. Hedrick, July 22, 1874, Hedrick Papers, Southern Historical Collection.

Editorial Method

Between June 10, 1862, and May 7, 1865, John A. Hedrick wrote 225 letters to his brother Benjamin and his brother's wife, Mary Ellen, with all but a handful being written to Benjamin. All but three of these have been included in this volume. The missing letters contain trivial information regarding office supplies. The few letters and enclosures in this volume that are not from John Hedrick to his brother Benjamin have italicized headings identifying the letter writer and recipient; all documents without headings are from John to Benjamin. The remarkably well-preserved letters are located in nearly equal numbers in the Southern Historical Collection at the University of North Carolina at Chapel Hill, and the Special Collections Department at Duke University. In this volume *SHC* and *Duke* are used to identify the repository for each letter. Unfortunately, attempts to locate Benjamin's letters to John during this same period, which, inferring from John's letters, were nearly as numerous as his own, have been unsuccessful, suggesting that they were not preserved.

The editors have selected letters beginning with June 10, 1862, when John was en route to Beaufort, and ending with May 7, 1865, when John wrote his first letter to Mary Ellen after Benjamin's arrival for a visit in North Carolina. This was the first time the brothers had seen each other in three years. The final letter followed the surrenders of Gen. Robert E. Lee and Gen. Joseph E. Johnston, which signified for all intents and purposes the war's end. Thus these letters present a North Carolina Unionist's observations during the actual time frame of the Civil War.

The Hedrick letters have been transcribed and printed as faithfully as possible. However, a few editorial adjustments and devices appear throughout the volume to assist the reader. Misspellings and punctuation eccentricities have been retained, except where the punctuation was so unusual as to confuse the reader. In such cases, silent corrections have been made. Flourishes and other extraneous marks have been removed. Superscript characters have been converted to a standard font followed by a period. Angle brackets (< >) enclose letters and words canceled by the writer but still legible. Interlinear insertions appear within solidi (/ /). All editorial insertions have been italicized and placed within square brackets ([ ]). All notes immediately follow the document to which they refer.

The editors have also noted enclosures with the heading [*Enclosure*] and placed them immediately after the correspondence that they accompanied, regardless of the date on which the enclosure was written. Finally, John Hedrick generally used the same headings and closings to begin and end each of his letters, but there is some random deviation in his style. These inconsistencies have been transcribed and presented to the reader just as he wrote them.

Letters from a
North Carolina Unionist

1862

Near Lewistown, off the
Delaware Breakwater,
June 6/62
6 P.M.

Dear Brother:

The Cossack[1] left New York according to appointment at 4 P.M. and has sailed ever since at a jog trot with the intervention of several stops. The weather was cloudy and I guess the Captain was some what afraid to venture out to sea. We stopped two or three times before we got out of New York Bay and I do not know whether we stopped any last night or not but this morning we came to anchor off the Delaware Breakwater about 10 o'clock and remained there till about five this evening when we again weighed anchor and sailed about an hour and are again at a dead halt. The watch has just struck six, so I was not far wrong in saying we had sailed an hour; for it struck five about the time we left the Delaware Breakwater. I understand that we are to take the Mail aboard at Fortress Monroe and hence I am writing this to put off there if I can so that you may get it as soon as possible. I am getting on very well though I might be doing better if I had exercised more care in selecting my stores. I did not lay in enough of variety, and some of the articles that I have are of inferior quality. I obtained them for convenience on Cedar Street whereas I should have gone on Broadway or to Fulton Market.

I find upon going out that we are again at the place we left an hour ago. The C. Vanderbilt, several ships and quite a number of schooners are lying in sight. It is getting too dark in my room to write and hence I shall close for the night.

June 7, 9 A.M.

We left the Delaware Breakwater last night after I went to sleep. This morning is very fine and we seem to be sailing at a pretty good speed. I heard some of the passengers conjecturing that we would get into Newbern by Sunday noon but it seems to me that we will have to do good sailing if we do.

The boat keeps <a> rocking all the time but I am not afraid that you will not be able to read my writing.

We have aboard about 100 soldiers, 20 or 30 marines, a few Army officers, some half a dozen Navy officers, one preacher, who seems to be well acquainted about Norfolk, a couple of dozens of private individuals and some contrabands.[2] One of the the last is from Norfolk and another from New Bern. They are genuine contrabands. <One ca> The one from Newberne calls himself Major and say that he is the crew. The one from Norfolk is waiting on some Army officers. His name is Charlie. He is the pure Guinea nigger style, full of talk and I think a little impudent. Last night he and our parson, whom has struck up a kind of second handed acquaintance with him, both being from the same neighborhood, came very near of having a quarrel. The boy was lying on a seat at the side of the hall <and> covered up ready to go to sleep and the parson /sitting/ on a chair in the middle of the hall. I was not present at the beginning and did not hear<d> a word that Charlie said but as I came near I heard the parson say to him, "If you give me any more of your impudence, I will slap your jaws." Upon this an officer said, "You let the boy alone. He is not giving you any impertinence. I will tend to the boy." Nothing further was said. Thus ended the parsono-negro-machy

I hear the dishes rattling out/in/ the hall and this reminds me that I have not eaten my breakfast yet.

I wrote you three times while in New York. Once only a few minutes before the boat left New York. This letter I put in a lampost box, so I guess you did not get it before the next evening. Mr. Johnston gave me the letter from Col. Tompkins. If I get this letter off at Fortress Monroe you will probably get it to-morrow morning.

Your brother,
John A. Hedrick.
12.30 P.M.

We have just passed the Sea Shore empty and the Kennebec with Secesh prisoners going north.

---

[1] The USS *Cossack* was initially scheduled to be part of the "Stone Fleet" sunk by the U.S. Navy in Charleston harbor in December 1861 as part of the blockade. The *Cossack* escaped this fate and was subsequently employed as a troop transport. *Official Records of the Union and Confederate Navies in the War of the Rebellion*, ser. 1, 12:418 (hereinafter cited as *ORN*); John D. Hayes, ed., *Samuel Francis Du Pont: A Selection from His Civil War Letters*, 3 vols. (Ithaca, N.Y.: Cornell University Press, 1969), 1:195.

[2] Benjamin F. Butler coined the use of the term "contraband" for fugitive slaves seeking refuge with the Union army. James M. McPherson, *Ordeal by Fire: The Civil War and Reconstruction* (New York: Alfred A. Knopf, 1982), 267.

Duke
Union Hotel,
Newbern, N.C.
June 10, 1862,

Dear Brother:

I arrived here yesterday about noon. We had no bad luck though we ran ashore in the Sound and had considerable trouble in getting in at Hatteras Inlet. Dr. Page[1] is gone to Roanoke Island and an old negro woman at his <his> office says that he will be back when Gen. Burnside[2] returns but she did not know when that would be. Gov. Stanley[3] is in Beaufort but is expected back by the first boat from that place.

The city is pretty much occupied by soldiers and negroes. All of the nice houses are taken up by the soldiers. There seems to have been a general stampede of the respectable citizens when our troops entered the city. What few white folks remain here have a pale sallow look. There are some very good houses here. They are not much fine but they have a neat appearance about them not common to any other Southern town, that I have seen. There are many houses of the style that you see in Salisbury south of the place that Mr. Rankin[4] lived on. Newbern is situated on a point /of/ land between the Neuse and a little river the name of which I have not learned. It is pretty level, well shaded, and not many feet above high water mark. The Union Hotel was formerly the Gaston House, as the old sign over the door, which has been imperfectly covered by the paint of the new one, indicates. The city is lighted by gas and every thing shows that there have been nice folks living here. Quite a number of squares have <either> been burnt down /either/ by the taking of the city or by the Rebels as they left. Since the occupation of the city by our troops, I think that there has been but little damage done. The houses occupied /by/ the soldiers seem to be neat and to have nearly all of the window panes whole. I expect to leave here for Beaufort to-morrow morning but perhaps will not get away before the next day. The boat that I am to go down on has not come in yet. It was expected last night but it stormed so that it was dangerous for a <u>Government vessel</u> to run. The cars between here and Beaufort have not commenced to run. The bridge burnt by the Rebels over the little river is nearly completed but I heard yesterday that the cars were not ready for the road. It takes a long time to have any thing done by our public functionaries.

Money seems to be plenty here and the negroes thriving. Sutlers stores and candy shops may be found all over the city. Cider is the most common drink for sale. I have not drunk any of it so that I cannot tell what it tastes like. The Provost Marshal has forbidden the sale of brandy and whisky to citizens, negroes and soldiers. Officers may order them for their own account and be responsible for their use.

I have seen military protections struck on some houses but I don't /know/ the circumstances under which they were placed there.

There are a great many schooners, perhaps fifty or sixty, lying in the harbor, apparently for no purpose. There are also quite a number of steamers here. It rained pretty hard last night and is cloudy and has the appearance of raining to-day. The weather here now is about as cold as it was in New York the day I left there. I have had my overcoat on all day. I hope it will clear up before I get to Beaufort. My passage down there is free but I have to find my own rations. Every thing here is done in military style. All of the baggage had to be sent to Adams Express Office[5] to be examined. They took it from the Cossack free. I have not been to see about mine yet: I thought that I would leave it there till I got ready to leave as It would be troublesome to have it carried from boat to hotel and from hotel to boat. The Mail will not leave before to-morrow and hence I will not close my letter till I learn when I shall leave.

June 11.

I leave here to-morrow morning at 8 o'clock on the Highland Light & will have about 10 hours sail to Beaufort.

Your brother,
John A. Hedrick.

---

[1] Dr. Jesse William Page, a graduate of Bowdoin College, was an agent of the U.S. Sanitary Commission in New Bern. John R. Barden, ed., *Letters to the Home Circle: The North Carolina Service of Pvt. Henry A. Clapp, Company F, Forty-fourth Massachusetts Volunteer Militia, 1862-1863* (Raleigh: Division of Archives and History, Department of Cultural Resources, 1998), 105; Jesse W. Page to Benjamin S. Hedrick, April 20, June 7, 1862, Benjamin Sherwood Hedrick Papers, Special Collections Department, Duke University Library, Durham.

[2] Ambrose Everett Burnside (1824-1881) commanded the successful Federal expedition to North Carolina that seized much of the state's coast between February and April 1862. *American National Biography*, s.v. "Burnside, Ambrose Everett."

[3] Edward Stanly, born in New Bern in 1810, represented North Carolina in Congress before moving to California in the early 1850s. Lincoln appointed Stanly military governor of North Carolina in April 1862, and he arrived in New Bern on May 26 to take office. *Dictionary of North Carolina Biography*, s.v. "Stanly, Edward."

[4] Jesse Rankin and his wife, Ann, ran a school in Lexington, N.C., which Benjamin Hedrick attended for a year before entering the University of North Carolina. Jesse Rankin was a Presbyterian clergyman and served as vice president of the Rowan County chapter of the American Colonization Society. Benjamin S. Hedrick to Benjamin Sherwood, July 1851, Hedrick Papers, Duke Special Collections; Monty Woodall Cox, "Freedom During the

Frémont Campaign: The Fate of One North Carolina Republican in 1856," *North Carolina Historical Review* 45 (October 1968): 358.

[5] Adams Express was one of the country's three largest express freight companies. They opened an office in New Bern in 1862, and employed several schooners and steamers in transporting goods between North Carolina and the northern states. Barden, *Letters to the Home Circle*, 63-64.

[*With enclosure*] SHC
Beaufort, N. C.
June 14. /62

Dear Brother:

Excuse me for writing on your friends' letter.[1] I arrived here on the 12th. and entered on the duties of my office[2] on the 13th. instant. I have not become fully installed in the business. Every thing about the office has to be rearranged. My predecessor[3] held over during the reign of Secessia here and when the city was taken, they captured him so that he did not have an opportunity to make returns. He was released and is now about 8 miles out in the country. He never comes to town. A Mr. Willis[4] held the office temporarily when I arrived. He was appointed by Gov. Stanley. I have not made any appointments yet. I recieved an applicant for <one> light house keeper this morning. I have not recieved all my papers from Washington. I am much in need of a list of articles considered contraband as well as a few other papers relating to the regulations to be observed at this port. Most of the citizens of this town are still here. The town is about a third as large as Newbern and there are, I guess, four times as many white folks here as there. This is a plain place with very few fine houses. Provisions are very dear. Chickens as large as <a> pa/r/tridges sell for 40 cts a pair. I do not know the price of board. The rail-road between this place and Newbern[5] was passed over /by/ a locomotive and one freight car for the first time, since the taking of the town,[6] day before yesterday. They do not yet carry passengers and mail. As soon as every thing is ready, the mail for the interior must pass through here.

Write as soon and as often as you can,

Your brother,
John A. Hedrick

[Enclosure: David H. Knapp to John A. Hedrick]

New York
June 1st. 1862

Professor Heidrick

Sir allow me to Congratulate /you/ on your appointment to the position of collector of the Port of Beaufort for it gives me much pleasure to see worthy young men move upward and onward with the wheels of progression & I have no doubt you will show Mr. <u>Secesh</u> that a yankey mud sill can collect for them as well as they can - - - -

I am out of Business & am living at Bloomingdale enjoying myself vary well. I was at the Cooper Institute a few days ago to the exibition of the drawing classes they made a fine show. I should like to hear from you if you get any spair time to write pleas direct, 161 Orchard Street N York

I remain your friend
David H. Knapp

---

[1] John Hedrick wrote this letter on the back of a letter sent to him by David H. Knapp, an acquaintance of Benjamin Hedrick from New York.

[2] Special collector for the port of Beaufort, N.C.

[3] Josiah F. Bell (1820-1890) served as a Confederate Secret Service agent during the war. *Cemetery Records of Carteret County, North Carolina* (Carteret Historical Research Association, n.d.), 148; Eighth Census of the United States, 1860: Carteret County, North Carolina, Population Schedule, National Archives, Washington, D.C. (microfilm, Genealogical Services, State Library of North Carolina, Raleigh, hereafter cited as Eighth Census, 1860, with appropriate county); Mamré Marsh Wilson, *A Researcher's Journal: Beaufort, North Carolina and the Civil War* (New Bern, N.C.: Griffin and Tilghman, 1999), 38-40.

[4] Stephen F. Willis (1813-1867) was a local Unionist. He had been a teacher and surveyor, and later served as a treasury inspector under the supervision of John Hedrick. *Cemetery Records of Carteret County*, 173; Norman D. Brown, *Edward Stanly: Whiggery's Tarheel 'Conqueror'* (University: University of Alabama Press, 1974), 244, 246-247; Seventh Census of the United States, 1850: Carteret County, North Carolina, Population Schedule, National Archives, Washington, D.C. (microfilm, Genealogical Services, State Library of North Carolina, Raleigh, hereafter cited as Seventh Census, 1850, with appropriate county); Eighth Census, 1860: Carteret County.

[5] The Atlantic and North Carolina Railroad.

[6] Beaufort was occupied by Union troops early in the morning of March 25, 1862. John G. Barrett, *The Civil War in North Carolina* (Chapel Hill: University of North Carolina Press, 1963), 109-110.

SHC
Beaufort, N.C.
June 20, 1862

Dear Brother:

I have been about the city considerably since I arrived and have become acquainted with quite a number of the citizens. Pretty much all of the citizens are still here as very few left when our troops came.

Some are Secessionists but the greater number are Union men now and I think always have been.

The notion of State Sovereignty is deeply rooted in the minds of the people, and hence they are very much afraid to do any thing contrary to State law. The last legislature of North Carolina passed an act making it treason to hold any office under the government of the United States;[1] and I was talking a few days since to Mr. James Rumley, Clerk of the County Court of Carteret[2] about the offices about here in the gift of the general government and he said the difficulty in the way of the Union men accepting those offices would be that they were afraid they would be punished under State law. But I think that I could get enough trustworthy men to take all of the offices in this part of the State.

Gov. Stanley's course has tended to make the people even more timid than they were before his arrival. He tells them that he has come to restore and not to disturb things. He was here only two days before I arrived and yet failed to tell them what the policy of the government was.

All of the County officers here still retain their places as they stand on a kind of neatral ground. I am stopping at the Ocean House, which is the only hotel in the place, that is open. The fare is very good but not stylish. We get butter, eggs, clams, soft crabs, oysters, scollops, ham, beef, lamb and pork. The weather here is very pleasant generally but there has been considerable rain during the last week. There is not much trade going on in the place. The country immediately round is not productive and we have not possession far enough interior for the produce to come in. The citizens cannot buy much from the vessels that come in because the Yankees are afraid to take N.C. money. I think that the old bank money will be good as soon as the war is over. Shinplasters[3] are plenty but no one will take them. I have seen quite a number of them. They are printed on poor paper and badly executed.

Shell hunting and fishing are very common pastimes for invalids and officers. They hire negroes with little sail boats and go down ten or twenty miles towards Cape Lookout. I have seen strands of beeds, made from small shells, which looked very pretty. On certain days there are pony-pennings at Shacklefoot banks on Smith Island. The ponies run wild there and when young are caught and branded by the natives. They are then turned into the range and when grown, are enticed into pens and sold to those wishing to buy. They bring from 15 to 60 dollars a piece. I have seen some quite pretty little ones. They are not at all afraid of the water but may be led by the halter into it by walking on the wharf. They swim without apparent trouble.

June 22, 1862

I have been waiting to hear from you before writing but as it takes a letter so long [*to*] reach this place from Washington, I have concluded that it would be better [*to*] write now. <as> I recieved yesterday the National Republican[4] of the 11st instant. I have just returned from church. I went /to/ hear the Methodiste. The exhorter prayed that the country might be delivered from this unnatural war. I think that the war is about as natural as any I ever heard of.

I had an application yesterday evening from a prisoner on parole taken at Fort Macon[5] for the inspectorship at this port. He said that he held the office in 1857 and that he was now out of employment. His name is Pigott[6] and is a cousin of our friend of the same name.[7] He regrets very much ever having entered the Confederate service.

It is very pleasant here now since the breeze sprung up but was quite sultry this morning before 10 o'clock. I recieved yesterday a permit from the Treasury Department for a man in New Haven Conn. to ship a cargo of rosin from this port and at the same time a letter from the man asking whether there was any turpentine to be had here, and the price. I have not heard of but one lot of turpentine and it was bought before I arrived and was cleared by me this first thing that I did on my arrival. Excuse my scratching.

Your brother
John A. Hedrick

---

[1] Hedrick is referring to an act passed on September 13, 1861, by the North Carolina General Assembly. Called *An Act to Punish Trading with the Enemy,* the law prohibited residents from trading with, purchasing bonds from, or collecting notes for the United States. Violators were subject to a two-thousand-dollar fine and six months imprisonment. *Public Laws of the State of North Carolina passed by the General Assembly at its Second Extra Session, 1861* (Raleigh: John Spelman, 1861), 15-16.

[2] James Rumley (1812-1881) served throughout the war as clerk of the Carteret County court. *Cemetery Records of Carteret County,* 162; Eighth Census, 1860: Carteret County; notarized document dated May 10, 1865, Alfred H. Martine Papers, Southern Historical Collection, University of North Carolina Library, Chapel Hill. Portions of James Rumley's Civil War diary were published in the *Beaufort Look Out,* January 7, 14, 1910.

[3] Shinplasters were currency of small denominations issued by the government or bank notes inadequately secured and of slight worth. Mitford M. Mathews, ed., *A Dictionary of Americanisms: On Historical Principles*, vol. 2 (Chicago: University of Chicago Press, 1951), 1521.

[4] A Washington, D.C., newspaper.

[5] Fort Macon, located on Bogue Banks, protected Beaufort harbor. Col. Moses J. White surrendered the Confederate garrison at the fort to Brig. Gen. John G. Parke on April 25, 1862. Barrett, *Civil War in North Carolina*, 10; E. B. Long, *The Civil War Day by Day: An Almanac, 1861-1865* (Garden City, N.Y.: Doubleday and Company, 1971), 204.

[6] Levi Woodbury Pigott, born in Carteret County in 1831, enlisted in Company H, Tenth Regiment North Carolina State Troops (First Regiment North Carolina Artillery) as a sergeant on May 25, 1861. He transferred to Company F, Fortieth Regiment North Carolina Troops (Third Regiment North Carolina Artillery) on November 1, 1861. Pigott was captured at the surrender of Fort Macon. Louis H. Manarin and Weymouth T. Jordan Jr., comps., *North Carolina Troops, 1861-1865: A Roster*, 14 vols. to date (Raleigh: Division of Archives and History, Department of Cultural Resources, 1966-), 1:134, 434.

[7] Jennings Pigott (1811-1882), a native of Carteret County, was a Whig member of the North Carolina legislature from 1846 to 1850. He subsequently worked as a claims agent in Washington, D.C., and become acquainted with the Hedricks. He returned to North Carolina as secretary to military governor Edward Stanly in 1862. William C. Harris, *With Charity for All: Lincoln and the Restoration of the Union* (Lexington: University Press of Kentucky, 1997), 70; *Cemetery Records of Carteret County*, 160; Norman D. Brown, "A Union Election in Civil War North Carolina," *North Carolina Historical Review* 43 (autumn 1966): 388.

SHC
Beaufort, N. C.
June 25, 1862.

Dear Brother:

I recieved yesterday your letter of the 19th. instant, which was the /first/ private letter that I have had since my arrival here. I am enjoying very good health. Every thing is quiet. The mail reaches here so seldom that we are not much troubled with the news. I have seen the New York Herald of the 16th and I believe that a few copies as late as the 19th. are in town. The regulations to be observed at this port and the President's proclamation opening the port to commerce has failed to reach /me/.[1] I have writen several letters to the Department in Washington for information and documents; none of which have come to hand. A list of articles considered contraband should be furnished me, so that I might know when a vessel was violating her license.

I am now wishing to know whether a vessel would be subject to arrest for going from this place to Newbern. The latest instructions on that subject are of the 12th. Sept. 1861. These say that permits can be granted only by the President through the Secretary of the Treasury, and yet Gov. Stanley has granted the Captain of a schooner permission to carry his cargo to Newbern. I am directed to keep a strict supervision over the unlading of every vessel that comes into this port, whether it be foreign or coastwise; and how I am to superintend a vessel at Newbern, which is out of my district, I don't know. I think the man smells some "tar, pitch and turpentine,"[2] whose owners are probably from home. Last week a vessel came in here with lager, ale, and wine aboard, which I think are considered contraband at Georgetown, D.C. but I would not do anything with her, without positive instructions. They were all down on the manifest, which was granted in New York. If it be not too much trouble for you, I would be glad if you /would/ call at the Treasury Department and see if they have recieved my letters. They may not have gone through as they were all free.

I am still boarding at the Ocean House. I am to pay not over twenty five and perhaps less than twenty dollars per month. Eatables are very dear here now. This is the only boarding house in the place that is open and I thought that I would not try to get boarding at a private house yet awhile. I have not made any inquiries but I think it probable that I might have to pay nearly as much at a private house, and not get near as good fare.

I cannot find fault with the fare at the Ocean House. H.R. Helper[3] arrived at Buenos Ayres on the 2nd. of April, having experienced a voyage of over 90 days. Have you had a letter from him since I left Washington?

I did not get a legal form book when I was in New York. I had forgoten the name of the one that you mentioned and also the place to get it at, but I tried at quite a number of stores on Nassau, and Park Row, but could not find one to suit me.

I have inquired about Foster[4] and can find no body here who knows any thing about him. Mr. Willis, who is assistant hotel-keeper, says that he has never been here. I think that this is the case. For in a little place like this, a man is soon found out, especially if he is a public character as Foster would be if he were to come. I have had very little to do so far. I entered three, and cleared three vessels; all engaged in the coasting trade, and granted one temporary register. I have not got my office fitted up yet. In fact I have not yet seen all that I have to put into it. The room that the old collector had is locked up and the key cannot be got, and the man that owns the room wished me to wait as long as I could before I would have him to break open the door. As I did not have a place prepared to put the property in, I thought that it would be as well to leave it where it is till I could have my room plastered <up>. If I had a list of the property and the seal of office, the rest might remain there some time for what good it would do me. I understand that a good safe, a desk, some chairs, the books and other documents belonging to the office, are in the old office.

Mr. J.H. Davis[5] says that Josiah F. Bell, the old collector, deposited what specie, there was in the office (about 2,000 dollars), in Wilmington and took Confederate Bonds for it.

I have found quite a number of Mr. [*Jennings*] Pigott's old acquaintances. Among them are James Rumley, Joel Davis, Mr. Whitehurst,[6] Thomas Duncan,[7] Robt. Chadwick,[8] and Benj. L. Perry.[9] Give my respects to Messrs. Goodloe,[10] and Pigott.

Your brother,
John A. Hedrick

---

[1] President Lincoln declared the port of Beaufort open for trade on May 12, 1862. Long, *Day by Day*, 211.

[2] The production of tar, pitch, and turpentine, or "naval stores," was one of North Carolina's most important industries until after the Civil War. William S. Powell, *North Carolina Through Four Centuries* (Chapel Hill: University of North Carolina Press, 1989), 135-136.

[3] Hinton Rowan Helper (1829-1909), a native of Rowan County, N.C., wrote the controversial book *Impending Crisis of the South* (1857). He became friends with Benjamin Hedrick after Hedrick's dismissal from the University of North Carolina. Lincoln appointed Helper consul to Argentina in 1861. Hugh C. Bailey, *Hinton Rowan Helper: Abolitionist-Racist* (University: University of Alabama Press, 1965), 27, 47, 51, 115.

[4] Charles Henry Foster (1830-1882) was born and raised in Maine. He moved south and in 1859 became editor of the *Citizen*, a newspaper in Murfreesboro, N.C., in which he expressed pro-Southern sentiments. By 1861, however, he had become an active Unionist in politics. He attempted unsuccessfully to win a seat in Congress from Union North Carolina during the war. Foster served as recruiting agent for the First North Carolina Union Regiment and as lieutenant colonel of the Second North Carolina Union Regiment until banished from the army in 1864. *Dictionary of North Carolina Biography*, s.v. "Foster, Charles Henry."

[5] Joel Henry Davis (ca. 1804-1868) was a local merchant who owned fifteen slaves at the outbreak of the war, yet became one of Beaufort's leading Unionists. Eighth Census, 1860: Carteret County, Population and Slave Schedules; *New Bern Progress*, September 13, 1862; John A. Hedrick to Benjamin S. Hedrick, August 18, 1868, Benjamin Sherwood Hedrick Papers, Southern Historical Collection, University of North Carolina Library, Chapel Hill.

[6] David W. Whitehurst (ca. 1810-1865) was a farmer who served three terms in the North Carolina House of Commons. Eighth Census, 1860: Carteret County; John A. Hedrick to Benjamin S. Hedrick, April 11, 1865, Hedrick Papers, Duke Special Collections, in this volume; John L. Cheney Jr., ed., *North Carolina Government, 1585-1979: A Narrative and Statistical History* (Raleigh: N.C. Department of the Secretary of State, 1981), 313, 321, 327.

[7] Thomas Duncan Sr. (1806-1880) was a Beaufort merchant. *Cemetery Records of Carteret County*, 153; Ninth Census of the United States, 1870: Carteret County, North Carolina, Population Schedule, National Archives, Washington, D.C. (microfilm, Genealogical Services, State Library of North Carolina, Raleigh, hereafter cited as Ninth Census, 1870, with appropriate county).

[8] Robert W. Chadwick (1826-1884) was director of the Beaufort Male Academy. *Cemetery Records of Carteret County*, 150; Eighth Census, 1860: Carteret County; *Halcyon and Beaufort Intelligencer*, November 7, 1854.

[9] Benjamin L. Perry (1811-1869) was a merchant, insurance agent, and former county clerk. *Cemetery Records of Carteret County*, 160; Eighth Census, 1860: Carteret County; *Halcyon and Beaufort Intelligencer*, October 10, 1854.

[10] Daniel Reaves Goodloe (1814-1902) was an antislavery author and editor who was born in Louisburg, N.C. He held several minor federal appointments during the war. Goodloe and Benjamin Hedrick became friends following Hedrick's dismissal from the University of North Carolina. *Dictionary of North Carolina Biography*, s.v. "Goodloe, Daniel Reaves."

———————

SHC
Beaufort, N.C.
July 10, 1862.

Dear Brother:

I have recieved three letters from you since I wrote last. I have forwarded the letter to Laura Stanford.[1] I have not recieved any instructions from Washington. I have writen twice asking whether vessels chartered by the Government are exempt from port fees but have recieved /no answers/. The Captain of the Cutter sent to my service is of the opinion that they are required to enter and clear like any other merchant vessels. I know that they were required to do so at Georgetown, D.C. for the day that I was there, the Collector was telling of a schooner whose <papers> license had run out while in the district and Mr. Brown[2] would not clear him till he paid hospital money, which amounted to about 40 dollars. So he left without clearing and was stopped down the Potomac and sent back and when he got back, Mr. Harrington[3] sent a note to the Collector at midnight requesting him to give a temporary register and clear /him/ so that he might carry government stores down to the lower part of the Potomac. The ships masters refered the question to Capt. Porter,[4] Quartermaster at Morehead, and he refered it to Capt. Biggs,[5] Quartermaster at Newbern and he refered it to Gen. Burnside, who was of the opinion that Government chartered vessels were not required either to enter or clear. I could have the vessels stopped by the Cutter but the Capt. & myself would prefer to have positive instructions from the Treasury Department before doing so.

Capt. Nones[6] of the Cutter advises me to go to Baltimore to find out what the regulations are there but I tell him that it would be of no use; because the Collector there is not in a situation similar to mine. I would be glad if you would call at the Treasury Department and get instructions from Sec. Chase[7] or Assist. Sec. Harrington or perhaps the Commissioner of Customs[8] would do as well, and send them to me by mail.

I recieved a letter day before yesterday from the Register of the Treasury[9] stating that he had transmitted to me blank registers, enrolments and licenses on the 3rd. of last month in care of the Collector at New York. I expect Mr. Barney[10] has enough of care of his own without taking any care of those blanks. I still live in hopes that they will come some time.

The details of the fighting at Richmond[11] have not reached here. I heard that Gens. Jackson & Hill were killed.[12] There must have been some very hard fighting done there. It is thought that Gen. McClellan[13] has a more advantageous position than he had before the battle.

The weather to-day is a little warmer than usual but not oppressively hot. We generally have a good seabreeze, especially during the night.

I have got into my new office at last but I don't like. It is not nice enough but owing to the number of houses occupied by troops I could not get a better one at present. It is back of Joel H. Davis' Store. It belongs to him.

Tell Mr. Pigott that he will probably get his old case of Stephen F. Willis applying for money due him as Inspector, Weigher and Guager in 1857 under Mr. Gibble,[14] who became stubborn and would not pay him. Mr. Willis expects to make application to the Department. I have not particularly examined the case. Mr. Thomas Duncan, one of Mr. Pigott's old friends obtained a license for a little schooner to-day.

I have sent to the Treasury Department the name of L.W. Pigott as weigher, guager, measurer and Inspector. At first I did not think that I would appoint him but I concluded that he would be about the best man for the place that I could get. He took the oath of allegiance to the United States the second day after he was released and has always been a Union man. Many men have been forced into the Rebel Army by circumstances. It was either join the army or be counted and treated as a traitor.

You wished to know whether I had any appointments in my gift. I have the nomination of Inspector, Weigher, Guager and Measurer (one office) and Light House Keeper at Cape Lookout. I have not learned when the L. H. Board expect to repair the light house so I have not sent in a nomination for that place. The light house is now in charge of Mr. I.S. Davis, who was put in charge of it last April by Gen. Park.[15]

Newspapers are very scarce here. The military mails come in open bags and the commissioned officers are permitted to rumage the mails when they are opened and take out whatever they think [*they*] would like to have.

Write soon.
Your brother,
John A. Hedrick

---

[1] Laura Stanford, a relative of Mary Ellen Hedrick, Benjamin Hedrick's wife.

[2] Thomas Brown (1819-1867), a longtime Ohio political associate of Salmon P. Chase, was a special agent for the Treasury Department, 1861-1867. *Appleton's Annual Cyclopedia and Register of Important Events*, vol. 1 (New York: Appleton, 1861), 411.

[3] George Harrington was assistant secretary of the treasury. Harry J. Carman and Reinhard H. Luthin, *Lincoln and the Patronage* (New York: Columbia University Press, 1964), 57.

[4] Capt. Henry Porter served as assistant quartermaster of the Department of North Carolina. *The War of the Rebellion: A Compilation of the Official Records of the Union and Confederate Armies*, ser. 1, 18:512 (hereafter cited as *OR*).

[5] Lt. Col. Herman Biggs (1851-1887) was chief quartermaster of the Department of North Carolina. He was promoted to colonel in August 1864. Francis B. Heitman, *Historical Register and Dictionary of the United States Army*, 2 vols. (Washington: Government Printing Office, 1903), 1:218.

[6] Henry B. Nones (1830-1905) was a naval engineer officer. Hayes, *Samuel Francis Du Pont*, 3:186.

[7] Salmon P. Chase (1808-1873), secretary of the treasury, was Benjamin Hedrick's political patron and largely responsible for Benjamin's Patent Office and John's Treasury Department appointments. Stewart Sifakis, *Who Was Who in the Civil War* (New York: Facts on File Publications, 1988), 117; Benjamin S. Hedrick to Salmon P. Chase, Sept. 14, 30, 1861, Abraham Lincoln Papers, Library of Congress, Washington, D.C. (microfilm, D. H. Hill Library, North Carolina State University, Raleigh).

[8] Nathan Sargent (1794-1875), a longtime political associate of President Lincoln, served as commissioner of customs from 1861 to 1871. *Dictionary of American Biography*, s.v. "Sargent, Nathan."

[9] Lucius Eugene Chittenden (1824-1902) was a prominent Vermont Republican. John Niven, ed., *The Salmon P. Chase Papers*, 5 vols. (Kent, Ohio: Kent State University Press, 1993-1998), 1:360.

[10] Hiram Barney (1811-1895) was collector of customs in New York City from 1861 to 1864. Carman and Luthin, *Lincoln and the Patronage*, 60-62, 278-280.

[11] The Seven Days' Battles around Richmond, June 25-July 1, 1862.

[12] Confederate generals Thomas Jonathan "Stonewall" Jackson and Ambrose Powell Hill were not killed in the battle.

[13] Maj. Gen. George Brinton McClellan (1826-1885) was commander of the Army of the Potomac. *American National Biography*, s.v. "McClellan, George Brinton."

[14] James E. Gibble (b. ca. 1785). Eighth Census, 1860: Carteret County.

[15] John G. Parke (1827-1900) served as a brigadier general in Burnside's North Carolina expedition. Ezra J. Warner, *Generals in Blue: Lives of the Union Commanders* (Baton Rouge: Louisiana State University Press, 1964), 359-360.

SHC
Beaufort, N.C.
July 20, 1862.

Dear Brother:

I am well, as <u>usual</u>, and have gained about four pounds since I arrived. We have had very hard rain during the last two days and it is now warm and cloudy. I did not get any summer clothing except a coat as I came through New York and have not needed any. It is generally very pleasant here. I have been told that the Atlantic House two years ago had at one time eight hundred visitors and that the other two hotels and all private houses that would take boarders were full too. The seabreeze at times is delightful but then the dulness of the place pays for all the pleasure. Since Burnside left Newbern there has been less shipping done at this port than there was before.[1] Only two vessels came in during last week. One was a trading vessel from Boston with ten barrels of whiskey on board as shipstores. This seemed like a very large allowance for so short a trip; as there were only four men aboard. I had a very strong notion to send the vessel to New York, but as the man seemed to be honest and open about it, and as his manifest showed that it was aboard and reported when he was cleared at the Custom House at Boston, I permitted him to land the rest of his cargo. He had an old Newbern Progress,[2] which quoted from the regulations that the Collector at New York prescribed for vessels clearing for the Southern ports before the regulations of the Secretary of the Treasury had reached him. This paper said that vessels clearing for ports recently opened to commerce, would be permitted to take a small quantity of whiskey (not exceeding ten barrels). It seems to me that the Collector of Boston should have recieved his instructions before now.

The supercargo of this vessel says that they told him at the Custom House in Boston that ten barrels were allowed, to each vessel coming here, as shipstores. The instructions to the different collectors are to refuse clearance to any vessel having on <u>board</u> any of the articles mentioned as contraband, and whisky is among them. I saw yesterday the New York World of the 16th. which gave an editorial on the confiscation bill. I hope that Uncle Abe will sign it. It is much better than I thought, a month ago, could have passed the Senate.[3]

There are not many niggs here and what there are, are fewer than the whites.

Gov. Stanley made only one appointment when here was here. He called him Harbor Master but he has none of the duties of a Harbor Master to perform. Negro Searcher would be a more appropriate title for him.

He has to examine the vessels as they leave to see that no 'niggs' are aboard. It don't amount to much: for any body disposed to take them away, can easily box them up, till they get to sea. When the 4th. Rhode Island Regiment left here, they took about a dozen, some barrelled up, others boxed, and others concealed among the vessels cargo.

You asked in one of your letters whether I had seen Governor Stanley? I saw him as I came through Newbern. I had only a few moments conversation with him. He was very busily engaged with his constituents. One was wanting an order from him that he might get his negro woman back home to do cooking and housework. The soldiers had killed a hog for another and he wished pay for it. And so on.

It seems to me that the Governor should have a clerk <should> to hear all of these little claims, and devote himself to more important matters. He made a speech in Washington, N.C. about three weeks ago. I did not get a chance to read it but heard part of it read. I thought it was as good as might be expected from him. It savored a little of "your institutions." The speech was well writen. My official fees up to this time amount to about twenty five dollars. This belongs to me. I guess that Congress will have adjourned before this letter reaches you.

I heard that there was an official letter for me at the Post Office for me. But it is Sunday and the Office is closed.

Mr. D.W. Whitehurst is our Harbor Master. He is a very fine man. He has been a member of the N.C. Legislature twice.

Give my respects to Messrs, Goodloe, Underwood,[4] Pigott & c.

Your brother,
John A. Hedrick

W.W. Holden,[5] Johnston of Mecklenburg,[6] and Vance,[7] are candidates for Governor in this State.

---

[1] Burnside left North Carolina on July 6, 1862, for Virginia. William Henry Singleton, *Recollections of My Slavery Days*, ed. Katherine Mellen Charron and David S. Cecelski (Raleigh: Division of Archives and History, Department of Cultural Resources, 1999), 95-96.

[2] A Unionist newspaper in New Bern, N.C.

[3] Hedrick is referring to the Second Confiscation Act, which Lincoln did sign on July 17, 1862. The bill stated that slaves belonging to rebels could gain their freedom when they came under the Union army's control. The difficulty of determining the loyalty to the Union of each individual owner rendered this law ineffective. Lincoln declared in September 1862, "I cannot learn that that law has caused a single slave to come over to us." Phillip Shaw Paludan, *The Presidency of Abraham Lincoln* (Lawrence: University of Kansas Press, 1994), 145-146.

[4] John C. Underwood, a Virginia Republican, was the fifth auditor of the U.S. Treasury. In 1863, he was appointed judge for the Eastern District of Virginia. Carman and Luthin, *Lincoln and the Patronage*, 59, 222.

[5] William Woods Holden (1818-1892) was editor and publisher of the *North Carolina Standard* of Raleigh and leader of the state's wartime peace movement. In 1856, he campaigned to have Benjamin S. Hedrick dismissed from the University of North Carolina, and as a result, the Hedrick brothers detested him. Holden served as provisional governor of North Carolina in 1865. He was elected governor as a Republican in 1868 and served until impeached and removed from office in 1871. *Dictionary of North Carolina Biography*, s.v. "Holden, William Woods"; Cox, "Freedom During the Frémont Campaign," 368, 369, 372-373, 377, 379.

[6] William Johnston (1817-1896) was president of the Charlotte and South Carolina Railroad and a friend of former governor John W. Ellis. *Dictionary of North Carolina Biography*, s.v. "Johnston, William."

[7] Zebulon Baird Vance (1830-1894) was a popular Whig/Conservative Party leader and colonel of the Twenty-sixth Regiment North Carolina Troops. He would serve as governor until the end of the war. Vance was elected governor again in 1876 and later served in the U.S. Senate. *Dictionary of North Carolina Biography*, s.v. "Vance, Zebulon Baird."

SHC
Beaufort, N.C.
July 27, 1862.

Dear Brother:

I have writen to you twice since I heard from you last. Every thing here is quiet. Gen. Foster[1] has placed an embargo on all vessels in port. I have not been able to learn the object of. Last Friday the Rebels attacked our pickets between here and Newbern. It was reported by a darky that they were Eleven Hundred strong but the report is not credited. Washington, N.C. has furnished a few companies of Volunteers[2] for our army but I do not know the number. The people about here are so so. They profess to be Union, but are not fighting Union men. Some have taken the oath of Allegiance, others the oath of Neutrality, and others still, have refused to take any oath.[3] Paper is scarce. I run out yesterday and did not think that I would write any today. So I did not buy any. If you have not already obtained me a form book you need not send one for I have as many forms I need.

Your brother,
John A. Hedrick.

---

[1] John G. Foster (1823-1874) was a brigadier general in Burnside's North Carolina expedition. In July 1862, Foster was assigned as commander of the Department of North Carolina. Warner, *Generals in Blue*, 157-158.

[2] For the First North Carolina Union Regiment. See Judkin Jay Browning, " 'Little Souled Mercenaries'? The Buffaloes of Eastern North Carolina during the Civil War," *North Carolina Historical Review* 77 (July 2000): 337-363.

[3] These were oaths required of Confederate citizens in order to receive rights and services provided by the occupying Union forces. Stephen V. Ash, *When the Yankees Came: Conflict and Chaos in the Occupied South, 1861-1865* (Chapel Hill: University of North Carolina Press, 1995), 44-45.

SHC
Beaufort, N.C.
July 29th. 1862.

Dear Brother:

I recieved by yesterday's mail your letter of the 18th. inst. and three packets, from the Register of the Treasury, containing Crew Lists, Enrolments, Licenses and Registers. I wrote a letter to you last Sunday but neclected to put it in the post office, so that it did not leave here till this morning. The mail leaves this place for Newbern every morning at 7 o'clock and Newbern for the North about once a week. My last letters and documents from Washington have reached me in ten days. When I first arrived here they generally came in 7 days. I thought when I left New York that we would soon have a regular Mail between here and New York but from some cause the Government has failed to establish the line of Steamers. Sometimes steamers leave here for New York but the Post Master has not been instructed to send letters that way.

I told you in my letter of Sunday last that Gen. Foster through the Quartermaster at Morehead City had requested me not to clear any more vessels from this port until otherwise directed by the general. Every body here is at a loss to know the meaning of this embargo. I cannot see the reason for it; but then there may be things behind the scene, which justifies it.

There are only two trading vessels in port that wish to leave now. There are four in all but the others are not quite ready to go to sea. There have been eight cargos brought into port and mostly disposed of since I arrived and two before my arrival. The number of cargoes dispatched is somewhat greater; because some of the Chartered vessels have carried private property from here.

The usual number of inhabitants in this town is about 2000 and there are now about 1500 here. The country around is thinly settled and the houses often widely separated by bays, branchs, and rivers, so that it would be difficult /to estimate/ the number of people within our lines; but our lines extend from Morehead with the Rail-road to Newbern and round to Washington &c. East /and North/ of this line, I think there are no Rebel troops and the people are mostly loyal. Slavery is not highly valued in this part of the State and the slaves are about as free as their masters, or a little more so now because the niggs can go without passes, while the whites have to have them. I have not heard any thing from Gov. Stanley lately. He keeps himself very quiet. Doctor Evans,[1] Gov. Morehead's[2] son-inlaw skedaddled a few days after the taking of Newbern and has not returned since. I understand that he was a strong Secesh. News from the army of the Potomac is very slow getting here.

We have nine Sisters of mercy at the general Hospital in the place.[3] They came a little more than a week since and I understand are doing good service. There are about 400 soldiers in the hospital. Most of them were convalescent when sent here from Newbern. It is so much more healthy and pleasant here that all that are able to bear the transfer are sent here to get well.

> I am your brother
> in the dark,
> John A. Hedrick

---

[1] Peter G. Evans was married to Ann Eliza Morehead, daughter of John M. Morehead. Evans later served as colonel of the Sixty-third Regiment North Carolina Troops. Burton Alva Konkle, *John Motley Morehead and the Development of North Carolina, 1796-1866* (Philadelphia: William J. Campbell, 1922), 399.

[2] John Motley Morehead (1796-1866) was governor of North Carolina from 1840 to 1844. *Dictionary of North Carolina Biography*, s.v. "Morehead, John Motley."

[3] The wife of Maj. Gen. John G. Foster arranged for members of the Sisters of Mercy of New York's St. Catherine's Convent to come to Beaufort in the spring of 1862 to tend the sick and wounded. Stevenson L. Weeks, "The Federal Occupation of Morehead City and Beaufort," and Virginia Pou Doughton, "The Atlantic Hotel," in *North Carolina's Coastal Carteret County During the Civil War*, ed. Jean Bruyere Kell (n.p.: Jean Bruyere Kell, 1999), 19, 86-87.

SHC
Beaufort, N.C.
Aug 4, 1862,

Dear Brother:

Your last letter (July 18) was recieved on the 28th. of last month. I recieved at the same time some blanks from the Register of the Treasury. We have had rain every day and night for the last week. I have felt a little unwell to-day but I ascribe it to the weather. There are more folks here with the jaundice than I ever saw at one place before. It is a common complaint among the army officers. I have not seen as much of it among the privates.

To-day I granted Capt. Nones of the U.S.C. "Forward" leave of absence to return North to recruit his health. He has been down with the fever for the last two weeks and Dr. Potter[1] said that it might result fatally if he remained here longer. There has been quite a number sick aboard the Cutter- but the others are getting better.

We have had no recent war news. Two papers of the 29th. of last month are here. Perhaps you have heard that Newbern has been taken by the Rebels. The steamer Baltimore from Fortress Monroe brought that news, or we would never have heard of it. I was at Newbern last Thursday and all was quiet.

The cars run from Morehead to Newbern and back everyday. It has been rumored here that this port would be closed soon, but I guess that it arose from the embargo. There was no arrival of any merchant vessel from the North during last week.

All government transports have been detained here; but for what purpose I do not know.

Business is very dull.

Write often,
Your brother,
John A. Hedrick

---

[1] Albert Potter was assistant surgeon of the Fifth Regiment Rhode Island Heavy Artillery from October 1861 until December 1863, when he became regimental head surgeon. John K. Burlingame, *History of the Fifth Regiment of Rhode Island Heavy Artillery, During Three Years and a Half of Service in North Carolina* (Providence: Snow and Farnham, 1892), 265, 373.

SHC
Beaufort, N.C.
Aug. 11th./62

Dear Brother:

Your letter of July the 18th. was recieved in due time. I have just seen the N.Y. Herald of the 7th. inst, which was brought by a Steamer this morning. An account of the great Union meeting in Washington City was given. Some fighting had occurred near Richmond and our forces had in part advanced within ten miles of that City.[1]

There has nothing of importance occurred here for some time. Gov. Stanley was here last week. He expects to go to Washington City in a fortnight. The Johnson, who was ultra Secession Candidate for Governor in this State, is President of the Charlotte and S.C. Rail Road. He lives in Charlotte but is a native of South Carolina. The Election for Governor in this State came off last Thursday. Its result I have not heard. There was no attempt to run a Union Candidate here. There is not enough of territory within the Union lines to justify the attempt. The Herald says that Gov. Sprague[2] offers to raise a regiment of negroes and accompany it in person in the field. Hurrah for him if he is a Democrat. I have learned that our old friend Amos Wade[3] abscotulated with his negroes to High Point on the approach of our forces to Newbern. I have not had any letter from Laura Stanford in reply to Sis. Ellen's[4] letter. A flag of truce went up the next week after I sent the letter but I cannot vouch for <its> the letter reaching its destination.

In this general exchange of prisoners I guess that William Gaston,[5] and Forest will be included.

Gen. Danl. Harvey Hill[6] has been appointed on the part of the Confederates to make the exchange. I prefer exchanging to paroling soldiers. A soldier on parole is good for nothing. We expect another northern mail shortly. It usually arrives at Newbern about once a week and it has been a little over a week since the last arrived.

I have writen twice since I recieved your last.

Are they raising any Volunteers in the District of Columbia? If they will give me a first or second lieutenants place in the District or Virginia Volunteers, I will accept of it. How is Mr. Goodloe getting on?

Give my respects to all friends and enquirers:

Write all the time.
Your brother:
John A. Hedrick.

---

[1] Hedrick is referring to some minor skirmishes that occurred at Malvern Hill, Va., on August 5, 1862. The two armies sparred after the Seven Days' Battles before the Union army abandoned the Peninsula. Robert E. Denney, *The Civil War Years: A Day-by-Day Chronicle of the Life of a Nation* (New York: Sterling Publishing, 1992), 200-201.

[2] William Sprague (1830-1915), governor of Rhode Island from 1860 to 1863, served as an aide to Burnside at the First Battle of Bull Run in July 1861. *Dictionary of American Biography*, s.v. "Sprague, William."

[3] Amos Wade (1803-1879) resided in New Bern's First Ward in 1860. At that time he owned twenty-six slaves. *Cedar Grove Cemetery* (New Bern, N.C.: Historical Records Survey of North Carolina, 1939), 64; Eighth Census, 1860: Craven County, Population and Slave Schedules.

[4] Mary Ellen Hedrick (b. ca. 1830), daughter of William Thompson of Orange County, N.C., was the wife of Benjamin S. Hedrick. They were married in Chapel Hill on June 3, 1852. Seventh Census, 1850: Orange County; John Spencer Bassett, *Anti-Slavery Leaders of North Carolina* (1898; reprint, Spartanburg, S.C.: Reprint Company, 1971), 30; *Hillsborough Recorder*, June 16, 1852.

[5] William Gaston Sanford, Mary Ellen Hedrick's nephew, had been captured by Union forces in the summer of 1862. He was imprisoned first in Washington's Old Capitol Prison and thereafter at Governors Island in New York harbor. W. Gaston Sanford to Benjamin S. Hedrick, June 14, 1862, Hedrick Papers, Southern Historical Collection.

[6] Confederate general Daniel Harvey Hill (1821-1889) commanded the Department of North Carolina from July to September 1862, and again from February to July 1863. *Dictionary of American Biography*, s.v. "Hill, Daniel Harvey."

SHC
Beaufort, N.C.
Aug, 15, 1862.

Dear Brother:

I recieved your letter of Aug. 5th. two days ago. I do [*not*] know of any thing that I wish to be brought to North Carolina by Dr. Page. Tell him that I would be happy to see him in Beaufort on his return to this State if he can make it convenient to come here. I called at his office when I came through Newbern and also two weeks /ago/ when I was up there but found him absent both times. Every thing is quiet at this place. Five small steam gun-boats from Newbern and two large once from Fortress Monroe arrived this morning. I guess some expedition is under contemplation but I do not know to what place. There are not many troops here now, only enough to do police duty. The weather has been quite warm for the last week, but not so as to be oppressive.

I have not heard the result of the election in this State but think it probable that Vance is elected. My weight is one hundred and thirty pounds. I recieved from Washington D.C. day before yesterday the Tribune of the 30th. ultimo. I am very much obliged to you for it. Papers of the 9th. inst are here and I have read the Herald of the 7th. yet I like to read those back papers to see what has been done. We get a Mail about once a week. There is no cotton near here. The land is too poor to produce it. People here don't raise much of any thing. They have been accustomed to fish for their living, but now if they have North Carolina money or no money at /all/ they are furnished from the Commissary Department. Before the war broke out, men used to dig clams for eight cents a bushel and now it is hard to get them for forty cents. Men are not anxious to work when Uncle Sam will feed them for nothing. Chickens as big as partridges bring forty cents a pair and every thing else in proportion. Write soon.

Your brother-
John A. Hedrick

SHC
Beaufort, N.C.
August 17, 1862

Dear Brother:

I have <of> the pleasure of reporting the safe return of the first vessel that I cleared for a foreign port. On the 5th. of July I cleared the Schr. Pacific of Washington, Capt. Farrow[1] for the Island of Guadaloupe West Indies. Yesterday she returned with a cargo of salt, sugar & molasses. The duties on them will be about three hundred dollars: Last week I cleared two other schooners for the West Indies, which on account of the weather have not left the harbor. Their cargoes are shingles and lumber. If the war was over so that the produce could come to the sea, there would be a considerable amount of shipping from this port. Naval stores are higher here than they are in the West Indies.

Tar here is worth ten dollars per barrel and only eight at St Martins West Indies. My official reciepts so far have been about enough to pay my board and lodgings.

My salary will be clear gain. News of the fight between Banks and Jackson has been recieved.[2] Nothing has been heard from the Expedition[3] which left here a few days ago nor is its destination known to the public.

The pickets continue to be fired on in Newbern by night. Persons near the place of firing have been arrested and in one instance six or seven houses were torn down in retaliation, but I have /not/ learned of any more severe punishment having been inflicted. Gen. Pope and the commissioned officers who serve under him will not be treated as prisoners of war if taken by the Rebels.[4]

Every thing is quiet in town. The ninth New Jersey is doing guard duty here. The people seem to be pretty well contented with their condition. There are some pretty strong secesh here but they dare not be much bold.

The other day before the Expedition left, the pilots were notified to hold themselves in readiness to go along, and it is said that one was attacked with a sudden cholic so that he could not go. I think that he has not taken the oath of Allegiance and has refused to take it. The others five in number have taken it but one of them Sam Howland held back a long time before he would take it. At last he caved in and took /it/ and then employed the pilot who was so suddenly /attacked/ with the choloc, as one of his boats crew. There are here now only this cholicy polit and a boy commissioned temporarily to pilot the vessels in till the regular pilots return.

Piloting is regulated by state laws but as the laws of the State are not in force, the military prescribe such regulations as they think necessary.

Write all the time
Your brother,
John A. Hedrick.

P.S. The Steamer Baltimore from Old Point arrived to-day with papers of the 14th. inst. I haven't had a chance to read one yet.

J.A.H.

---

[1] This is possibly a reference to Edward Farrow, who in 1874-1875 was captain of the *Nellie Potter*, a merchant ship. Fred M. Mallison, *The Civil War on the Outer Banks* (Jefferson, N.C.: McFarland and Company, 1998), 181.

[2] Hedrick is referring to the Battle of Cedar Mountain, Va., August 9, 1862, in which Stonewall Jackson's corps fought two Union divisions commanded by Nathaniel Banks. Denney, *Civil War Years*, 201.

[3] A minor raid to Swansboro, N.C., which encountered little resistance. Barrett, *Civil War in North Carolina*, 132. See the letter of August 21, 1862, in this volume.

[4] Hedrick is referring to John Pope, latest commander of the Army of the Potomac. Upon taking command, Pope had declared that civilians who harbored or aided Confederates would be held responsible for guerrilla actions and their property would be confiscated. In addition, any who refused allegiance to the U.S. would be driven from their land. Confederates, particularly Robert E. Lee, took umbrage at this and threatened to be just as

harsh on Pope and his army if the orders were carried out. Obviously, the rumors of all this had reached Beaufort, N.C., by this time. McPherson, *Ordeal by Fire*, 253.

SHC
Beaufort. N.C.
Aug. 21st. 1862.

Dear Brother:

As one of the gunboats is to leave at 1 o'clock today direct for Baltimore I take this opportunity to write you. The Expedition which I mentioned in my last letter returned day before yesterday, having gone to Swansboro, found nobody, destroyed some salt works, killed some hogs and stole a lot of chickens, ducks and geese. The Rebel home Guards about 250 in number had left before our gunboats arrived. We took one prisoner but I have not heard whether he was in arms or not. Vance has been elected Governor of the State.[1] I hardly know how to regard his election. The Union men here regard it as a Union victory.[2]

The weather is quite hot to-day with a northeast wind. We have have the most pleasant weather when the wind is south. There is a recruiting office opened here for the 1st. N.C. Reg.[3] but I do not think that many have e/n/listed. As the Government supplies a considerable portion of the country around here with provisions, I cannot see why it does not draft those fit for service into the army, and make them do service for their rations. The U.S. Transport Guide has been detained here for the last two days because, Gen. Burnside placed some contrabands aboard of her as a part of her crew. It seems that some of them belongs to citizens who live about here.

Your brother,
John A. Hedrick

---

[1] Zebulon B. Vance defeated William J. Johnston, 55,282 to 20,813. Cheney, *North Carolina Government*, 1401.

[2] Vance's opponent, William Johnston, advocated North Carolina's withdrawal from the Union following Lincoln's election. Vance, on the other hand, had been a vocal Unionist until the Confederates fired on Fort Sumter and Lincoln called for troops to put down the rebellion. Only then did he support secession. During the 1862 campaign, newspapers endorsing Johnston tried to shame Vance partisans by portraying support for Vance as support for the Union. Frontis W. Johnston and Joe A. Mobley, eds., *The Papers of Zebulon*

Baird Vance, 2 vols. to date (Raleigh: Department of Archives and History, 1963—), 1:xxxviii, xlii; *Dictionary of North Carolina Biography*, s.v. "Johnston, William," "Vance, Zebulon Baird."

[3] This refers to recruitment for Company F of the First North Carolina Union Regiment. Efforts to enroll recruits in the First North Carolina continued through 1862, and in November 1863, three companies of the Second North Carolina Union Regiment began recruiting. Browning, "Little Souled Mercenaries," 348; Compiled Service Records of Volunteer Union soldiers Who Served in Organizations from the State of North Carolina, Record Group 94, National Archives, Washington, D.C. (microfilm, State Archives, Division of Archives and History, Raleigh).

SHC
Beaufort, N.C.
Sunday, Aug. 24th. 1862.

Dear Brother:

I am well. All is quiet about here. There has been a little skirmishing with the Rebels near Washington, N.C. but I heard a man say that an officer, who was just from there, told him that it did not amount to much. The Expedition that went to Swansboro returned to this place last week. The Rebels had skedaddled before they reached the place. The Expedition destroyed a small fortification and some saltworks near there. The duties on the cargo of the Schr. Pacific amounted to three hundred and twenty seven dollars and ninety cents. The Pacific is a small schooner of only eighty tons.

The other two schooners that I have cleared for the West Indies are considerably larger. One of them, /the/ Watauga, left this morning, and the other, the Marinah N. expects to leave in a day or two. No trading vessel has arrived for more than a week. The Barque, C.C. Merimon of Bangor, ran aground on the Cape Lookout shoals, Thursday night or <Sat> Friday morning. I heard that She was loaded with coal for Government and bound to Port Royal, S.C. How this man found out what she was loaded with and where bound, I don't know. No one has been able to get nearer than one hundred yards of her. The breakers are breaking all around her and over her decks. Some people down on the Banks saw the crew in two boats /bound/ towards Portsmouth. I can't see why they did not come in here. Perhaps the wind was wrong for that. It has rained a little today and is cloudy now, 5 P.M. Gov. Stanley will leave here next Tuesday on the steamer Baltimore of Baltimore for Baltimore. He will be in Washington City about Thursday evening. You must have mis<tarding>taken my meaning if you thought I intended to say that Newbern was taken.[1] I said that the boat from Fortress Monroe brought that news and that I had been at Newbern only two days before I wrote and that the cars had come from there only the evening before, and we had heard nothing of it.

Last Friday evening one of the citizens of this town stuck up posters for a Union meeting in the Court House yesterday evening. The Commandant of the post, Capt. Curlis,[2] advised him to defer the meeting till the last night of this week so that the Union men might have a chance to hear of it. So there was no meeting yesterday. The enlisting office has been open for a whole week but no soldiers obtained. There have been about a dozen in to see the conditions of enlistment but all seem to have some objection. Some would enlist if certain others would enlist first and others would enlist if they were certain that they would not be taken out of the State. It would be well to require the men, who are so an/x/ious to have their slaves <&> returned to them, to join the army as the first condition to any agreement on the subject. I am afraid that the oath of allegiance does not amount to much. A man, who is mean enough to be a rebel, will do most any thing to save his property.

<Ju>Aug. 25th. 1862.

There is nothing new this morning. The 9th. N. J. Reg. is doing police and guard duty here. It is not a very arduous service. As far as the citizens are concerned it amounts to almost nothing. The soldiers, when they get liquor, and it is very hard to prevent them from getting it, occasionally create disturbances. The sailors from the gunboats are the worst to manage. Let them have a little liquor and there is no keeping them quiet. They like to get into a mess. We have had papers as late as the 15th. There was very little news from Gen. McClellan. He had sent his transports to Hampton Roads but was still on the James himself.[3] It is thought that there will be no draft in the Northern States. If six hundred thousand men in addition to those in the field last Spring, can be raised without a draft, I think that the Government is in no great danger of overthrow.[4]

Your brother,
John A. Hedrick.

[1] See the letter of August 4, 1862, in this volume.

[2] William B. Curlis served in Company F of the Ninth New Jersey Regiment. He eventually attained the rank of lieutenant colonel. Janet B. Hewett, ed., *The Roster of Union Soldiers, 1861-1865, New Jersey and Delaware* (Wilmington, N.C.: Broadfoot Publishing, 1998), 69.

[3] After retreating from the outskirts of Richmond to the James River, McClellan was ordered to transport his army to northern Virginia to support John Pope's army. McClellan was slow to comply with this order. Kenneth P. Williams, *Lincoln Finds a General: A Military Study of the Civil War*, vol. 1 (New York: Macmillan, 1950), 330-332.

[4]During the summer of 1862, President Lincoln ordered each state to provide a certain number of militia to serve nine-month terms. Those states that could not meet their quotas with volunteers were to conduct a draft on August 15. The prospect of conscription prompted riots in Indiana and Wisconsin, and the threat of disturbances in Pennsylvania. Such strong public opposition resulted in the postponement of the draft. Some states eventually held a draft, while others did not. Mark M. Boatner III, *The Civil War Dictionary*, rev. ed. (New York: Vintage, 1988), 245; Benjamin P. Thomas and Harold M. Hyman, *Stanton: The Life and Times of Lincoln's Secretary of War* (New York: Alfred A. Knopf, 1962), 245-246.

SHC
Beaufort, N.C.
Aug. 29th. 1862.

Dear Brother:

Your letters of the 18th. and the 23rd. inst. came to hand to-day. I had writen to Mr. Watkins[1] about my debt to him but if Mr. Berney[2] pays him it will save me the trouble and danger of sending the money. I am sorry to hear that Sis Ellen is sick, and hope that she will recover shortly.

I wrote to Mr. Goodloe and gave the letter to /the/ pilot to put it aboard the Baltimore when she went out and yesterday I saw him put it in the Post Office. Gov. Stanley went aboard the Baltimore and expected to be away about a fortnight. He will be in Washington before this letter reaches you.

All is quiet here. There have been no arrivals of merchant vessels in more than a week. They must be taken up for other purposes or afraid to come. The last of the two West Indies vessels has left. If they have luck to get back with good cargoes, their duties together with those already collected will be sufficient to pay all expenses of collecting the Revenue in this district.

The duties and hospital money in this district, to date, amounts to three hundred and fifty-three dollars and fifteen cents. I have just bought a Revenue Boat for the use of the Inspector, for Ninety dollars. I found that he required a boat nearly every day and that I could not hire one for less than fifty cents per day, and that it was sometimes difficult to get one even at that price. People here do not know how to charge less than 50 cents.

The boys have shell beads for sale but they won't take less than 50 cts per string of a yard, whether you take one or fifty strings.

I had heard that the President had authorized Gov. Stanley to hold an Election in the 1st. and 2nd. Congressional Districts of North Carolina for Members of Congress but do not think that the Governor made any arrangements to that effect previous to his departure for Washington. We are to have a Union meeting in this town next Saturday, the 30th. inst. I would like to do all I can to put down this infamous rebelion and for that purpose I would be glad to have a Commission in the Union Army, but should our army be victorious in the battle that is likely to come off shortly between Washington and Richmond, I hardly think that I could do much good by joining the Army. My services here might be of more service to the Union cause by remaining in my present position than they would be in the military service. I know very little about military tactics but I have no fear that I could not soon post myself up in them.

In a list of N.C. officers in the Rebel service, which appeared in the Newbern Progress of the 26th. & 27th. insts, I find the names of E.G. Morrow,[3] James R. McAuley,[4] E.N. Dickey,[5] Yancey M. Wilfong,[6] Wallace Rheinhardt,[7] J.D. McIver,[8] D.J. Devane[9] and a host of other old school mates and acquaintances of mine.

E.G. Morrow was 2nd. Leit. in the 28th. Regiment N.C. state Troops. This list was taken from the N.C. Register and is of course a long way behind time. H.L. Roberts[10] and Hamilton C. Long[11] of Salisbury and Daniel R. Roseman[12] of Rowan are put down as 2nd. Lieutenants'.

John J. Hedrick[13] is Captain of artillery. I think that he is a Commission Merchant of Wilmingto[n] N.C. and was born in Maryland. It looks bad to see so many of my friends in the Confederate service but I see no way to bring them to their senses but by whipping them and that well. They must be whipped if it takes every loyal man in the United States to do it.

Papers from New York to the 25th. came on to-day's Mail. Up to that time no fight had occurred between Pope and Jackson. There has been a rumor here that McClellan was going to resign but the latest papers do not confirm the rumor. I have writen quite a number of letters to you lately. Two <beside> I guess, have not left Newbern.

Write often
Your brother,
John A. Hedrick

---

[1] Thomas Watkins was a New York City tailor. Thomas Watkins to Benjamin S. Hedrick, September 18, 1862, Hedrick Papers, Duke Special Collections.

[2] Alfred Berney was a New Jersey inventor. Alfred Berney to Benjamin S. Hedrick, January 12, 20, 28, 1863, Hedrick Papers, Southern Historical Collection.

[3] E. Graham Morrow, Mary Ellen Hedrick's stepbrother, briefly lived with Benjamin and Mary Ellen in Washington, D.C., before the war. Morrow rose to the rank of captain in the Twenty-eighth Regiment North Carolina Troops and was mortally wounded at Gettysburg. Benjamin S. Hedrick to Eliza J. Thompson, July 21, August 12, 1863; obituary enclosed in Eliza J. Thompson to Benjamin S. Hedrick, August 26, 1863, Hedrick Papers, Duke Special Collections.

[4] James R. McAuley, a native of Iredell County, was a teacher before the Civil War in either Burke or Iredell County. During the war he served as captain in Company I, Seventh Regiment North Carolina State Troops. He was wounded at Gaines' Mill and Chancellorsville

and was killed August 25, 1864, at Reams Station, Va. Manarin and Jordan, *North Carolina Troops*, 4:493.

[5] This is possibly a reference to William N. Dickey, a first lieutenant in Company I, Seventh Regiment North Carolina State Troops. *New Bern Progress*, August 26, 1862.

[6] Yancey M. Wilfong (b. 1840) of Catawba County attained the rank of captain in Company A, Twelfth Regiment North Carolina Troops. He was killed at Spotsylvania Court House, Va., on May 12, 1864. *Catawba County Cemeteries*, vol. 7 (Hickory, N.C.: Catawba County Genealogical Society, 1991), 9; Manarin and Jordan, *North Carolina Troops*, 5:118.

[7] Wallace M. Reinhardt of Lincoln County was a first lieutenant in the First Regiment North Carolina Infantry and was mustered out November 13, 1861. Manarin and Jordan, *North Carolina Troops*, 3:51-52.

[8] James D. McIver of Moore County rose to the rank of captain in Company H, Twenty-sixth Regiment North Carolina Troops. He resigned from the army on June 17, 1864, to become solicitor in the Moore County court. Manarin and Jordan, *North Carolina Troops*, 7:561.

[9] Duncan J. Devane of Sampson County was at the time of this letter captain of Company I, Twentieth Regiment North Carolina Troops. On May 12, 1864, he was promoted to major. Devane was wounded three times. Manarin and Jordan, *North Carolina Troops*, 6:433, 512.

[10] This is possibly a reference to H. Roberts (b. ca. 1840) of Salisbury, who was a "machinist," and a native of New York. Eighth Census, 1860: Rowan County.

[11] Hamilton C. Long of Rowan County served as a second lieutenant in Company K, Fourth Regiment North Carolina State Troops. He resigned from the army on November 6, 1863, because of illness. Manarin and Jordan, *North Carolina Troops*, 4:104.

[12] This is possibly a reference to Daniel F. Roseman, who was born in Catawba County and served as an officer in Company F, Thirty-eighth Regiment North Carolina Troops. He resigned on March 12, 1863, because of disability resulting from wounds. Manarin and Jordan, *North Carolina Troops*, 10:58.

[13] John J. Hedrick of New Hanover County was by the time of this letter a major in the Thirty-sixth Regiment North Carolina Troops (Second Regiment North Carolina Artillery). On December 1, 1863, he became colonel of the Fortieth Regiment North Carolina Troops (Third Regiment North Carolina Artillery). He was wounded in the left thigh in March 1865. This Hedrick appears to be no relation to John A. Hedrick. Manarin and Jordan, *North Carolina Troops*, 1:219, 374.

SHC
Beaufort, N.C.
Sept. 4th. 1862,

Dear Brother:

I recieved last Saturday the Republican of the 21st. ultimo, containing internal Revenue Taxes. New York papers of the 1st. inst. came yesterday on the Steamer, "Guide." There had been considerable fighting near Manassas.[1] Jackson's army was between Pope's and Washington. The prospect for the Union forces seemed to be fair. Gov. Stanley left here for Washington City about a week ago. The Union meeting at this place last Saturday was pretty well attended. Speeches were made by Mr. Congleton[2] of this town and Capt. Arnold[3] of the U.S. Steamer, "Mystic." Ten volunteers were obtained. The<re> whole number of volunteers obtained here is fifteen.

Times are very dull. There is some stir about the return of the Rebel soldiers captured at Fort Macon. Some have taken the oath of allegiance to the United States and others do not wish to go back to the Rebels. Out of three hundred taken I do not believe that there are more than 20 who wish to go back. If we are successful in the coming battle between Pope and Jackson, very few will return to the Rebel army but should we be repulsed, most of them will return. The "Guide" brought in some troops. I understand that about 30,000 of the last draft are to be sent to this place and Newbern. There have been no arrivals of Trading Vessels for about two weeks. It has been quite cool during the last three days. I wrote to you last Saturday and gave the names of some of the Rebel Army Officers. Uncle Mike[4] has been elected to the House of Commons from Guilford County.

Your brother,
John A. Hedrick.

---

[1] The Second Battle of Manassas, or Bull Run, August 29-30, 1862.

[2] Abraham Congleton, sixty-four years old, helped recruit the First North Carolina Union Regiment and served as a private in Company F. He was president of the Free Labor Association in Carteret County and in 1868 represented that county at the state constitutional convention. He also served as mayor of Beaufort after the war. Mallison, *Civil War on the Outer Banks*, 117; Brown, "A Union Election," 395; Cheney, *North Carolina Government*, 846; John A. Hedrick to Benjamin S. Hedrick, January 8, 1869, Hedrick Papers, Duke Special Collections.

[3] Lt. Cmdr. Henry N. T. Arnold. *ORN*, ser. 1, 8:92-93.

[4] Michael S. Sherwood was editor of the Whig *Greensboro Patriot*. He was a member of the North Carolina House of Commons during the 1862-1864 session. He died September 19, 1868, at the age of fifty-three. Sherwood was the brother of John Hedrick's mother. *Patriot and Times* (Greensboro), September 24, 1868; Cheney, *North Carolina Government*, 330.

SHC
Beaufort, N.C.
Sept. 4th. 1862,

Dr. Brother:

I wrote to you this morning but since then the humbug [*Charles Henry*] Foster has arrived. He is a Candidate for Congress in this district.

He says that he brought down dispatches from President Lincoln for Gov. Stanly, whom he met at the Astor House New York. It would be well for you to call on Gov. Stanley and see whether he is going to hold an election in the 1st. & 2nd. Congressional districts in this state and if so at what time. I would like to have what papers you can furnish me with in relation to Foster's rascality. I do not wish to run for Congress if I can get a good man to run against Foster but if no one else will oppose him, I guess I must. If Mr. [*Jennings*] Pigott was living here, I have no doubt but that he could beat Foster.

Should he come down before the election and make it his home, I guess that he would be allowed to take his seat in Congress.

It would be well for Messrs Pigott & Goodloe to see Gov. Stanley and tell him what a humbug Foster is.

He will use all of the means that rascality can devise. I shall do all that I can to defeat him.

All quiet.
I am your brother,
John A. Hedrick.

P.S. Foster has a pass from President Lincoln to pass him around on his campaign.

J.A.H.

SHC
Beaufort, N.C.
Sept. 7th. 1862.

Dear Brother:

I presume that you will not object to reading this letter because it is writen on foolscap.[1] My health is good. The weather is quite warm to-day, much more so than it has been for the last week.

We have just heard of a battle near Washington, N.C.[2] The Confederates about 2,000 strong came down upon that place, yesterday, and were repulsed after having taken two pieces of our cannon. A small gunboat, named, "Picket," stat/ion/ed there was blown up yesterday through some carelessness. The Captain and nineteen of the men were killed. She was not in the engagement.[3]

The last news from Washington City is very gloomy. Burnside is said to have evacuated Fredericksburg, and fallen back on Aquia Creek.

McClellan has avanced two miles from Centreville, in the direction of Jackson's Army. Our loss in the last Bull Run battle is stated to be 5,000 killed and, 4,000 wounded, taken prisoners. This I learned from a Navy Officer, who came through the canal from Norfolk to Newbern[4] and on the train from Newbern this morning. He had had a New York Herald of the 3rd. inst. but had loaned and lost it at Newbern.

Our last New York paper, is dated the 1st. inst. This Navy Officer said also that 50,000 Confederates were advancing on Cincinatti and that the City was under Marshal Law.[5] If this be so, the Government of the United States had better draft 50,000 more men. There is not much danger of having too many troops in the field. It would be much better to have too many than not enough. If the white men will not fight, make a draft on the contrabands. Some of them, at least, will make good fighting material. I do not believe that they are all cowards, though it would seem from their present condition that they were. Most of the Army and Navy officers here are bitterly opposed to arming the negroes. They are always cursing the negroes and the Abolitionists. They make the latter mean as the former is low.

I have not heard from Foster since he left here last Friday. I have been thinking that if Gov. Stanley should order an election in this district that Jennings Pigott would run as well as any man that I know. In this County, I have been told that he could carry the entire Union vote. Suppose you get him to come down and run for Congress, if Mr. Stanley concludes to hold an election.

You or he can find that out before I can and it may be necessary for him to be here pretty soon. I do not wish to see Foster elected. Men about here are rather timid in expressing their Union Sentiments and Mr. Pigott, being acquainted with all of them, would have much influence in bringing them out. I do not think that it would be absolutely necessary for him to move his family to this State though it might be better for him to do so.

The Constitution requires a Representative, when elected, to be an inhabitant of that State from which he shall be chosen. He may come and reside here even if his wife cannot come with him. He is more of an inhabitant of this State now than Foster is, though I do not know whether he would be so regarded in law. He can make all of that right, if he wishes, to be a Member of Congress.

My business for the last two weeks has nearly died out altogether. There has been only one arrival and two departures during that time.

Do you know whether Congress increased my salary? The papers came here so seldom that I could not tell what they had done about it.

Sept. 8th. 1862.

It rained last night and is somewhat cloudy this morning. I could not learn how many or whether any were killed in the battle near Washington N.C, last Saturday. The messenger that brought the news to Newbern could not tell. It seems that on Saturday morning about 5 o'clock, about a thousand cavalry & the same number of infantry, made their way into Washington without being discovered. The first that was known of their approach, was made in their surrounding the hotel in which most of the officers were quartered. There were about 400 Union troops at Washington. These, it is thought, would all have been captured, had not the gunboat, Louisiana come to their rescue. She got her guns to bear upon them and drove them away. How she could do this without killing our own men I cannot understand. The story is very vague and I think very much exagerated.

The messenger from the scene of action is said to be a very excitable man. He said that he would rather go through three Newbern battles[6] than /the/ melee at Washington, yet he did not know whether any one was killed or not. It is thought here that there is not a body of Rebels soldiers two thousand strong nearer than Goldsboro. I can not see where they get all of their men from. It seems that they are a match for us at every point.

The Union voluntiers at this place amount to about twenty. I beleive that this twenty have put their names down but some may be rejected on examination by the Surgeon.

Men of property and influence are afraid to do any thing for the Union cause. There are about four good Union men who are men of considerable property. Mr. Joel H. Davis, Mr. Rigor and a few others of some wealth and standing have contended for the Union all the time but I can tell that men of their stamp are few and far between.

Write soon and often,
Your brother,
John A. Hedrick

---

[1] The letter is written on a long legal-sized piece of paper.

[2] A skirmish took place at Washington, N.C., on September 6, 1862. A small Confederate force launched a surprise dawn attack on the sleeping Union garrison. A Union force that had just departed the town heard the firing and returned. After a fight of two and a half hours, the Confederates retreated. *OR*, ser. 1, 18:4-7.

[3] The magazine of the Union gunboat *Picket* exploded. Capt. Sylvester D. Nicoll and nineteen men were killed; six others were wounded. *OR*, ser. 1, 18:5, 7.

[4] Hedrick is referring to either the Dismal Swamp Canal, completed in 1828, or the Albemarle and Chesapeake Canal, which opened in 1859. In subsequent letters, Hedrick refers simply to "the canal." Clifford Reginald Hinshaw Jr., "North Carolina Canals Before 1860," *North Carolina Historical Review* 25 (January 1948): 24; Alexander Crosby Brown, *Juniper Waterway: A History of the Albemarle and Chesapeake Canal* (Charlottesville: University Press of Virginia for the Mariners' Museum, Newport News, Va., and the Norfolk County Historical Society, Chesapeake, Va., 1981), 1.

[5] This refers to Edmund Kirby Smith's army, which spearheaded a Confederate invasion of Kentucky. The army was neither as large as Hedrick reports, nor as near Cincinnati as rumors stated. Boatner, *Civil War Dictionary*, 776-777.

[6] There had been a short but sharply contested battle at New Bern on March 14, 1862, which resulted in the capture of the city by Union forces. Barrett, *Civil War in North Carolina*, 96-106.

SHC
Beaufort, N.C.
Sept. 12, 1862.

Dear Brother

There has been very little news afloat since I wrote you last.

The Steamer, "G.C. Collins" brought in last week 250 recruits for different regiments at Newbern, and about 150, which she carried to Port Royal, S.C.

The steamer "Albany," left New York for Newbern the day before the "Collins" did, but had not arrived at Newbern yesterday. It is feared that she has been lost. A tug left Newbern day before yesterday for Hatteras in search of her but had not returned when the train left Newbern yesterday morning at 9 A.M.

The N.C. troops are highly praised for their gallant conduct in the battle at Washington N.C.

I am getting sick of hearing the Yankees wish that the Rebels would take Washington City. They say that that would wake the North up; that they have been only playing with the rebillion so far. If they are not waked up by the reverses that we have already suffered, I am at a loss to know what would wake them. Are they so stupid as not to be aroused by the slaughter of fifteen thousand of their fellow citizens in a single series of battles? Does the investment of the Nation's Capital by a victorious army seeking our destruction, not disturb them? I have seen some so insane as to wish the Northern States themselves to be invaded.[1]

C.H. Foster addressed the Union meeting at this place yesterday. I was not present at the commencement of the speech. He narrated the events of the past year and appealed to the Union men in this County to join the 1st. N.C. Regiment, for self protection. He said that he did not ask them <them> to do what he would not do himself; that he had been sent here on a mission which would last during the next three months and that then he would enter the Regiment with them. He said that he was acquainted with every body in the north counties and he was going to visit them. He praised the President and the course he had persued towards the Southern States. He said that the President had it in his power at any time to cause their women and children to be slaughtered by the negroes.

In relation to European interferance, he said that the probability was that England and France would assist the North in as much as it was the stronger side: because in this way the war could be stopped and cotton obtained easiest.

I have heard him say last night that he had given up a two thousand dollar situation in the General Post Office at Washington, but for what purpose I did not understand. He said in his speech that he had never asked the President for an office. I thought that it might be true and that it might not.

The weather is quite warm to-day. We have had considerable rain during the last four days.

The fishing season has arrived. Mullets are the principal fish caught. As many as five hundred barrels have been caught at a single haul, at a fishing place about six miles from here. The mullet is, when fresh, the best fish I ever ate. I do not like them so well when corned. They ran from the 1st. of September to the last of October and during these last two months the people of this County lay up their meat and bread for the year. They send their fish to Hyde and exchange them for corn. There will not be so many caught this Fall for various reasons. In the 1st. place, hands are not so plenty as usual, 2nd. salt is scarce and hard to obtain, 3rd. twine is very high, and 4th. the market is obstructed.

It has been some time since I have had a letter from you. Your last if I mistake not, was dated the 18th. of last month, perhaps the 23rd. I have writen you quite a number of letters lately. Two on one day. One in relation to C.H. Foster's history during the last winter. If Mr. Pigott concludes to come down here, it would be better for him to have all of the documents. I would like to hear as soon<er> as possible whether Mr. Pigott can come.

I have not heard from Gov. Stanley since he left except through Foster, who met him at the Astor House, New York.

> Write all the time,
> Your affectionate
> brother,
> John A. Hedrick.

---

[1] These statements of disappointment are a result of Lee's first invasion of the North. He marched the Army of Northern Virginia into Maryland on September 4, 1862. Denney, *Civil War Years*, 209.

SHC
Beaufort, N.C.
Sept. 16. 1862,

Dear Brother:

I recieved last Friday your letters of the 30th. of August and the 2nd. of Sept. 1862, and on Saturday five Tribunes. Our last news from the seat of war is very unsatisfactory. The principal part of the Rebel army was in Frederic and Hagerstown, Maryland. The exact whereabouts of McClellan was not known but when last heard from he was on his way to Damascus. The Rebel General Lee had issued a proclamation to the people of Maryland inviting them to his standard, provided it was their will to <do so> /come/.[1]

Our latest papers from New York are those of the 12th. of September. It seems to me that the Rebels have placed themselves in a close corner. I can not see how they can escape it if our generals use rightly the forces at their command.

Every thing is quiet in this department. The force at the place has been increased. There are five companies of the 9th. N.J. Regiment here now and the balance of the Regiment in Morehead and Caroline City. The steamer "Wilson" mounting two guns and carrying one company of infantry left here yesterday for some place not yet known, but thought to be Swansboro. The boat is rather trifling, being an old vessel captured on the Neuse above Newbern and used during the last two months as a ferry boat between here and Morehead. I guess Gen. Foster thinks it time to send some body round to Swansboro <round to Swansboro> to see what they have been doing there since the visit by the Expedition that I mentioned some time ago.

The health of the people here is good. There are between three and four hundred soldiers in the hospital — most of them brought down from Newbern. The weather is a little cloudy to-day, with very little air stirring. The Steamer "Star of the South" Capt. Woodhul,[2] arrived here yesterday morning. He left New York on the 12th. He brings a few soldiers and some quarter-master stores. Business is still dull in my office. Only two arrivals and two departures in about three weeks. It was rumered here yesterday that Gov. Stanley would not return to this department. I have not found who brought the report and am inclined to discredit it.

Recruiting progresses rather slowly in this place. If our army should gain a few decisive victories the people would be encouraged to enlist; but under present circumstances I think we will not get many volunteers.

Write often.
Your brother,
John A. Hedrick.

---

[1] Lee issued a proclamation of deliverance on September 8, 1862, hoping that Marylanders would rise to the aid of the Confederacy. The results were disappointing to the South, as few natives joined Lee's army. E. Merton Coulter, *The Confederate States of America: 1861-1865*, vol. 7 of *A History of the South*, ed. Wendell Holmes Stephenson and E. Merton Coulter (Baton Rouge and Austin: Louisiana State University Press and the Littlefield Fund for Southern History of the University of Texas, 1950), 355.

[2] Maxwell Woodhull (1813-1863) was killed in February 1863 in Baltimore harbor by the accidental discharge of one of his ship's guns. Hayes, *Samuel Francis Du Pont*, 1:54, 2:483.

SHC
Beaufort, N.C.
Monday, Sept. 22nd. 1862,

Dear Brother:

I recieved last Friday your letter of the 6th. inst. and three Tribunes. I cannot tell the exact date on which Mr. Berney first came into your office nor the day on which he brought the first specimens of Asphalt. I have a vivid recollection of his taking me from the Patent office in his buggy drawn by a fine black-bay horse for which he was trading with a Virginia refugee, down to his room on Penn. Avenue, where we got some specimens of Asphalt, which I placed in the window behind my desk. On his return to the Patent office, he did not stop, but promised me to call at Mr. Maukins that evening after four o'clock, to see you. He did not fulfill his promise. This I think was about the 1st. of May, and just after I had got over the measles. I have been consulting my account of clothing sent to the washerwoman's to find when I had the measles but I cannot find any diminution in the number of clothes sent out during each week for April and May — it is two shirts and one pair of socks throughout the whole chapter. The writing on your record of Specifications will tell when I had the Measles, as you recorded a few of the Specifications during the time. It might have been just before I took the measles that I obtained the specimens. Mr. Berney showed me the day that he took me to his room a recommendation from some officer at the Navy Yard, which I believe was dated that morning. I came from Rhode Island to Washington on the 28th. of March and /it/ was shortly after then that Berney first came to your office but I think that he mentioned by name only the "Tube and Shell" which was greatly needed then to sink the "Merrimac." It was about the middle of April when I first learned what Berney was to fill his "Schrapnell" with. When Berney and I were going to his room we passed two Express wagons, the driver of one of which, he stopped and asked whether he was done hauling his asphalt to the Navy York. So that if you can obtain the bills of lading for this asphalt, you will have very nearly, within three days at least, the date of my obtaining the specimens. It was some time before this that he first mentioned asphalt for filling shells, and it was two or three weeks before I got all of the facts to complete his specification and then about a week after I had it completed before he filed it. You know I had the middle before I recieved the two ends of the specification. There may be some of my first writing on this Specification with the date on it in my drawer, on the left side of the desk, though I think that I burned them all up.

It rained all day yesterday and all night last night and is cloudy to-day. There have been a great many rumers from the war in Maryland. The Rebel Army has been reported as having left Maryland altogether and to have lost a great many men in the Potomac by Gen. Miles firing into them from the Maryland side while in the river. The next rumor was that Gen. Miles and 8,000 of his men had been captured by the Rebels.[1] The last rumor was that Jackson was attacked in the front by Burnside <by> and in the rear by McClellan.[2] It is very hard to get a trustworthy story from the seat of war. New York papers to the 12th. have been recieved.

Last Saturday, the steamship "Star of the South" left here with 57 Rebel prisoners taken at Washington N.C. about three weeks ago. They will be taken to New York. Some of them have been captured the second time, but I believe that all had been exchanged before they went into the Rebel service a second time.

All is quiet in this department.

Write often
Your brother,
John A. Hedrick.

---

[1] Col. Dixon S. Miles surrendered his surrounded and outnumbered Harpers Ferry garrison of ten thousand men to Confederates under Stonewall Jackson on September 15, 1862. Boatner, *Civil War Dictionary*, 20.

[2] McClellan's Union army attacked Lee's much smaller Confederate force at the Battle of Antietam, September 17, 1862. After bloody but inconclusive fighting, Lee withdrew and McClellan did not pursue.

Duke
Beaufort, N.C.
Sept. 25th. 1862,

Dear Brother:

I recieved day before yesterday your letter of the 18th. inst. and two Republicans of the 2nd. of January last. The U.S. transport steamer Geo. C. Collins with about 400 calvarymen arrived here yesterday evening. She brings New York papers of the 21st. inst. The Herald contains an important Rumor from Hagerstown from a reliable man that Jackson and his whole army had surrendered.

[*Charles H.*] Foster did not fulfil his appointment to speak here last Saturday. He came down from Newbern last Thursday, to-day a week, and went to the Banks with the recruiting Sargeant for the purpose of getting enlistments and did not return until Monday. I do not know what kept him there so long. He had also advertised in the Newbern Progress to speak at Cape Lookout banks on Monday, at a church on the Island, Tuesday and at Cedar Island on Wednesday. I think that he did not fulfil any of his appointments. He stopped here on his return but was so offended about something that he would not come to the hotel to get his dinner. I understood that he was angry with the Secessionists and was going to Newbern to get orders to punish them.

I have not heard from Gov. Stanley since he was in New York. It is generally believed here that he will not return to this State. It seems very queer to me that he should leave as he did, if he did not intend to return.[1]

He told me about a week before he left that he had writen to the President for leave of absence to go /to/ Washington; that he wished to see the Administration personally in order that he might know what their policy was on the slavery question; and that he would be gone about a fortnight. He said he could learn more by talking with /the/ President two hours than by writing a week.

Foster seems to be very intimately acquainted with the <u>President</u>. To hear him talk about Uncle Abe, you would think that they had been bed-fellows all of their lives. Foster says that the <u>Black</u> Republicans were willing to admit him to a seat in Congress as a Delegate from the territory of North Carolina but that he was unwilling to disgrace the State to the condition of a territory. I believe this to be a lie and that the Republicans nor no one else <every> with authority to do so ever offered him a seat in Congress.

In his speech before the Union meeting held in the Court House a couple of weeks ago, he did not mention his being a Candidate for Congress. Of course these speeches are mere fore-runners of his campaign harrangues.

Your brother,
John A. Hedrick.

---

[1] Though Stanly did return to North Carolina in the autumn of 1862, he eventually resigned as military governor of North Carolina on January 15, 1863, because of his opposition to the Emancipation Proclamation. Harris, *With Charity For All*, 69-71.

SHC
Beaufort, North Carolina,
Sunday Oct. 5th. 1862,

Dear Brother:

I recieved last Friday your letter of the 23rd. ultimo, two papers and the Patent Office Report for 1861. A mail from the north is expected in, every day.

There are rumors of a delegation having been sent by Jeff. Davis to Washington to propose a compromise. The truth of the rumor I doubt.

I understand that Gov. Stanley is to return to North Carolina Shortly. I do not know where the humbug Foster is. It has been quite warm for the last week. It is hard to tell from the papers what either army is doing. My thoughts brake off to-day so that I had better stop writing. All is quiet in this department.

Your brother,
John A. Hedrick.

Oct. 6th. 1862,

It is considerably cooler this morning. The Rebel paroled prisoners of this place were sent to Wilmington last. There were fifty eight out of one hundred thirty two, who were left here last Spring. I do not know the number that refused to go but not as great as the numbers above would indicate.

I saw last week a young man, who escaped from prison in Wilmington last Thursday a week. He represents that he was taken under the conscript act[1] and refused to serve and was therefor put in jaol. He says that he is the son of the <the> Sheriff of Sampson County. Flour sells at $40 per bbl. salt, $25 per bushel, coffee $2.50 per lb.

I thought that these things were cheap at the prices given, considering the money paid.

The Yellow Fever was in Wilmington at the time he left.[2] He says that there are between 4,000 & 5,000 troops in the forts around Wilmington.

Your brother,
John A. Hedrick.

---

[1] The Confederate Congress passed a conscription act on April 16, 1862, requiring white men between eighteen and thirty-five to serve in the army for three years or until the war's end, whichever came first. There were legal exemptions, and individuals could avoid service by providing someone to take their place. Coulter, *Confederates States of America*, 314.

[2] A yellow fever epidemic began in Wilmington in late summer 1862 and continued to November. About fifteen hundred people contracted the disease. Andrew J. Howell, *The Book of Wilmington, 1730-1930* (n.p., n.d.), 124-128.

Duke
Beaufort, N.C.
Oct. 13th. 1862,

Dear Brother:

I recieved last week two letters from you informing me that Gov. Stanley and Mr. [*Jennings*] Pigott were coming to N.C. Gov. Stanley arrived last Saturday and proceeded to Newbern and Mr. Taylor[1] my landlord recieved a letter from Mr. Pigott informing him that he would have come along with Gov. Stanley if he could have got ready in time.

The Steamer, "United States," which brought Gov. Stanley, proceeded to Port Royal with Gov. Saxton.[2] We have recieved N.Y. papers of the 8th. inst. which give a account of a second battle at Corinth, in which the Union forces, under Gen. Rosencrantz were victorious over the Confederate forces under Gen. Price. Between seven hundred and one thousand prisoners were taken by our arms.[3] We have no news of Gen. McClellan's army. All is quiet in this department, with the arrival of some new troops and more expected. The "Guide" is expected in, every day with a lot of horses.

Refugees come here from Swansboro occasionally. There is one here from Alamance. His name is Sellers.[4] His father lives near Graham and not far from the "Company Workshops." He has joined the Company of Union Volunteers which is raising here. The company has increased to thirty two and has recieved its arms and uniforms. The men look first rate with their sky blue pants and dark blue coats and caps on. I believe that they make a better appearance than the Yankee Soldiers do. Their uniforms make them appear so large that the people call them the<n> "Buffaloes." I think that they like to be called buffaloes. They go about in gangs like herds of buffaloes.

This old man Congleton, whom Mr. Pigott thinks "all talk," was the principal man in getting up this company. He held the two first Union meetings here and although 64 years old was among the first to put his name down on the volunteer list. I find that the old man is not popular here but his being ahead of the times, I believe to be the cause of his unpopularity. He is a strong Abolitionist, and that is enough to damn any man in the estimation of the people here. He was the first man in the State who ran on the Free Suffrage ticket and obtained only about a half of a dozen votes. Davie Reid afterwards took up the same hobby and rode into the gubernatorial chair on it.[5] I think that Mr. Congleton would not get many votes on an Abolition ticket in this County but in the course of ten years some body else will.

The humbug Foster according to the Newbern Progress was going over to Washington and the north Counties last week. If Mr. Pigott comes, you need have no fears about Foster.

Your brother,
John A. Hedrick.

---

[1] George W. Taylor (b. ca. 1814) was a farmer and the proprietor of the Ocean House Hotel. Eighth Census, 1860: Carteret County.

[2] Rufus Saxton (1824-1908) of Massachusetts, a graduate of the United States Military Academy, was commissioned brigadier general of U.S. Volunteers in April 1862. In 1863 and

1864, he served as military governor of the South Carolina and Georgia sea islands, overseeing the employment and enlistment of a large number of African American refugees. John T. Hubbell and James W. Geary, eds., *Biographical Dictionary of the Union: Northern Leaders of the Civil War* (Westport, Conn.: Greenwood Press, 1995), s.v. "Saxton, Rufus."

[3] William S. Rosecrans's Union force defeated the Confederates under Earl Van Dorn and Sterling Price at Corinth, Miss., on October 3-4, 1862. Richard N. Current, ed., *Encyclopedia of the Confederacy*, 4 vols. (New York: Simon and Schuster, 1993), 1:413-415.

[4] Thomas Sellers Jr. (b. ca. 1823) of Alamance County was a farmer. Eighth Census, 1860: Alamance County; Compiled Service Records, Record Group 94.

[5] David S. Reid, a Democrat, was elected governor in 1850 largely due to his advocacy of suffrage reform. Powell, *North Carolina Through Four Centuries*, 301-302.

Duke
Beaufort, N.C.
October 16, 1862,

Dear Brother:

I wrote you last Sunday and informed you that Gov. Stanley had arrived at Morehead and proceed to Newbern last Saturday. The "Guide" has not yet arrived but it is expected every day. I think that Mr. Pigott will come in her. All is quiet here. The weather is cloudy and chilly. Our latest news from the north is that the Confederates had taken Chambersburg, Pa, but with how many troops it is not known. I presume that it amounts to nothing more than /a/ Cavalry raid.[1]

One of the West India vessels returned yesterday with nine puncheons of molasses and thirteen barrels of sugar. The duties will amount to about one hundred and twenty-five dollars. The Captain was directed by the owner of the vessel to bring a cargo of salt but he was afraid to bring salt on account of the leakiness of the vessel. He brought a little more Sugar and Molasses than was ordered but still had to take in stone ballast to keep the vessel on her bottom.

Salt is needed here now very bad. This is the fishing season and the people have not enough of salt to preserve the fish they catch.

The other schooner is expected back in the course of a week or two and will bring a full cargo of salt. I collected during the quarter ending on the 30th. of September, 1862 from Duties on Imports $327.90

Hospital Money . . .	$23.17
Fees for clearances &c. .	$66.40
	$417.47

The fees recieved have heretofore belonged to the Collector as a part of the emoluments of his office but the Commissioner of Customs has directed me to bring them into my Customs Account as the Secretary has fixed a Salary as a compensation for my services. If he has made it $400 per annum, the minimum that I should have for coming here, I will recieve about $40 less for last quarter than the compensation heretofore allowed. During the next three quarters if the war continues I think it probable that the reciepts will not be so large as they were last quarter. I have not yet learned what my Salary is, but have writen to the Commissioner of Customs to let me know.

I wrote to Mr. Goodloe sometime ago but have not recieved any letter from him. I did not make any inquiries so I guess he thought that it did not require an answer. I have not heard any thing from the humbug Foster lately. The Tribune correspondent who calls him the "Administration Candidate" for Congress is mistaken for Foster is a strong proslavery man and says that he does not wish the slavery question discussed until the war is over. He wants slavery to be let alone. He says that all that he has, is in that species of property.

> Write often,
> I am your Brother,
> John A. Hedrick.

---

[1] J. E. B. Stuart led eighteen hundred Confederate cavalrymen in a raid on Chambersburg, Pa., on October 9, 1862, inflicting considerable damage. This daring raid, known as Stuart's "second ride around McClellan," greatly embarrassed the commander of the Army of the Potomac. Boatner, *Civil War Dictionary*, 814.

> *Duke*
> Beaufort, N.C.
> Oct. 20th. 1862,

Dear Brother:

Mr. & Mrs. Pigott arrived here last Saturday evening on the Steamer "Guide." Mr. Pigott is complaining of sickness a little but I think that he will be all right in a day or two. He has not been confined by his sickness at all. Mrs. Pigott was sea-sick pretty much all the way but is now as well as ever. The sea had not quit rolling yet. She says that she can feel the boat rock. All is quiet here. This morning is very nice. It is just about cool enough to be pleasant.

Mrs. Pigott brought me a letter from Mr. Goodloe, I was very glad to get it. Tell him that I will answer it shortly.

Custom House business has been more brisk during the last week. There were four arrivals last Saturday. It seems that the vessels always come in gangs.

I wrote you last week by the steamer "Baltimore" which was going direct to Baltimore. For the last three or four weeks except yesterday I have been writing to you every Sunday. I do not usually have much to do on Sunday. Sometimes I go to church. Yesterday in the forenoon I heard a sermon from the Rev. Mr. Van Antwerp,[1] Episcopal Minister of this place, then dined with Mr. Pigott at one of his Cousin's and spent the greater part of the afternoon with them.

And that caused me to fail to write to you.

Write often,
Your broth,
John A. Hedrick.

---

[1] The Reverend D. D. Van Antwerp (b. ca. 1823), a native of New York, was minister of St. Paul's Episcopal Church in Beaufort and later chaplain of the town's hospital. The *New York Herald* noted that "the Sunday before the landing of our troops, [he] prayed for the safety of and prolongation of Jeff. Davis and his tribe, and the following Sunday the good old prayer for the long continuance of the United States." Eighth Census, 1860: Carteret County; *North Carolina Times* (New Bern), January 23, 1864; *New York Herald*, March 31, 1862.

Duke
Beaufort, N.C.
Oct. 21st. 1862,

Dear Friend:

I recieved last Sunday by the hand of Mrs. Pigott your letter of the 5th. inst. which I was very glad to get. Mr. Pigott was sick yesterday but is out to-day. He knows every body and every thing that has happened here for the last twenty years.

The weather is cloudy and a little chilly. The health of Beaufort is good. I have gained about eight pounds since I left Washington. I weighed this morning 133 pounds. This is my winter weight while I usually weigh in Summer about 125 pounds.

Times are very dull. We have had no news of interest lately. In fact we have quit noticing battles unless there has been at least 2000 killed on each side. Stuart's raid into Pennsylvania created no sensation here. Buel's fight with Price at Corinth made a little fuss when the news first came, but that soon passed away. I can't see how Stuart got into and out of Pennsylvania without meeting with more opposition than he did. Some body is at fault. Mrs. Pigott says that she heard that Stuart was on his way into Pennsylvania again. I guess he gets better provisions and more of them among the

Pennsylvania Dutch than he has recieved during the last six months among the F.F.Vs.[1] of the Old Dominion.

The report of a battle between McClellan and Jackson near Winchester has been expected for the last few days.

You wish to know how the President's Proclamation takes in North Carolina? I have not heard much said either for or against it. I think that it will not make many Secessionists. There are many here who seem willing that the negroes should be freed, provided they be removed from the country. How to get rid of the negroes is the only question with them. They say that if Mr. Lincoln liberates the slaves among them that as soon as the war is over, they will take up arms to exterminate the negroes. I think that they would in time become reconciled with the change and lose their resentful feelings.

The U.S. gunboat Ellis returned from an expedition to New Topsail Inlet yesterday. She found a schooner loaded with Turpentine and Cotton ready to go to sea. Upon seeing the gunboat, the crew of the schooner, ran her aground, set fire to a barrel of Turpentine and deserted the vessel. Men from the gunboat succeeded in extinguishing the flames, but being unable to get the vessel off, fired her again.

A Small expedition started for Swansboro yesterday on a flat but has not been heard from since. It was sent out to see what the secesh were doing around Swansboro.[2]

I am respectfully,
Your friend,
John A. Hedrick.

---

[1] First Families of Virginia.

[2] This expedition is not mentioned in the *Official Records*.

SHC
Beaufort, N.C.
Oct. 27th. /62,

Dear Brother:

I wrote you last Monday. I have recieved no <letter> letter from you since Mr. Pigott arrived. Mrs. Pigott wishes you to tell Mr. Goodloe, to tell his French teacher to inform Nancy[1] that her old master and mistress have arrived here in safety and are in good health. Mr. Pigott has not gone to Newbern yet but expects to go in a few days. The weather is quite cold and blustering to-day. The steamers, Mississippi and Merimac arrived here yesterday with troops and Geo. Peabody[2] is expected with horses. There is no news to write.

> Your brother,
> John A. Hedrick.

---

[1] Nancy Page (b. ca. 1843), an African American and a native of Virginia, was a member of the Pigott household in Washington, D.C. Eighth Census, 1860: District of Columbia, City of Washington, Fourth Ward.

[2] The *George Peabody* was a large steamer that housed Burnside's headquarters during his North Carolina campaign and was thereafter used as a transport. William Marvel, *Burnside* (Chapel Hill: University of North Carolina Press, 1991), 43.

> *SHC*
> Beaufort, N.C.
> Oct. 31st. /62,

Dear Brother:

It has been a long time since I have recieved a letter from you. Pigott and his wife are well. They have not been to Newbern yet but will go shortly. I have just completed my account of Customs for the month of October. I owe the United States $917.33 on account of Collections and $47.29 on disbursements.

> Write oftener,
> Your brother,
> John A. Hedrick.

> *SHC*
> Beaufort, N.C.
> Nov. 2nd. /62,

Dear Brother:

I have written you five letters since I recieved your last. It is probable that you are not altogether to blame for my not getting letters from you; For last Friday a Steamer arrived at Newbern with a Northern mail, just as Gen. Foster was leaving on an expedition up Neuse River,[1] which the general took from the boat and carried with him. He has not returned it yet. It may have been very important that Gen. Foster should get any dispatch that the mail might contain but I think that he could have done so without taking all the mail with him. You may expect to hear of a battle up towards Goldsboro soon.

Mr. and Mrs. Pigott are well and still here. They have determined not to go to Newbern until they learn the result of the expedition now under way. There are about fifty soldiers in town. All that could be spared, were sent to Newbern last week, to go with Gen. Foster.

Our latest Northern papers are of the 28th. of last month. There are only two of them here and I have not been able to get hold of them but I understand that there has been no recent fighting on the Potomac.

We have news of a meeting shortly to take place in Washington City, of the Governors of some of the loyal States, for the purpose of considering certain propositions offered by <u>influential</u> <u>Southern</u> men.[2] If the meeting should /be/ held, which I think very doubtful, in my opinion, it would result in no good. It is also reported that Halleck[3] is to be sent West again and that McClellan is to be made General-in-Chief with Hooker,[4] General-in-the-field.

I moved my office yesterday. I am in very nice quarters now. All I lack now is a few chairs and /a/ bookcase. Then give me a good Salary and I would be at home. By the way I have not learned, what my Salary is.

Mrs. Pigott wishes you to see Mr. Marribone and write me in your next letter. Mrs. & Mr. Pigott send their repects to you, Sister Ellen and Mr. Goodloe. Gov. Stanly writes Mr. Pigott that Sister Ellen's letters have been sent through the military lines.

Nov. 3rd. 1862,

The weather is very fine this morning. The Steamer Guide is coming into the harbor. I hope she will have some late news.

The humbug Foster has not been here lately. There is no danger of his being elected if Mr. Pigott is in the field.

Your brother,
John A. Hedrick

---

[1] This expedition, made up of five thousand men and twenty-one pieces of artillery, departed Washington, N.C., on November 2, to capture three Confederate regiments collecting forage in Hyde and Washington Counties. Foster had traveled to Washington to head the expedition a few days before. Troops in the expedition destroyed the towns of Williamston and Hamilton, contrary to Foster's orders. Barrett, *Civil War in North Carolina*, 136-138.

[2] Twelve governors met in Altoona, Pa., September 24, 1862. After pledging their support for the administration and the Emancipation Proclamation, they traveled to Washington and

met with Lincoln on the afternoon of September 26. William B. Hesseltine, *Lincoln and the War Governors* (New York: Alfred A. Knopf, 1948), 253-261.

[3] Henry Wager Halleck (1815-1872) was general-in-chief of the Union army from July 1862 to March 1864. Boatner, *Civil War Dictionary*, 367.

[4] Joseph Hooker (1814-1879) commanded the Army of the Potomac from January 26 to June 28, 1863. Sifakis, *Who Was Who in the Civil War*, 317.

SHC
Beaufort, N.C.
Nov. 9th. 1862,

Dear Brother:

I recieved last week your letter of the 24th. ult. which is the only letter that I have had from you during the last three weeks. Your letter of the 18th. has not reached me. It has been more than a week since we have had a Northern Mail. The last arrived in Newbern last Friday a week [*ago*] but did not get here till Tuesday, because it was carried away by Gen. Foster on his Expedition. I have not yet learned where the Expedition has gone: It is probable that they intend to menace Weldon in the rear while the forces from Suffolk attack the town in front. The Expedition started from Washington, N.C. and had a skirmish with the enemy about 15 miles N.W. from that place, where 11 of our men were killed. They may be making a feint towards Weldon with the intention of attacking Goldsboro.

We have had very cold weather for the last three days. There was considerable frost last night. I presume that you have felt colder weather than I have, this Fall, but it is so damp here that the cold air affects a person much more than it does in Washington. Our coldest weather is when the wind is from the South.

Lieut. Gladding[1] of the 5th. R.I. Battalion, for whom I brought a packet from Mr. Gilson, died a little over a week ago at the Hospital. His Battalion was sent to Newbern about the 1st. of August and some time in September he was down here, and I saw him and asked him how Newbern agreed with him and he said that he liked it very well. I had not seen or heard any thing further from him till about a month ago when I learned that he was at the Hospital and in a critical condition. I saw Dr. Babbit[2] of the Hospital a few days afterwards and he told me that the Lieutenant had been very low but was getting better. I put off going to see him from day to day till last week, when I inquired about him and was told that he was dead. Some of the men that have been sent there from Newbern, Havelock Station and Newport, have died very suddenly. Lieut. Springer[3] of a N.J. Reg. came down on the cars one evening and stopped at the Hotel <one evening>, somewhat sick at the time, but was not thought to be dangerously so, was carried to the Hospital next morning and died the following evening.

Mr. Pigott and lady are still here. Mrs. Pigott did not come to the table at breakfast and dinner, but I guess she is not seriously ill. I am in good health.

> Your brother,
> John A. Hedrick

---

[1] Munro H. Gladding, quartermaster of the Fifth Regiment Rhode Island Heavy Artillery. Burlingame, *History of the Fifth Regiment of Rhode Island Heavy Artillery,* 97, 265.

[2] Robert A. Babbitt later became surgeon of the First North Carolina Union Regiment. He died of yellow fever in Beaufort in October 1864. John A. Hedrick to Benjamin S. Hedrick, October 18, 1864, Hedrick Papers, Duke Special Collections, in this volume; Janet B. Hewett, ed., *The Roster of Union Soldiers, 1861-1865, . . . North Carolina . . .* (Wilmington, N.C.: Broadfoot Publishing, 1998), 533.

[3] This is probably a reference to 2d Lt. Charles B. Springer of Company I, Ninth New Jersey Infantry. Hewett, *Roster of Union Soldiers, New Jersey and Delaware,* 275.

SHC
[Nov. 14th, 1862]

Statement of money received from and paid to B.S. Hedrick, from Sept. 22nd 1859 to June 2nd 1862.

				Received	Paid
1859,	Sept.	22nd	By Cash	— —	256.00
"	"	24th	" "	5.00	— —
"	"	28th	Suit of Clothes	25.00	— —
"	Oct.	5th	Oedipus Tyrannus	.75	— —
			Loomis Nat. Philos.	1.00	— —
			Walker's Reid	.75	— —
			Sophocles	.75	— —
			Whateley's Rhetoric	.38	— —
			Contingent Expenses	5.00	— —
			French book	1.25	— —
			Guizot	1.00	— —
			Overcoat & C	30.00	— —
1859,	Dec.	29th	Cash	5.00	— —
1860,	Jan.	28th	"	1.00	— —
"	"	31st	"	5.00	— —
"	Feb.	25th	"	1.00	— —

"	March	31st	"	1.00	——
"	April	7th	"	3.00	——
"	"	12th	"	1.00	——
"	May	3rd	"	7.00	——
"	"	17th	"	1.25	——
"	"	18th	"	——	35.00
"	"	"	Gray's Anatomy	5.00	——
"	July	19th	Cash	1.00	——
"	Aug.	27th	"	——	51.00
				$102.13	$342.00

[*End of page of original document*]

Continued.

				Received	Paid
1861			Amt brought forward	102.13	342.00
"	Jan.	8th	By Cash	——	80.00
"	"	15th	"	——	5.00
"	"	16th	Sis Ellen	——	.25
"	Feb.	5th	"	——	.25
"	"	6th	"	—.50	——
"	"	8th	"	——	—.04
"	"	14th	By Cash	——	1.00
"	"	"	Sis Ellen	——	—.25
"	"	17th	By Cash	1.00	——
"	"	22nd	Sis Ellen	——	—.05
"	March,	1st	P. Stamps for Sis Ellen	——	—.12
"	"	9th	Sis Ellen	——	3.00
"	"	"	" P. Stamp	——	—.03
"	"	18th	2. 3s & 1. 2ct Stamp	——	—.08
"	"	29th	Sis. Ellen	—.02	——
"	Apr.	9th	"	1.25	——
"	"	13th	"	7.00	——
"	"	17th	"	——	—.03
"	"	22nd	"	——	—.03
"	"	24th	"	—.06	——
"	"	25th	"	—.06	——
"	"	27th	"	—.25	——
"	"	30th	"	—.25	——
"	"	"	"	2.00	——
"	May	6th	Breakfast at St. Germain	—.30	——
"	"	7th	" "	—.30	——
"	"	8th	By Cash	20.00	——
"	"	10th	"	——	—.50

"	Aug	10th	Washing	— —	2.00
"	"	30th	By Cash	—.25	— —
				$135.37	$ 434.63

[*End of page of original document*]

Continued.

				Received	Paid
1861.	Oct.		Amtt brought forward	135.37	434.63
"	"		By Cash	—.50	— —
"	Dec.	4th	"	25.00	— —
"	"	23rd	"	— —	12.00
1862,	March	27th	Fixing Trunk Lock	— —	—.25
"	"	"	Carrying Trunk to Depot	— —	—.25
"	"	28th	"　　　"　from "	— —	—.25
"	June	2nd	By Cash	10.25	— —
				$171.12	$447.38

The above is as accurate as my account book will give.

I owe you for Board, Lodging & Washing while in New York, at $5 per week, from the 21st. of September 1859 to the 1st. of May 1861. From this is to be deducted by agreement, $3.50 for Board 1 week while at Mr. Pierces. I owe you for Board, Lodging & Washing, price not stated, while in Washington City, from the 18th. May to the 6th. December 1861; from the 18th. to the 28th. December 1861, and from the 28th. March to the 2nd. June 1862. It would have been better If I had left the $2, out of my cash account, that I paid towards washing, and had you to deduct it from my Board, Lodging and Washing account while in Washington City, but I did not think of it when I was drawing off the account.

I have given above, statements of the amounts recieved from and paid to you, and of the several periods for which, I owe you for Board, Lodging and Washing. If there be any items, which I have omitted, you will please bring them into your account and forward the account to me at your earliest convenience.

I have not the money to pay you now, but it will be some satisfaction to me to know how much my indebtedness is.

I have been sick for the last three days and am not well now. I took cold during the cold weather that we had at the beginning of the week, and it has not worked itself out yet. Besides I have a painful bile arising in my lower lip, which is very slow in coming to a head. I have some fever withal, but I apprehend nothing serious from it.

The Herald Special Correspondent was right about Foster's making a speech here on the 21st. <of> Ult. I wrote you the same morning but did not know at the time that a meeting was to be held and so did not mention it. When I wrote next, it had all escaped my memory. The meeting did not amount to much. I was not there but learned from Mr. Davis, who was, that he was the only citizen present. Foster had his Sancho Panza,[1] Carpenter.[2] There were a number of soldiers in attendance. You my regard nearly all the dispatches from this section to Northern papers, either as falsehoods or exagerations. You need have no present fears about Foster. The Expedition that I mentioned in my last, has returned, having gone as far as Hamilton. It seems to have been a failure as far as this department is concerned. There seems to be a general skedaddling by the Rebels, both citizens and soldiers, on the approach of our soldiers. The Rebels drove in our pickets at Newbern and killed three day before yesterday morning. There had been no further disturbance when the train left Newbern yesterday morning.

I am you brother,
John A. Hedrick

---

[1] Sancho Panza was the hero's loyal companion in Cervantes's *Don Quixote*.

[2] Ed W. Carpenter (b. ca. 1833) was a New Bern attorney and president of the local Free Labor Association. During Reconstruction he served several times as Republican clerk of the Craven County Superior Court. *New Bern Progress*, October 25, December 18, 1862; Alan D. Watson, *A History of New Bern and Craven County* (New Bern, N.C.: Tryon Palace Commission, 1987), 430, 475-476, 482, 492; Ninth Census, 1870: Craven County.

SHC
Beaufort, N.C.
Nov. 18th. 1862,

Dear Brother:

By reference to Statement in my letter of Friday last you will percieve that I have omitted an item of $40 that I paid you on the 25th. Sept. 1860. The whole amount which I have paid you is $487.38. I owe you for Board while in New York,

Eighty-three weeks, 3 days at $5 per week . . .	$417.14
In Washington Board &c 38 weeks & 6 days	
Money recd. from 22nd. Sept. 1859	
to the 2nd. June 1862	171.12
You owe me for money received from	
21st. Sept. 1859 to the 2nd. June 1862 . . .	$487.38
Board 1 week at Pierces . .	3.50
	$490.88 [*total*]

I feel quite well to-day. My lip is subsiding somewhat so that I can eat and drink again. I have been very much bothered about drinking. My lower lip was so thick in the middle that a hole was left on each side of my mouth for the liquid to run out. Mr. & Mrs. Pigott went to Newbern last Friday and I have not heard from them since. I recieved yesterday the Tribune of the 5th. inst for which I am obliged to you.

> Your brother,
> John A. Hedrick

SHC
Beaufort, N.C.
Nov. 23rd. 1862,

Dear Brother:

I recieved yesterday your letters of Oct. 18th. and Nov. 11th. 1862.

The humbug Foster made a speech here on the 21st. October, which I did not hear. There were only a few people at the meeting and most of them were soldiers. Carpenter was with him and made a few remarks at the close of Foster's address, and begged to be excused from further remarks as he wished to go to Newbern on the train that afternoon. Carpenter has opened a law office in Newbern and is a correspondent of the N.Y. Tribune, so I have been told by Dr. Page. Foster also advertized himself in the Newbern Progress as Attorney at Law and solicits patronage. You need never expect any truth in the news, in the Tribune, from N.C. so long as Carpenter and Foster, are the correspondents.

Dr. Page arrived here from N.Y. about the middle of last week. He says that he is at a loss to know how to attack Foster. He is such a scoundrel that he would be hard to hurt. I do not think that an article in the Tribune would do any good at present. Besides I doubt whether the Tribune would publish the articles. You did wrong in not exposing his rascality the time he was before the Committee of Elections.[1] I never could see how it would disgrace us as /a/ nation to let the world know that we would not admit impostors into our national legislature.

Mr. & Mrs. Pigott went to Newbern last Friday was a week and have not returned <yet>. I saw a letter last week from Mr. Pigott. He seemed to be well pleased with Newbern and expected to stay there longer than he intended when he left here. The election seems to progress very slowly and it looks rather doubtful whether any will be ordered. I am sure that I will not object to its postponement till after the 1st. of January 1863, <that>

so that this whole state will be included in Mr. Lincoln's Emancipation proclamation. I have seen others of the same way of thinking. So/me/ of the<se> Union Volunteers had their names taken from the list of petitioners to Gov. Stanly to order an election because they were afraid that an Election might have an evil effect on emancipation. I do not believe that there is a single proslavery man in this State who is sound on the Union question. Some have negroes, who are not proslavery in their views. Some of these are trustworthy; but not all. The poor people seem to be well contented and say that they are doing as well as they have ever done. The way produce is selling now I think that they ought to be satisfied.

Turpentine is selling for $12 whereas it used to bring about $1.50 per barrel, Grown hens are worth 80 cts a pair.

I recieved yesterday a letter from Mr. Harrington, Dated Oct. 28th. 1862, in which he says that the Salary of the Collector of Beaufort, by Act. 3 March 1803 is $200, with emoluments.

I was aware of that before writing to the Secretary about my Salary. I knew moreover that by the Act of May 7th. 1822, the Salary of the Collector of Beaufort, N.C. was raised to $250 per annum: but by the letter of the Commissioner of Customs of Oct. 1st. I was instructed to bring my Fees into my collection accounts as the Sec. had fixed me a Salary. This is a thing which I think he has no right to do, and having found himself in a scrape he is trying to get out of it, the best way he can.

Mr. Harrington says that if there has been any mistake on this point, referring to my salary &c, in the rendering of my accounts, it will be rectified hereafter in their settlement.

The Sec. should have had a special act of Congress increasing my salary. The duties are much greater than they were before the war and the responsibility four times what it was. Together with the Confederate Bonds, I have about $3000 of money in my hands.

The only Act of Congress, passed by the last session, that I /have/ seen, relating to the southern ports is one enabling the Sec. to appoint Temporary Collectors at ports, which may hereafter be opened, with a Salary not exceeding that recieved in 1859. Of course that does /not/ effect my Salary; because I am not a Temporary Collector and my appointment was made before the passage of the Act.

You need not tell the Secretary that I said that he had no right to raise my Salary but that is my belief. Mr. Harrington promised us in the passage of the Treasury Department that he would see that my Salary was raised. I think that he should have done so.

My present Salary and the old emoluments will amount to more than $400 per annum, so that if you go to see Mr. Chase about my Salary don't mention the $400 but try to get him to raise the Salary part to $800 or $1000 with the Fees usually allowed besides. Then I think that all will amount to $1000 or $1200. I should by rights have that much at least. I think that I will be in Washington about the middle of January. I was instructed to cause my Demand Notes to be deposited at the nearest U.S. Depositary when /ever/ they amounted to $300. I have $680 of them and there is no express here by which to send them.

Your brother,
John A. Hedrick

[*P.S.*]: (I would be pleased if you would get and send me a bunch or two of large Envelopes. They can't be obtained here.)

---

[1] Charles Henry Foster claimed that he was entitled to a seat in the Thirty-seventh Congress based on an election held November 28, 1861, on Hatteras Island. The Congressional Committee of Elections rejected Foster's claim, partly due to information supplied to them by Benjamin Hedrick. Norman C. Delaney, "Charles Henry Foster and the Unionists of Eastern North Carolina," *North Carolina Historical Review* 37 (July 1960): 359-362.

SHC
Beaufort, N.C.
Nov. 26th. 1862,

Dear Brother:

I wrote you last Sunday a long letter on short paper and now I expect to write you a short letter on long paper.

Nothing of interest has happened in this department since I wrote you last.

Dr. Page was here yesterday looking up some goods shipped to the Sanitary Commission on board the Strs. Mississippi, and Merrimack. He came in about 12 M, stayed half an hour, left for Morehead, and as he did not come back in the evening, I presume, he went on the train to Newbern. He said that he found Foster and Carpenter comfortably ensconced in his quarters on his arrival in Newbern. They have left them.

Some time since you wished to know what I did for clothing? I do without. One pair of pants, one colored shirt and ten paper colars are <the only> all the clothing that I have bought since I came through New York. Had I known, a few weeks before you went, that you were going to N.Y. I would have sent with you for a suit of clothes. I do not understand how it is that Mr. Watkins has mixed our names. My clothing bills always came properly directed.

I have not heard any thing from Mr. Pigott since I wrote you last. Dr. Page said that he had been so busy since his return to North Carolina, that he had not had time to call on any one. My lip has assumed its natural dimensions and feels quite comfortable. The weather is clear with a strong S.W. gale blowing.

Your brother,
John A. Hedrick.

SHC
Beaufort, N.C.
Nov. 30th. 1862,

Dear Brother:

I wrote you about the middle of last week and also last Sunday. The last letter that I have recieved from you is dated 11th. Nov. 1862. Our Mail facilities are getting worse all the time. It has been over a week since we have had a Northern Mail. We however have New York papers of the 26th. and the Baltimore Sun of the 27th. inst. which were brought by the Str. Guide, She arrived here yesterday, I have not seen the papers but I understand that there is nothing of importance in them.

The Strs. "Mississippi" and "Merrimack," of Boston, and from Boston arrived off the bar yesterday morning. A strong N.W. wind blowed all day yesterday and lowered the water so much on the bar that they could not come in. Besides there was a pretty heavy sea on. They measure 2000 tons and draw 16 feet of water. They have been in here twice before and brought 3000 troops each time. I have not heard how many they have on board now. All has been quiet in this Department since I wrote you last.

I have not heard from Mr. and Mrs. Pigott for nearly two weeks. I presume they are fareing so well at Gov. Stanly's that they do not wish to come back to this old town.

I mean to write to Sec. Chase again concerning my compensation for services. I wish him to permit me to make a change in my subordinates. I wish to perform the duty of Inspector in connection with that of Collector. The Inspector's pay is three dollars per day when employed. This additional duty at present would employ about half of my time and I could easily spare three fourths of it, unless the duties of the Collector's office greatly increases. I would then have the Custom House Boat at my own command and would then <I> have /a/ chance to visits the vessels as they come in. The offices of Inspector, Weigher, Guager, and Measurer are now combined in one but there was a time when the offices of Collector and Inspector were combined.

I am well,
Your brother,
John A. Hedrick,

SHC
Beaufort, N.C.
Dec. 7th. 1862,

Dear Brother:

Your letters of the 14th. 21st. & 26th. /Nov./ reached me yesterday. I shall hereafter acknowledge each of your letters by date, so that if you will keep a record of letters sent me, by date, you can tell whether I get them all. I am pretty sure that I have not recieved any thing like one per week. It had been over two weeks since we had the previous Mail. The boat that brought our last mail arrived at Newbern last Friday and another got in yesterday, so that we will have another mail to-morrow. The cars run but carry no mail on Sunday.

I have forgotten what Mrs. Pigott wished you to see M. Maruel for. I guess she merely wished to know how they were getting on. I am sure she had no message to send him.

The humbug Foster did make a speech here on the 21st. of last October.

You are to understand from my letter that at the end of the month of October, I had over $900.00 of Uncle Sam's money in hands, which I had collected between the 1st. of June and the 31st. of October, 1862. I retain the money collected by me subject to the orders of the Secretary of the Treasury. I intend to ask the Secretary's permission <to deposit> to allow me to deposit it in Baltimore or Washington. Ten cents per mile is allowed for travelling to deposit money.

Thanks to you for your kind remembrance of me on Thanksgiving day. We kept the same day in this Department but it did not amount to any thing so far as I was concerned.

In the first statement of our accounts, I omitted $40.00, which I brought into the second. At the end of this quarter, I think I shall have some money for you and the University.

I wrote you sometime ago what Mr. Harrington said in relation to my Salary. I wish the Secretary would settle difinitely what he intends to do about it. It would relieve me from a great deal of suspense. Because if I should pay out the Fee Money, which legally belongs to me, and then he should draw on me for the amount, it would place me in a bad situation. This money at present is doing me no good whatever and I should know whether I am to have it or some other and if other, how much. I have been in the United States service a little over six months and the amount, that I have recieved from the Treasurer for my own use, is $83.79. Another quarter's Salary ($62.30), however will be due at the end of this month.

The latest paper here, is the New York Herald of the 2nd. inst. which I have not read. I learn that there is no war news from the Potomac.

I saw this morning a letter dated Dec. 2, 1862, from Jennings Pigott. He is Gov. Stanly's Private Secretary, says that Mrs. P. is well pleased with Newbern and that there will be no election in this State for some time.

Foster made a speech here at the Court House a few days ago. I did not feel enough of interest in it to go to hear him. Carpenter also made one. A report of them was given in the Newbern Progress. Foster says that he is no Abolitionist and never will be, but that he is in favor of Free Labor and of delivering the poor "white trash" from beneath the yoke of the Slave Oligarchy. Should a person, not acquainted with the parties, see the report of the meeting, he might think that there was a powerful Union party here. The report says that it was <the> acknowledged by the oldest citizens to have been the largest meeting ever held in the town of Beaufort.

It claims to have been held under the auspices of the Free Labor Association[1] of Beaufort, which elected Abraham Congleton, President and a Mr. Babbitt,[2] Secretary. Foster has a law office in Newbern but is down here quite often. When here, however, he does not come round to the Hotel and consequently I have not seen him in about two months. He stays at the quarters of the N.C. Volunteer Company raised at this place

Dr. Page has called to see me twice since his return to North Carolina. He looks harty and stout. I did not recognize him immediately the first night he came. I thought that it was he but was not sure until I saw his name on the Hotel Register. He did not know me either for some time. I guess I had changed more than he had since we saw each other last.

He says that he is at a loss to know how to attack Foster. He thinks that it must be done here and not in any of the Northern papers. If he is let alone awhile he will kill himself. I have no fear of him. You think that Mr. Pigott ought to show him up in the Newbern Progress. That would be difficult to do at present. Because in my opinion he and Carpenter have the principal management of the paper. I know that they write a great many editorials for it. Besides he pretends to be busily engaged in raising his Regiment of N.C. Volunteers,[3] which I believe would have been nearer full now had he remained out of the state, than it is; yet it would look wrong to attack a man engaged in so good a cause, and /it/ would have a bad effect. You will have to wait for events to take their course and I have no doubt but that you will see him take the downward one never to come up again. I shall write you from time to time what news I can about the scoundrel.

I have not heard of the arrival of the metalic coffin for the remains of Lieut. Gladding. Prof. Jillson[4] said that it would leave in a steamer the same week he wrote.

The weather is very cold to-day for this latitude. The ice over ponds back of town was half of an inch thick this morning.

I am well and weigh about as much as usual.

> Write often and long
> letters,
> Your brother,
> John A. Hedrick.

---

[1] The Free Labor Association membership consisted almost exclusively of nonslaveholding whites who wished to free slaves in order to deport them. They disapproved of both slave owners and African Americans. Many members of the association also served in the First North Carolina Union Regiment. Brown, "A Union Election," 391.

[2] Samuel Babbitt. *New Bern Progress*, December 4, 1862.

[3] Charles Henry Foster had been promised that he would be appointed lieutenant colonel of the Second North Carolina Union Regiment if he could enlist enough volunteers. Delaney, "Charles Henry Foster," 365.

[4] Professor Jillson was the head of the U.S. Patent Office Library. *Scientific American*, April 27, 1861.

SHC
Beaufort, N.C.
Dec. 10th. 1862,

Dear Brother:

I wrote you on the 7th. inst. and recieved by Monday's Mail yours of the 29th. ultimo, and by yesterday's yours of the 17th. of November last.

I computed the time for my boarding in New York thus: [*His computations totaled eighty-three weeks and three days.*]

I have not counted over the days and weeks from Sept. 21, '59 to May 1, '61 and so you may be right.

On the 8th. of September last, the Commissioner of Customs directed me to charge myself in my collection account with the amount of Fees recieved. Upon the reception of his letter, I wrote him, asking whether the fees did not form a part of the emoluments of my office. He then wrote me, "I have in reply to your letter of the 24th. ultimo, to iform you, that the compensation authorized by the Secretary of the Treasury to be paid to you, is a fixed Salary, and therefore it is considered proper that the fees should be accounted for in the manner stated in my letter of 8th. Sept." I then wrote him, asking him what that Salary was, and about two weeks ago recieved from Mr. Harrington the following reply: "The Salary of the Collector of Beaufort is fixed by the act of March 3, 1803 at $200 = per annum, in addition to the fees and other emoluments established by law, resulting from the business transacted at your port. Should there have been any mistake on this point in the rendering of your accounts, it will be rectified hereafter in their settlement."

Two hundred dollars was the Salary by the Act of March 3, 1803 but it /was/ raised to $250 = by Act of May 7, 1822. This is all that I have recieved in relation to my Salary. You wish to know the amounts total collected by me for the different months. I can do this best by giving you the following tabular statement.

	Duties on Imports.	Hospital Money.	C. House Fees.	Total.
June, 1862	——	2.48	10.00	12.48
July, "	——	4.70	34.00	38.70
August "	327.90	18.10	27.00	373.00
September "	——	.37	5.40	5.77
October "	448.13	8.15	31.30	487.58
November "	38.64	6.25	18.80	63.69
	$814.67	$40.05	$126.50	$981.22

The amount of the column, headed "Custom House Fees," by law belongs to me and three per cent of the balance when deposited <and>/or/ paid by order of the Secretary of the Treasury. The first column is composed of gold, silver and Demand Notes, the rest, Legal Tender Notes.

There is an Expedition[1] on foot but I don't know against what point.

A new Captain for the Cutter arrived here today and hence my time has been occupied all the evening, so you must excuse me from writing more.

The weather is pleasant and I am well and the supper bell is ringing. Good evening to you -

Your brother,
John A. Hedrick.

---

[1] This expedition would leave New Bern on the morning of the next day, December 11, for Goldsboro. Barrett, *Civil War in North Carolina*, 139.

SHC
Beaufort, N.C.
Sunday, Dec. 14th. /62,

Dear Brother:

I wrote you on the 7th. & 10th. insts. and have had no letter from you since the latter date. I am well and the weather is warm and pleasant.

The Str, "Guide," arrived here this morning, bringing Baltimore papers of the 11th. The bombardment of Fredericksburg had commenced, and the City was reported in flames.[1] I did not hear any other news of much interest. We have had no news from the N.C. Expedition, since it left Newbern three days ago. It is probable that Goldsboro will be taken before this reaches you, unless this fizzles out like [John G.] Foster's other Expedition did.[2]

Gov. Stanly has ordered an election for a Representative from the 2nd. Congressional district to be held on Thursday, the 1st. day of January 1863. To-morrow at 2 o'clock a meeting is to be held at the Court House to nominate a Candidate. I guess that Mr. Pigott will get the nomination.

Your brother,
John A. Hedrick.

---

[1] He is referring to the Battle of Fredericksburg, Va., December 13, 1862. Beginning on December 11, Union artillery shelled the city to drive out Confederate sharpshooters. Denney, *Civil War Years*, 240.

[2] This expedition, over ten thousand strong, was to destroy the Wilmington and Weldon Railroad near Goldsboro, in particular the bridge over the Neuse River. The Union force inflicted only superficial damage, however, which the Confederates quickly repaired. Barrett, *Civil War in North Carolina*, 138-148. For John G. Foster's report on the expedition, see *OR*, ser. 1, 18:54-59.

SHC
Beaufort, N.C.
Dec. 16th. / 62,

Dear Brother:

I wrote you Sunday Dec. 14th. /62. We have had no Northern Mail in more than a week. The news from the N.C. Expedition is meager. It was reported here yesterday that our troops had taken Kinston, which is midway between Newbern and Goldsboro. There were various reports about Bank's Expedition[1] being off Wilmington, the taking of Weldon and Halifax &c, which need confirmation.

We had a meeting at the Court House, yesterday and a speech from Mr. Pigott. He announced himself, a Candidate for Congress. There was no formal nomination of a candidate made, as there were so many factions in the meeting that they could not agree upon any person. Messrs. Pigott, Willis and [*Charles H.*] Foster, have announced themselves as candidates. The election will take place on the 1st. of January 1863 and therefore very little time is left for electioneering. Mrs. Pigott came down with her husband and sends her respects to you and family.

Your brother,
John A. Hedrick.

---

[1] Hedrick is referring to an expedition that was outfitted to assault Wilmington in a joint land and naval attack. Twelve thousand men assembled in Beaufort in January 1863 in preparation for the attack, but authorities in Washington abandoned the venture in favor of an assault on Charleston, S.C. Nathaniel Banks was one of the commanders involved in the preparations. Barrett, *Civil War in North Carolina*, 150 n.

SHC
Beaufort, N.C.
Sunday, Dec. 21st. / 62

Dear Brother:

I recieved yesterday yours of the 6th. inst. If you go to New York, I wish you to pay the amount of my bill to the University[1] and obtain my Diploma.

Dr. Ferris[2] told me last Summer that it was ready for me. If it had not already been made out I would have preferred Mayor Opdyke's to Mayor

Woods name to it.[3] I wish you also to get Mr. Watkins to make me a full suit of Every day clothes. Tell him to have no binding about the coat & vest, and lining that will last well. I leave the color to you and the style to him. I want a nice suit. If he can get them done while you are in the city, take them with you to Washington; if not, have them sent to you, as I expect to be in Washington some time during next month. You may pay him for them or not, as can be agreed upon between you. I can pay either of you for them at any time. My last measure, I think was taken in March, 1861. The bill that you paid will give the date.

We have N.Y. papers of the 17th. inst. They contain very sad news from the Army of the Potomac. Burnside's attack, repulse, loss and retreat are given.[4]

When last heard from, Gen. Foster had taken a small town half way between Kinston and Goldsboro, and expected to return to Newbern without taking the latter place.

Gov. Stanley came down yesterday and is here now. He offers me the position of Private Secretary and thinks he can give me $1200 or $1500 per annum. He is authorized to employ a Private Secretary with a compensation equal to that allowed the Private Secretary of the civil Governor of this State.

By the law of N.C. the Governor's Private Secretary recieves a Salary of $300 and fees for issuing commissions to different State and Federal officers &c, which all together, usually amounts to $1200 or $1500 a year. The fees, at present, would amount to nothing, while the work to be performed, would be much greater than that performed by the civil Governor's Private Secretary, so I presume that Mr. Chase would allow me as much as the Private Secretary usually recieves. I ask your opinion about my taking the position offered, though I expect to take it any how, if the Governor will insure me $1200. It is better than my present position, which has a great deal of responsibility and very little pay. If I take the position, I cannot enter upon the duties of my office, before the 1st. of next February. I cannot get any percentage on the money I have collected until it is deposited; and besides I would like for Uncle Sam to pay me 10 cts per mile for riding to Washington and back. I have to employ a Special Deputy at my own expense during my absence. I expect to send in his name and official oath sometime next week and apply for leave of absence. Then I shall have to wait for my leave to come, which I think will not be before the middle of January next. Then should a steamer happen to be here, I will be in Washington before the last of the month. The Secretary may be unwilling to grant me leave, and then I shall have to resign without making the deposit.

Christmas will soon be here and I wish a happy Christmas to you all.

The election, as stated in two previous letters, will take place on New Years day. I have no doubt but that Mr. Pigott will be elected.

It is quite cold to-day. Last night, I have been told, the thermometer went down to 24° F. We had no snow the time you mention your having some.

I do not know how many brothers the humbug Foster has. He told me the first time I saw him in N.C. that he had one on Gen. McClellan's Staff,[5] and another in the Rebel army. I have been told by some gentlemen from Maine that he has a brother in that State, a Methodist preacher, who is as grand a scoundrel as the Hon. C.H.F. himself.

> Write often,
> Your brother,
> John A. Hedrick.

---

[1] Cooper Institute.

[2] Isaac Ferris (1798-1873) was chancellor of the University of the City of New York from 1852 to 1870. *National Cyclopedia of American Biography*, s.v. "Ferris, Isaac."

[3] Incumbent Democrat Fernando Wood lost a closely contested election for mayor of New York in 1861 to Republican George Opdyke. Wood had dismissed Benjamin Hedrick from his clerkship in the mayor's office after his 1859 election. Edward K. Spann, *The New Metropolis: New York City, 1840-1857* (New York: Columbia University Press, 1981), 358-397; Samuel Augustus Pleasants, *Fernando Wood of New York* (New York: Columbia University Press, 1948), 126.

[4] Hedrick again refers to the Battle of Fredericksburg. The Union army suffered 12,653 casualties, the Confederates 5,309. Long, *Civil War Day by Day*, 296.

[5] Benjamin B. Foster (b. ca. 1832), brother of Charles Henry Foster, entered the army on November 1, 1861, as a first lieutenant in the Eleventh Maine Infantry. He was promoted to major and became an assistant adjutant general on October 7, 1862. He later served in that capacity under Maj. Gen. John J. Peck, and in his absence, Brig. Gen. Innis Palmer. Seventh Census, 1850: Penobscot County, Maine; Heitman, *Historical Register*, 1:431, *OR*, ser. 1, 33:54, 61.

SHC
Beaufort, N.C.
Dec. 25th. 1862,

Dear Brother:

We have had quite stirring times during the last two days. The Congressional campagne is in full blaze & you, Mr. Goodloe, and myself are getting all the vituperation that a vile tongue can heap upon us. The humbug Foster made a speech last night at the Court House. He commenced at 6 ½ P.M. and was continuing at 9, when I left there. He said that Mr. Pigott was an Abolitionist and as proof of this, he said that he had never seen Mr. Pigott but once and then he was in company with you and Mr. Goodloe. Said that Mr. Goodloe had been driven from the state sixteen and you six years /ago/ for your abolition sentiments — that he had some respect for a Mass. Abolitionist, but none for one from a slaveholding State — that he was no abolitionist, yet was in favor of Free Labor and was pledged to put an end to slavery before the war ends — that he was the poor man's friend and was going to array the poor against the rich. He is the completest demagogue I ever saw.

A man was there by the name of Bowen,[1] who lives near Plymouth, but happened to be down here last evening, and on learning that Foster was to make a speech, said he would go and hear him, as he had heard him make a bitter Secesh speech in Plymouth before the war broke out. Mr. Bowen stayed at the Court House about 2 ½ hours to get a chance to reply to him, but getting tired of waiting he left and had it announced this morning that a meeting would be held at 10 A.M. at the Market. Foster was invited to be present. He came at the appointed hour and on introducing Mr. Bowen to the audience, he took occasion to say that Mr. Bowen has for several years been the worst enemy he had. (He afterward said that you and Mr. Goodloe were the worst.). Mr. Bowen knew the whole of Foster's political history and Foster took this opportunity to prejudice the audience against him as much as possible, so that they would not believe him. Mr. Bowen is an old stump speaker, was born in Rowan and could not be bluffed off in that way. He had taken notes the previous evening and so was prepared to sift Foster's speech. He did it effectually. He showed Foster to have been one of the bolters at the Baltimore Convention[2] in 1860, a Secessionist of the blackest dye and a latter day convert to the Union cause.

In the beginning of his speech, Foster said that the election ordered by Gov. Stanly was all a humbug and a swindle. Mr. Bowen replied that, if it were a humbug and a swindle, it was very queer that he should have any thing to do with it. Foster asserted that Mr. Pigott was ineligible to a seat in Congress and seemed to lay great stress upon the fact that his wife was a North Carolinian whereas Mr. P's was not.[3] Bowen replied that he did not see what a woman's nationality had to do with her husband's right to a seat in Congress, and that respect for the female portion of our county should have left them entirely out of the question; but as gentlemen had tried /to/ cast a slur upon Mrs. Pigott's character by saying that she was not a native of North Carolina, he would say that she was born and raised in North Carolina, that he had a high opinion of Mrs. P's character as a lady, and that he did not believe that she would publish a card denouncing her husband as unworthy of her <affections>/confidence/. This last remark cut Foster to the quick. He here interrupted Mr. Bowen and begged leave to make an explanation, which was granted. Before this however he asked whose wife had denounced her husband in a public journal. Mr. B said that last Summer a year there appeared in the Raleigh Standard, a card, which no doubt the gentleman had seen. He did not have to mention the parties. Foster then recollected all about it and said that he had seen the card, with his wife's name to it but that he did not believe that she had signed it and if she had; it was under compulsion. He then went into a long explanation to prove that his wife was loyal to him now and to do this, read from a letter recently recieved from his wife, in which she addresses him as "My Dear Charlie." He spoke over a half hour on his wife's loyalty, and nearly tired the audience out of all patience. Capt. Bowen then attacked him upon the insinuations that he had cast upon the good people of Carteret County by supposing that their votes could be bought by a drink of whiskey or a shake of the hand. Mr. Taylor, my landlord, has been treating his friends on the election during the last week and no doubt the slur was meant for him but Foster dinied that he had him in view, and said that he meant some liquor, which had been sent to Washington, N.C. Capt. Bowen <had> said that he did not see what a barrel of whiskey in Washington had to do with the voters of Carteret County. Foster said in his speech last night that salt was being distributed for electioneering purposes.

Capt. Bowen said that he guessed the remark was intended for Mr. [*Levi W.*] Pigott, the Inspector of the port and indirectly for Mr. [*Jennings*] Pigott, the Candidate for Congress, but that he would take upon himself all the responsibility and would explain why the salt was given away. He said that he had brought a cargo of salt here and not finding sale for it, he had told Mr. [*Levi W.*] Pigott and others that if they knew any poor meritorious persons, who needed salt and could not pay for it, that they should send those persons to him and he would give them small quantities for their own use. It seems that Mr. Pigott had brought some salt ashore for some poor widow ladies, in the Revenue Boat, and hence arose all of this fuss. The two points that Foster made against Mr. [*Jennings*] Pigott were that he was an Abolitionist and ineligible to a seat in Congress. He says that he will contest the election if Mr. Pigott is elected.

He says that he can keep Mr. Pigott out of Congress till the end of the session by doing so — that any body can <test> contest another's eligibility to a seat in Congress, by merely notifying the Speaker of the House that he intends to do so before he takes his seat, and then he has twenty days to appear in, and then he can summon his opponent for twenty days. The scoundrel is mean enough for any thing and I have no doubt that even if Mr. Pigott is elected by a large majority that he will try to keep him out of his seat. It would be well for you and Mr. Goodloe to see how this is and apprise Mr. Dawes[4] of the game that the rascal wishes to play.

Foster wishes it distinctly understood that he is the poor man's friend and that he intends to array the poor man against the rich man.

I will not attempt to give you an account of the abuse that he heaped upon you and Mr. Goodloe, because I do not know enough of his vile epithets in connection with Abolitionists to express it. Hell-begotten and a many more similar expressions were used.

I to-day sent a letter to Mr. Chase asking leave of absence to deposit the money that I have and if he sees fit to grant it I will try and be in Washington between the middle and last of January next. Considering all of the excitement we have had to-day from speech making, I think to-day has been a very nice Christmas. The weather was almost as warm as it is in May. We have Northern papers of the 21st. inst, in which, it is rumored that Gen. Burnside has resigned. I hardly think it probable. I think that the loss of a battle should not cause a General to resign.

I could not find out whether Seward's resignation had been accepted or not.[5] Mr. Lincoln ought to appoint Gen. [Nathaniel] Bank's, Secretary of War. We need a man there of energy and ability and I think that Banks has those attributes.

I have strung out this letter to a much greater length than I had expected when I began, and still it is not as full, not as lucid as I could wish. I recieved a few days since your letter of the 14th. inst, and 25 large envelopes for which I am more than obliged. I am going to Newbern day after tomorrow. Write often.

Your brother,
John A. Hedrick

[1] Capt. M. Bowan was a Unionist planter from Washington County. Wayne K. Durrill, *War of Another Kind: A Southern Community in the Great Rebellion* (New York: Oxford University Press, 1990), 17, 135-138, 169-170, 177.

[2] The Democratic Party held a convention in Baltimore after the unsuccessful convention in Charleston, S.C. Many southern delegates left this second meeting after it became apparent that their platform would not be approved. Richard B. Morris, ed., *Encyclopedia of American History*, rev. ed. (New York: Harper and Row, 1965), 226-227.

[3] Charles Henry Foster was married to Sue Agnes Carter of Murfreesboro, N.C. Jennings Pigott's wife, Ann Eliza Pigott (1818-1870), was born in Virginia. Delaney, "Foster and the Unionists," 350; Eighth Census, 1860: District of Columbia, City of Washington, Fourth Ward; *Cemetery Records of Carteret County*, 160.

[4] Henry L. Dawes (1816-1903) of Massachusetts was chairman of the House Committee on Elections from 1861 to 1869. *American National Biography*, s.v. "Dawes, Henry Laurens."

[5] After repeated calls by congressional Republicans for his dismissal, William H. Seward tendered his resignation as secretary of state in December 1862. President Lincoln refused to accept it. Glyndon G. Van Deusen, *William Henry Seward* (New York: Oxford University Press, 1967), 344-347.

SHC
Beaufort, N.C.
Dec. 31st. 1862,

Dear Brother:

I recieved day before yesterday your letters of the 18th. and 21st. insts. the latter inclosing a letter of Dec. 1st. from Sister Sarah.[1] I could swear to the authorship of that letter. It reads like Sarah's composition from beginning to end. I was very glad to see the original. Tell Sister Ellen that I think the letter was misdirected. It should have been sent to me, instead of her. It contains news most interesting to me. However, I will return the letter when I go to Washington.

All is quiet in this Department or rather Army Corps.[2]

The election comes off tomorrow and I think Mr. Pigotts' prospects are good. He has not visited the people as much as I could wish, on account of bad health of his wife. I wrote you a few days ago an account of the speaking here on Christmas day and the night before Christmas. I also informed you that Foster said that he would contest the election if Mr. Pigott recieved a majority of the votes. Should Mr. Pigott be elected, the House of Representatives ought to let him take his seat and then let Foster contest it. For, Foster says that he will contest it for the purpose of preventing any one from taking his seat. I mentioned that he said that he would have twenty days to appear in, after notifying the Speaker that he intended to contest the seat, and that then he could notify Mr. Pigott for twenty days, which would carry them to the close of the session and then niether would get his seat. I <would>/was/ told by Gov. Stanly that if the House does its duty, they will admit Mr. Pigott to his seat and let Foster contest it afterwards. Foster wishes /to/ make an impression among the people that Mr. Pigott is ineligible to a seat in Congress because he is not intitled to a vote. Voters have a State qualification whereas a representatives have a Constitutional qualification. A representative must be twenty five years old, seven years a citizen of the United States and an inhabitant of the state at the time he is chosen. Mr. Pigott, if elected, will hardly be able to be in Washington before the middle of January next. You seem to fear that the fact of the election being held on the 1st. day of January 1863, might interfere with President Lincoln's Emancipation Proclamation. I think you need apprehend no danger on that account.

I told you in one of my letters a short time ago that Governor /Stanly/ had offered me the position of Private Secretary with a Salary of $1500. I have accepted it and will enter upon the duties of my office about the 1st. of Feb. 1863.

He wished me to resign my present office now and he would give me my appointment on the 1st. of next month, and let me go to Washington on leave of absence, but I prefered to wait till the 1st. of Feb. as in that way I would have time to deposit the money that I have collected, and close up my accounts. I was in Newbern last Sunday. Mr. & Mrs. Pigott were complaining of sickness. The Mr. Willis, who is a Candidate for Congress, is a native of this County, has lived in the town Beaufort for the last twenty years, is a man of pretty good common sense, a /land/ survor by trade, and is hardly known out of the county. The furthest he was ever from home, was in 1860 when he went to the Douglas convention in Raleigh. He tells a joke about trying to go into the Caucus at Raleigh. He went to the door and knocked. The door keeper <ask> opened the door, whereupon <the> Mr. Willis said, "Can I come in." Door-Keeper, "If you have got undisputed credentials, you can come in." Mr. Willis, "I have no creditials. I am a committee of one self-appointed." Door-Keeper, "If you are an undecided Douglas Democrat, you can come in." Mr. Willis, "I am not an undecided Douglas Democrat. I am a decided Douglas Democrat." The doorkeep closed the door and Mr. Willis did not get in. I have just recieved your letter of the 20th. inst. which is the latest. New York papers of the 27th. are here. I have just read the Herald of the 27th. It contains nothing of especial interest. I made an acquaintance last evening with a lady whom I guess you know. She is the wife of Mr. E.H. Norcum[3] of this place and the daughter of old Mr. Dusenbury[4] of Lexington N.C. Her name is Laura. She was married to Mr. Norcum in 1847, and has, I believe, six children. I learned from her that there was another Davidson lady here. I have not called on her yet but expect to go to see her shortly. This lady, is the wife of Col. Taylor[5] of this place, and her maiden name was McIver. Her folks live at Clemonsville, Davidson County, N.C.[6] I do not think that I ever heard of the family before but yet she may know persons with whom I am acquainted. I have collected $395 from duties on Imports this week. Coastwise trade is very dull at present. There have been no coastwise entries in more than a week.

Tell Mr. Goodloe that I have been expecting a letter from him some time. Mr. Pigott recieved one from him a short time ago.

> Write often,
> John A. Hedrick.

[1] Sarah Hedrick was one of John's younger sisters. She lived with the Hedrick family in Davidson County, N.C. Sarah Hedrick to Benjamin S. Hedrick, December 8, 1865, Hedrick Papers, Southern Historical Collection.

[2] On December 24, 1862, the Federal troops in the Department of North Carolina were officially designated the XVIII Corps, under the command of John G. Foster. Boatner, *Civil War Dictionary*, 197-198.

[3] Edmund Halsey Norcum (1824-1867) was an 1847 University of North Carolina graduate, former state legislator, and merchant. *Cemetery Records of Carteret County,* 160; Kemp P. Battle, *History of the University of North Carolina*, vol. 1 (Raleigh: Edwards and Broughton, 1907), 801.

[4] Henry R. Dusenbury (b. ca. 1794). Sixth Census of the United States, 1840: Davidson County, North Carolina, Population Schedule, National Archives, Washington, D.C. (microfilm, Genealogical Services, State Library of North Carolina, Raleigh.); Seventh Census, 1850: Davidson County.

[5] James H. Taylor (b. ca. 1802) attended the University of North Carolina from 1827 to 1828 but did not graduate. Eighth Census, 1860: Carteret County; Daniel Lindsay Grant, ed., *Alumni History of the University of North Carolina*, 2d ed. (Durham: Christian and King, 1924), 611.

[6] Mrs. Taylor's father had evidently died by 1860, but her mother, Eliza McIver (b. ca. 1812) of Clemmonsville, was working as a "domestic" by that time. Eighth Census, 1860: Davidson County.

1863

SHC
Beaufort, N.C.
Jan. 1st. 1863.

Dear Brother:

We have just learned the result of the election at this place. Mr. Pigott received 94 votes; Foster, 61; and Willis, 57,—making a majority of 33 for Pigott. Foster is here today and I think he considers this his stronghold.

I must say that I had some fears of his getting a majority at this place, but I never thought that Mr. Pigott would be beaten. I told you that Foster said that he would contest Mr. Pigott's right to a seat in Congress.[1] All that Mr. Pigott has to do to take his seat, is to prove that he was an inhabitant of the State at the time of the election. You and Mr. Goodloe can show that he rented out his house before he left Washington D.C. Holding an office at Washington does not bar a man of his right to vote at his former home but as Mr. Pigott lived in Washington part of the time without being in office, I do not know whether he would be excluded /or not/. I say that Mr. Pigott is an inhabitant of this State now and, that with being 25 years old, and seven years a citizen of the United States, are the only Constitutional qualifications. Tell Mr. Goodloe that I have been trying to obey his instructions and that I think, we have "sent Mr. Pigott to Congress." I have just heard the result at this place and should I hear from any other precinct before the Mail closes in the morning I will let you know it. Excuse bad English.

Your brother,
John A. Hedrick

P.S. At the Banks, Mr. Pigott recieved 21 votes, Mr. Willis, 26; and Foster, none.

J.A.H.

Jan 2nd. 1863

We have one Monitor and quite a fleet in the Harbor. They arrived here yesterday. This Department has been turned into the eighteenth Army Corps. Gen. [*John G.*] Foster is to have 50,000 men.

Bear in mind that [*Charles Henry*] Foster's avowed object in contesting Mr. Pigott's right to a seat in Congress, is to keep the latter out of Congress till the end of the session and then neither can take his seat.[2] All went off quietly at the poles yesterday but the Fosterites tried very hard to get up a row. I shall write again soon.

> Your brother,
> John A. Hedrick

---

[1] Voting occurred only in Carteret, Craven, and Hyde Counties, and of the 864 votes cast, Jennings Pigott received 595. Charles Henry Foster and his supporters did challenge Pigott's election. They complained to the chairman of the House Committee on Elections, Henry Dawes, that pro-Southern officials had permitted Confederate sympathizers to vote while prohibiting some Unionists from casting ballots. The question of Pigott's residency was also raised. The committee and subsequently the House voted against seating Pigott. Brown, "A Union Election," 394-400.

[2] The final session of the Thirty-seventh Congress ended on March 3, 1863. *Biographical Directory of the United States Congress, 1774-1989, Bicentennial Edition* (Washington, D.C.: U.S. Government Printing Office, 1989), 171.

> *SHC*
> Beaufort, N.C.
> Jan. 4th. 1863.

Dear Brother:

I have recieved no letter from you, since that dated Dec. 25th. 1862, and have answered that.

I have writen you quite a number of letters <to you> lately about the Humbug Foster. I told you that he said in his speech here the night before Christmas that if Mr. Pigott got a majority of the votes cast on the 1st. of January 1863, he intended to contest the election, and thereby delay the time of Mr. Pigott's taking his seat till the end of the present session of Congress, and then no one /would/ get into Congress. I saw five letters in the Post Office yesterday, addressed by the same person to Hons. H. L. Dawes, Ch. Com. Elections, Kelly, Pomeroy, Sumner, and Rice.[1] They were sent away from here by yesterday's Mail, and I have reason to believe that the one addressed to Mr. Dawes, contained a protest from Mr. Foster's constituents against Mr. Pigott's taking his seat in Congress. The ground of Foster's protest is, as I told you, that Mr. Pigott is a non-resident of the State. The Constitution says that a Representative must be an inhabitant of the state in which he is chosen at the time of the election. If Mr. Pigott is not an inhabitant of this State now, I can not see by what means he can be one. His wife is here and he is here, and part of his land is here. According to Foster's notion, I guess he would have to sell his houses and lots in Washington D.C. or move them down here, before he could become an inhabitant of this State. The friends of Mr. Willis said on the day of the election that they would contest Mr. Pigott's right to a seat in Congress, on the ground that the Secesh voted for him. I have not heard them say any thing about do/ing/ so since then.

In this County, Mr. Pigott received 369 votes; Mr. Willis, 100; and Foster, 73. I think that Mr. Pigott will receive over three fourths of the votes cast. We had quite warm times during election week. The Fosterites challenged every man, whom they thought would vote against Foster. They even went so far as to challenge Capt. Fulford's votes, a man who is at least 75 years old and was born, raised, and lived among them during his whole life.[2] They wished to make it appear, /that/ they were the only Union men.

All is quiet here now, and the weather is pleasant. There are about fifty vessels in the Harbor. Among them are two iron clads—the Passaic and the Montauk. The latter ran aground on the bar this morning by trying to come in without a pilot. They succeeded this evening by the aid of two tugs in getting her off. I was aboard the Passaic day before yesterday. She has two guns—one, a fifteen inch.

I have not heard when Mr. Pigott will leave for Washington City, but I guess he will be along in a few days. I will go with him if he does not leave before I can get ready. I wish to get back here by the 1st. of February, and in order to do so, I must go on shortly. I have twelve hundred and fifty three dollars to deposit. I get three per cent on the amount deposited and 10 c per mile for the distance travelled over to and from the place of deposit.

Give Mr. Goodloe my respects and tell him that I will call on him for an answer to my last letter.

> Your brother,
> John A. Hedrick

P.S. The Monitor was lost in a gale 30 miles this side of Hatteras last week. A part of her crew were saved.[3]

---

[1] William Darrah Kelley (1814-1890), a U.S. congressman from Pennsylvania; Samuel Clarke Pomeroy (1816-1891), a U.S. senator from Kansas; Charles Sumner (1811-1874), a U.S. senator from Massachusetts; and Henry Mower Rice (1816-1894), a U.S. senator from Minnesota. *American National Biography*, s.v. "Kelley, William Darrah," "Pomeroy, Samuel Clarke," "Sumner, Charles"; *Dictionary of American Biography*, s.v. "Rice, Henry Mower."

[2] William Fulford (b. ca. 1786) had been a lighthouse keeper in 1850. Seventh Census, 1850: Carteret County; Eighth Census, 1860: Carteret County.

[3] The USS *Monitor* sank in stormy weather at about 1 A.M. on December 31, 1862. *ORN*, ser. 1, 8:346.

SHC
Beaufort, N.C.
Jan. 5th. 1863.

Dear Brother:

I recieved to day your letter of the 27th. ultimo, inclosing a letter clipped from the New York Tribune of the 25th. of last month. The inclosed letter was written either by Foster or Carpenter.[1] There are two sentences identical, verbatim et literatim, with two spoken by Foster at the Court House, the night before Christmas. The part of the letter on Free Labor, is the same as the sentiment expressed by Foster here. Carpenter may have writen Foster's speech and this letter also; and I do not care who wrote them, the language and sentiment is substantially the same. Gov. Stanley has greater forbearance to/ward/ the scoundrel Foster than I would have. I would hang him or send him out of the State before three days, if I had the Governor's power.

Most of this letter is based on facts. For instance, it speaks of the vessels seized by Capt. Ottinger[2] of the Revenue Marine at Newbern under Governor Stanly's permits. These vessels will be released as soon as the Secretary learns the circumstances under which they were seized. It has caused considerable delay to the shippers and as I think a great deal of trouble and loss of property for no purpose. Secretary of the Treasury knew that Governor Stanly was permitting vessels to go from point to point within the limits of his jurisdiction; for shortly after I came down here the Governor gave the Brig L.P. Snow permission to go to Newbern from this place, and I refused to let her go, because my instructions said that I could not permit a vessel to go to Newbern & other places on the Sound, unless I had special instructions from the Secretary in each case. The shipper did not insist on taking his vessel to Newbern <did not> and so the matter rested till the Governor recieved a letter from the Secretary of the Treasury.

The Secretary declined deciding whether the Governor of North Carolina had a right to permit a vessel to go from point to point within the limits of his State. The Governor considered that I had not the right but that he had under the power given him by the Secretary of War.[3] The whole fuss has arisen, and will again arise, from not knowing the Governor's position, every time there is a change of authorities in this Department. Such a position as he holds is an anomaly in this country.

People cannot understand it. It is neither military nor civil but a mixture of both. If Foster had the least spark of honesty about him, he might do some good. He gets hold of a great deal of news but always perverts it so that no one unacquainted with the facts, can tell the truth from /the/ Falsehood. This letter says that the petitions to Governor Stanly were for an election for a member to next Congress. I never saw any such petitions and I helped get up two. It would seem strange to petition for an election for next Congress when the election day is eight months off.

The following are returns of the late election so far as heard from

	Pigott	Foster	Willis
Newbern	78	21	-
Portsmouth	40	-	-
Newport	56	-	-
Smyrna	40	-	1
Beaufort	94	61	57
Cape Lookout Banks	21	-	26
Morehead City	30	-	1
	359	82	85

The middle column represents Foster's 600 Free Labor votes, which he said the night before Christmas, were pledged to be cast for him! I sent in my application for leave of absence on Christmas day. I wrote you yesterday. Write often.

Your brother,
John A. Hedrick

P.S. I told you that a letter had been sent from this Post Office to Mr. Dawes and supposed to contain a notification that Foster intended to contest Mr. Pigott's election. I also mentioned that five other letters, to Mssrs. Kelly, Sumner, Pomeroy and Rice, were sent away last Saturday. You will have to have my clothes in Washington pretty soon, as I will try to go to Washington and back before the end of the month.

If Pigott does not leave too soon, I will go with him. I have another cargo of salt to enter to-day. It was seized by blockaders off some thirty miles but has been released by the Navy Department. The vessel has five hundred sacks and the duties will amount to about two hundred dollars.

J.A.H.
Jan 6th. 1863.

<hr />

[1] This letter, which appeared on the front page of the *Tribune*, attacked Governor Stanly, characterizing his policies as "a complete failure," and praised the leaders of the Free Labor movement. *New York Tribune*, December 25, 1862.

[2] Douglass Ottinger was commander of the U.S. revenue cutter *Forward*. *ORN*, ser. 1, 8:608-609.

[3] Edwin McMasters Stanton (1814-1869) was secretary of war from 1862 to 1868. Sifakis, *Who Was Who in the Civil War*, 616-617.

<hr />

SHC
Beaufort, N.C.
Jan. 7th. 1863.

Dear Brother:

I recieved by to-day's Mail your letter of the 3rd. inst. It came through the Canal and made a very quick passage. My letters seem very slow in reaching you. I /have/ written five or six since the 21st. ultimo. So far as heard from, Pigott has 347 majority. As soon as the returns are complete, I will send you a list of them. I think that Foster has already notified the Speaker of the House that he intends to <protest> contest the election, on the ground that Mr. Pigott is a non-resident of the State. I have written you quite a number of letters on the subject, and give you about all the facts in the case. I do not know whether Foster has gone on to Washington or not. He may not intend to go but only notify the Speaker that he intends to contest Mr. Pigott's seat and thereby get forty days, which will keep Mr. Pigott out of his seat till the end of the present session of Congress.

Last Monday, I wrote Pigott to let me know when he expected to leave for Washington, but have received no answer. We are all shut up here now. No vessel is allowed to leave the Harbor until further orders from Gen. Foster.

There are about 40,000 troops in this Army Corps now; and two iron clads in the Harbor. The old Monitor was lost about 30 miles this side of Hatteras on its passage down here. Preparations are making for an advance both by land and water. The destination of the Expedition, is not known, but it is thought to be Wilmington. It looks now like I would not be able to get back to Washington and back by the 1st. proximo.

It seems that Dr. Ferris did not bring into my account, the Contingent Expenses for the last term, I was at the University.

I hope that the Expedition on foot m[a]y drive the Rebels back so that Gov. Stanly and I can go to Raleigh. I think that we could do more good if we could get into the Capitol of the State. The President's 1st of January

Proclamation reached here yesterday.[1] There is some talk against it, but I have heard no bitter opposition to it. Write soon.

Your brother,
John A. Hedrick

---

[1] This is a reference to the Emancipation Proclamation, which was issued on September 22, 1862, to go into effect on January 1, 1863. Boatner, *Civil War Dictionary*, 265.

SHC
Beaufort, North Carolina,
Saturday, Jan. 10th., 1863.

Dear Brother:

I recieved your letter of the 3rd. inst. and wrote you on the 7th. Nothing of interest has transpired since then. Gen. Foster has placed an embargo on vessels leaving here and therefore I expect that you have not had any of my late letters.

The returns of the late election in the State are reported in the Progress of yesterday as complete. There are no returns given for Beaufort County.

The following are the returns as taken from the Progress.

Election Precincts	Candidates & No. votes for each.		
	Pigott	Foster	Willis
Newbern	78	21	
Portsmouth	38		
Newport	56		
Smyrna	40		5
Beaufort	95	61	57
Cape Lookout Banks	21		26
Morehead City	31		1
Trent	35	13	
Kinnakeet	12	30	
Chickamacomico	3	23	
Lake Landing	12		
Ocracoke	44	1	
Hunting Quarters	19	2	7
Cedar Island	19		
Straits	22		4
Darr's Shore	16	6	

Harlow's Creek	8		
Currituck	3		
Swan Quarter	42		
	594	157	100

I wrote Mr. Pigott last Monday and asked him when he expected to go on to Washington, but have recieved no answer. It seems strange that he does not let some one know what he intends to do. If he wishes to take his seat in Congress, it is high time that he should be going on. The embargo on vessels leaving here may prevent his going. I do not know whether vessels are allowed to go through the Canal to Norfolk or not.

I have not heard from the humbug Foster in the last few days. It is hardly probable that he will go on to Washington to contest Pigott's right to a seat in Congress, but I think that he has already notified the Speaker of the House that he intends to contest it. I wish Gen. Foster would make haste and do what he intends to do. I am getting tired of being blockaded here. Besides I somewhat doubt the propriety of stopping all communication with the north. If he thinks that he will prevent the Rebels from knowing what is going on here by that means, he is certainly mistaken. For men from the country around are coming here and going away every day. It is rumored here that Stonewall Jackson is at Kinston with 40,000 men. If that be so I think that the sooner I go north, the better. I do not think that there is any danger of his taking this place; yet I would prefer to be away if he should try it. Gen. Foster in my opinion is not /a/ match for him.

Late New York papers report the taking of Vicksburg by the Union Army under General Sherman.[1]

There is a great deal of speculation here about what the Government intends to do with Gen. Butler. People do not know where they are going to send him.[2]

Sunday, Jan. 11th. 1863

We had quite a stormy time last night. It rained very hard from about 7 1/2 o'clock to 10 P.M. The wind shifted to the N.E. during the night, and the weather cleared off beautifully. It was a little cold this morning but now 2 P.M. it is quite pleasant without a fire. We have not /had/ any thing like cold weather this winter. There was ice about half an inch thick twice during the last month.

There is no news stirring to-day. The iron clads are still here.

There has been some stir created in this place by the seizure of the English Schr. Governor of Turks Island. On the 15th. of December 1862, she arrived here from Salt Cays, Turks Island, with a cargo of salt, bound to New York. The captain after leaving port was taken sick and ordered his mate to make the quickest port in the United States. On his arrival here he was suffering from fever and the jaundice and has since been under medical treatment. He stayed here about two weeks, and finding that he was not getting better fast, he concluded to sell his salt and send his vessel home by the mate. Mr. C.B. Dibble[3] of Newbern, N.C. made him an offer for the salt and he sold it. I then permitted the captain to enter it and pay the duties on the 29th. of last month. Since the salt was landed, the Captain of the Cutter, has seized the vessel, and ordered Capt. Duncan[4] to hold the salt till I shall have heard from the Secretary of the Treasury. He says that as the salt was not cleared for this port, it could not be landed here without special instructions from the Secretary of the Treasury. The captain of the schooner, C.F. Gardner, left here yesterday for Newbern on his way to Washington to see the English Minister.

He intended to stop in Newbern to see Capt. Ottinger of the Cutter, and probably they may arrange it, so that he will not have to proceed to Washington.

The Cutter to which Capt. Ottinger is attached is stationed here but he has charge of another little cutter stationed at Newbern, and since he has been down here he has spend most of his time at Newbern. It is most pleasant for him to associate with the Commodores and Generals around Newbern, than it is to stay aboard his vessel. Com. Murray[5] came down with him the time he seized the salt. Any thing the Commodore says, is law with him. The Commodore said that there was too much salt brought here for the health of the place, and that we ought to use every means to harass all who bring salt to this place, whether they do it legally or not. Therefore our model Revenue Officer seized the vessel and ordered the vessel to be detained, not, as he said, that he thought the owner of the salt had violated any law, but that he might be put to some trouble in going or sending to Washington to have his vessel released and his salt given up. I don't like any such work. If we are going to have an open port, I wish every one, who acts honestly, to be treated gentlemanly at it.

Dr. Page says that Prof. H.H. Smith[6] was a classmate of his at Bowdoin College. C.H. Foster is a graduate of the same college and was a class-mate of C.W. Smythe,[7] formerly of Catawba College, late teacher of a female school in Lexington and now a Captain in the Rebel Army.

Mr. Norcum of this place told me that Smythe raised a company in Lexington. Mr. Norcum graduated at Chapel Hill in 1847, and married Laura Dusenbury the same year.

I will try to get to Washington before the last of the month but may fail. I expect that three or four letters are in the Post Office at Newbern for you.

4 P.M. I have just received a letter from Mr. Pigott by private conveyance in which he says that he is anxious to go on to Washington by the first

steamer that sails from here or Newbern, but that he understands that the steamers will be detained for some days. The letter was written on the 5th. but did not reach me till to-day. Mr. Pigott was quite sick.

Write as often as your pens, paper, ink and postage stamps will allow; for mine are out.

Your brother,
John A. Hedrick

---

[1] William T. Sherman led thirty thousand Union troops in an unsuccessful campaign against the Vicksburg defenses in late December. Confederates under Martin L. Smith decisively repulsed Sherman's forces on December 29, 1862, at the Battle of Chickasaw Bluffs. Boatner, *Civil War Dictionary*, 153-154.

[2] Benjamin Franklin Butler (1818-1893) was recalled from his command in Louisiana in December 1862 after widespread criticism of his policies and actions. He did not receive another command until November 1863, when he became head of the Department of Virginia and North Carolina. *American National Biography*, s.v. "Butler, Benjamin Franklin."

[3] C. B. Dibble was a leading New Bern merchant and Unionist, who later in the war moved his business to New York. *Charleston Mercury*, September 12, 1861; *New Bern Progress*, April 16, 1862; *Old North State* (Beaufort), January 21, 1865; C. B. Dibble to Benjamin S. Hedrick, May 26, 1865, Hedrick Papers, Duke Special Collections.

[4] James M. Duncan (d. 1864) of the U.S. Navy was captain of the freighter *Norwich*. Hayes, *Samuel Francis Du Pont*, 2:61.

[5] Comdr. Alexander Murray's willingness to allow vessels with passes from Governor Stanly through the blockade, in defiance of orders from the Navy Department and his superior officers, led to his relief in February 1863. Robert M. Browning Jr., *From Cape Charles to Cape Fear: The North Atlantic Blockading Squadron during the Civil War* (Tuscaloosa: University of Alabama Press, 1993), 135.

[6] Hildreth Hosea Smith was professor of modern languages at the University of North Carolina from 1857 to 1868. Battle, *History of the University of North Carolina*, 1:659-660.

[7] C. W. Smith (b. ca. 1829) of New Hampshire. Eighth Census, 1860: Davidson County.

SHC
Beaufort, N.C.
Jan. 16th. 1863.

Dear Brother:

I recieved to-day yours of the 7th. which is the last I have had since that of the 3rd. inst. It is quite windy to-day but not very cold. I was in Newbern night before last and found Gov. Stanly and Dr. Page well. Mr. & Mrs. Pigott left Newbern for Washington D.C. last Saturday. They went off very unexpectedly to themselves as well as /to/ others. Gen. Foster sent a dispatch boat through the Canal and they went on it.

I am glad you have not ordered my clothes to be sent to Washington, as I may go to New York myself. Besides Adam's Express has started a line of Mail Steamers between here and New York and I can have them sent to Beaufort as easy as I could to Washington. My leave of absence has not arrived. I wrote for one on the 25th. ultimo. It is about time that it should be here.

Gov. Stanly told me not to be in any hurry about resigning, as it was very uncertain whether he would remain here much longer. He will let me know shortly what he intends to do. He has a hard row to weed and can't please every body.

There's no difficulty in sending letters by flag of truce to the interior of the state. If Sister Ellen will send me the letters that she wishes to go through the lines, I will try to put them on the right track.

I think you and I had better let the women do the correspondence for the present. Letters from us might create some difficulty at home.

The Expedition has not moved. The vessels are all in the harbor and it is very well that the ironclads are. There are about 10,000 troops at Carolina City.

Mr. Norcum wishes some cabbage and other garden seeds from the Patent Office. I was at Mr. Norcum's last night and she said that she would make out a list of them for me to send to you. Perhaps I will go round there to night, and if she has it ready I will get it and send it in this letter. If I do not send it you can have Isaac to send her such seeds as you think adapted to this climate. You will know pretty well what she wants. She has no seeds of any kind. Very little is going on in the shipping line as no vessels have been permitted to leave port for nearly two weeks.

State papers give bad news from Vicksburg and Galveston.[1] I hope future reports may give better news.

Have you read Gov. Seymour's Message.[2] It denounces the course pursued by the administration. The Times of the 9th. had a letter from Geo. N. Saunders[3] to Fernando Wood, Seymour and others. He congratulates them on the success of the Democratic Party in N.Y. I think that I would prefer to recieve praise from the Devil.

It is getting colder. It will be quite cold to-night. Has Mr. Goodloe recieved a letter from L.W. Pigott.

Write soon.
Your Brother,
John A. Hedrick

[1] This refers to Sherman's repulse at Chickasaw Bluffs and an action at Galveston, Tex., on January 1, 1863, in which Confederates under John Bankhead Magruder forced the surrender of the Union garrison. Boatner, *Civil War Dictionary*, 153-154, 322.

[2] In his annual message to the state legislature, Democratic New York governor Horatio Seymour rejected the possibility of a peaceful separation of the Union but denounced the Emancipation Proclamation. *New York Times*, January 8, 1863.

[3] George N. Saunders (1812-1873) of Kentucky acted as a Confederate agent in Canada and Europe. *Dictionary of American Biography*, s.v. "Saunders, George Nicholas."

SHC
Beaufort, N.C.
Jan. 18th. 1863.

My Dear Brother:

I recieved your letter of the 7th. inst. last Friday and wrote to you on the same day. Mr. Pigott left Newbern for Washington a week ago yesterday. He went on a dispatch boat through the Canal and is in Washington before now if the Rebs did /not/ gobble him up.

Part of the Expedition is under way. The two Monitors left here yesterday for parts unknown. Some land forces went with them and more are to leave soon. There are quite a number of schooners and one large ship outside of the bar. The schooners are thought to be from Newbern, as it is about time for those, that left there last week, to be round. Great preparation is making in Newbern for the reception of sick and wounded soldiers. I would infer from this that an advance by land would shortly be made.

In my last letter I requested you to get some <garden> /cabbage/ and other garden seed from the Patent Office and send to Mrs. E.H. Norcum. I have not been there since I wrote, and so have not obtained the list of seeds, which she promised to prepare for me. I saw Mr. Norcum himself this morning. His family is well. The weather has been cold during the last three days. We have had no snow worth naming this winter, but from the feeling of the wind, I would guess that there was some up in Virginia, and the western part of North Carolina.

Business has been very dull during this month. My leave of absence has not yet arrived. I hope that I may get it before the end of the month. I will hardly leave here before the first of next month, even if my leave comes before then. Because I ought to be here then to make out my monthly accounts. Besides as I told you in my last letter I am in no hurry to resign at present. The only thing that urges me to go on soon, is to get rid of some money which does not belong to me. I have about $1500 of U.S. Money. Of this amount $1381 is in specie and demand notes.

I do not know wheth the Secretary will allow me 3 per cent in kind of the amount collected by me, or 3 per cent in Legal Tender on that amount. The former would give me about $8. more than the latter, supposing gold, silver and demand notes worth only 20 per cent. I think that I will get 3 per cent on the amount collected. I send enclosed the last lief of Gov. Stanly's letter to Col. Gilliam.[1] If you will hunt up the other part, which I sent you some time ago, you will have the letter complete. You will perceive that this has been attached to the other wrong.

Write often.
Your brother,
John A. Hedrick

[1] This is possibly a reference to Alvan Cullem Gillem (1830-1875), a West Point graduate from Tennessee. Gillem served as colonel of the Tenth Tennessee until his promotion to brigadier general in August 1863. Warner, *Generals in Blue*, s.v. "Gillem, Alvan Cullem."

SHC
Beaufort, N.C.
Jan. 21st. 1863.

Dear Brother:

I wrote you last Friday and Sunday, and mentioned that Mrs. Norcum wished you to send her some cabbage, and other garden seed from the Patent Office. Yesterday she sent me a list of what she wanted and I inclose it in this letter.

I have heard nothing of interest from the Army since I wrote last.

Lieut. Whitcomb of the U.S. Rev. Cutter "Forward" died night before last. He had the consumption before he left Boston Harbor and came here because this was a milder climate. He was a very nice young man. I believe I have never mentioned to you that the metalic coffin for the remains of Lieut. Gladding arrived about the middle of December last and that his body had been sent to his relations at Providence R. Island. Mortification had set in before his body was taken up and his face was perfectly black.

The weather is quite blustery to-day, but not cold. It rained very hard last night.

We have had no mail since that which brought your letter of the 7th. inst. but one is expected every day.

We have a rumer here that Gen. Burnside has taken Richmond but no credit is given to it. It is probable that a fight has taken place in that Department. These rumers generally have some foundation in fact but the facts are sometimes very different from the rumers.

I am well with the exception of a cold. My leave of absence has not arrived. I hope it may be here by the end of the month so that I can leave on the first of next.

Write often.

Your brother,
John A. Hedrick

SHC
Beaufort, N.C.
Jan. 26th. 1863.

Dear Brother:

I wrote you two letters last week and thought yesterday that I would not write again till the middle of this; but as the Mail boat from Port Royal to New York is thought to be coming in, I take this occasion to write for fear I may not have an opportunity to send a letter soon again. The harbor is nearly full of vessels. About one hundred are here. The two iron clads left this place last Saturday was a week and we have not heard any thing from them further than that they were in a safe harbor. I cannot tell when the balance of the Expedition will move. From the amount of preparation it would seem that something great should be done.

We have had no northern mail in about 10 days. My leave of absence has not come. I am getting tired of waiting for it and am beginning to doubt my getting it.

Papers of the 22nd. inst. arrived yesterday on a steamer from Fortress Monroe. It was rumered at Old Point Comfort when the boat left, that Gen. Burnside had crossed the Rappahannock above and below Fredricksburg.[1] This I think very doubtful, and if it be so, I am afraid that we will lose by it. If it be meant for a feint to draw the Rebels from some other point, it may do some good.

The weather has been quite warm during the last three days, and would remind one more of Spring than Winter.

Write often.
Your brother,
John A. Hedrick

---

[1] On January 19, 1863, Burnside's army moved to cross the Rappahannock River and flank the Confederate left. Due to prolonged heavy rain, the campaign failed and has since become known as the "Mud March." Marvel, *Burnside*, 212-213.

SHC
Beaufort, N.C.
Jan. 30th. 1863.

Dear Brother:

I recieved yesterday your letter of the 17th., which is the last I have had since that of the 7th. inst. I cannot concieve why it is that you do not get more of my letters. There are about half a dozen due you, which you have not mentioned, since the 25th. ultimo. For sometime past I have never written to you less than one letter per week and sometimes as many as three.

Our Mail facilities are getting worse and worse especially for letters going north. Adam's Express Steamers have commenced carrying the mail between here and New York, but there is no certainty when or how often they will run.

My leave of absence has not come, and consequently I cannot tell when I will be in Washington or whether I will get there at all. In your letter of the 7th. inst. you said that you had not and would not order my clothes to Washington until it was certain that I would go there. I was in hopes that you would not order them till then, and upon the reciept of your letter, wrote you to that effect, but my letter could not have reached you before your last letter was written.

There is some expectation of an attack on this place, but I apprehend no danger at present. A couple of the gunboats have been stationed near the depot at Morehead City in such a position as to be able to rake the Rail Road.

The fleet left yesterday evening. It is not known where it has gone. It looked beautiful to see them as they went out. I hope that we may soon hear something from them worthy of such a fleet.

Write oftener,
Your brother,
John A. Hedrick

SHC
Beaufort, N.C.
Feb. 1st., 1863.

My Dear Brother:

I hardly know whether it's worth while to write you any more letters. It seems that you do not get more than half that I do write. I wrote you twice last week. One of those letters was put in the Mail, which left here on the Augusta Dinsmore, the same day the letter was written. I presume you have that letter. There is no news here. The fleet has not been heard from since it left here. It has had a very nice time with the exception of a little too much wind during the first night.

The weather is cloudy to-day. Business has been rather dull during the last month. I collected some what over three hundred dollars for Uncle Sam.

Is there any probability of Mr. Pigott taking his seat in Congress during the present session? How is Mrs. Pigott? She was ailing when she left Newbern.

Write still oftener.

Your brother,
John A. Hedrick

SHC
Beaufort, N.C.
Feb. 6th. 1863.

Dear Brother:

I recieved yesterday your letter of the 28th. ultimo. I guess your educated stomach has been overloaded by its civilized master. I am sorry for you but it can't be prevented now. You had better take more exercise hereafter. My leave of absence has not arrived. It has been raining like blazes for the last two days. I have not heard anything from the Expedition since it left here. It has doubtless gone further south than this State. The Mary Sanford is coming in from Port Royal and she will probably bring some news of its whereabouts.

Gov. Stanly has resigned but had not received an acceptance of his resignation on the 1st. inst. I have heard of no new movements in this Department since I wrote last. We have New York papers of the 2nd. inst. If I can get a good chance to go Baltimore and back right quick, I may do so without waiting for my leave of absence. I do not wish to stay in Washington City more than three or four days.

Continue to write whether I come or not.

Your Brother,
John A. Hedrick

SHC
Beaufort, N.C.
Feb. 8th. 1863.

Dear Brother:

I wrote you day before yesterday and my letter left here on the Mary Sanford yesterday about 2 P.M. The Mary Sanford brought some news from Port Royal but it is so mixed up that it is very unsatisfactory. The sum of the news, as near as I could learn, is that the Rebels at Charleston had sent out some rams, and butted some of our blockaders nearly to death,[1] and that we had taken an English steamer trying to run in at Charleston with a cargo of guns and amunition,[2] and that the Montauk was after the Nashville in Ossiba Bay.[3] The fleet that left here about a week ago is at Port Royal. There has been no news made in this Department lately. The weather is cloudy and somewhat cold. The past week has been exceedingly stormy with a great deal of rain. It looks now as if it would snow soon. We have had no snow worth naming this winter.

I mentioned sometime ago that Gov. Stanly had sent in his resignation. I have not heard whether it has been accepted or not. I guess you would know it sooner in Washington than we would here. Your letter of the 28th. ultimo was received last week. It is the latest that I have had from you. It seems from it that you got all of my letters in a bunch. It is queer to me how Foster's protest got to Washington sooner than my letters, which were written before it.

Business was a little brisker during last than during the week preceding.

Mrs. Norcum sends her best regards to you and wishes you to call and see her if you ever come down this way.

<u>My leave has not arrived.</u>

Write as often as you can.

Your brother,
John A. Hedrick

---

[1] On January 31, 1863, the Confederate rams *Chicora* and *Palmetto State* attacked ships in the Union blockade off Charleston, S.C. The Confederate vessels, which suffered little harm, seriously damaged two ships and inflicted lesser damage to others. *Civil War Naval Chronology*, pt. 3:18-19; Long, *Day by Day*, 317.

[2] On the morning of January 29, 1863, Union sailors captured the British steamer *Princess Royal* as it tried to run the blockade at Charleston, S.C. The cargo of the *Princess Royal* included rifles, powder, and two engines to be used in ironclads. *ORN*, ser. 1, 13:551-553.

[3] The Union ironclad *Montauk* destroyed the Confederate steamer *Nashville* near Savannah, Ga., on February 28, 1863. *ORN*, ser. 1, 13:704-705.

SHC
Beaufort, N.C.
Feb. 15, 1863.

Dear Brother:

Your letters of the 1st. and the 3rd. inst. have been recieved. I have also recieved a letter from Mr. Harrington directing me to send the money which I hold as Collector, to Mr. Jno. J. Cisco,[1] New York, by the first Government Steam Transport, which leaves my port. There are no Government Steamers running between this port and New York and have not been during the last three months. There are some running from Newbern to New York. Before the Expedition left the Guide and the Baltimore were making occasional trips from here to Baltimore but the Guide was taken for the Expedition and the Baltimore has gone north for repairs. The Adams Express Steamers are the only steamers, which run between here and New York. They leave here for New York once in about 10 days. They carry money for 1 $^1/_2$ per cent and passengers for $30 per head. The fare is nearly as much as the government mileage would amount to. I think that the government Steamers will be running between here and Baltimore shortly and should I get leave of absence I would wait for one of them. The clerk whom you mention is mistaken in the amount of money, that I hold. If he will refer to my collection account for the month of January, he will find that I had $1605.51 at the close of last month. By the end of this month I will certainly have $1700.

You said in your letter of the 3rd. inst. that you would see the Secretary of the Treasury, himself, about my leave of absence. If you have done so or if you hereafter do so, and he thinks that he cannot grant it, you may forward to me my clothes by Adams Express without prepayment and send me their receipt for the box. By the next mail steamer, which leaves for New York I will send you $40 and by the second $20 more or $60 in all, /with/ which you may pay Watkins and the University. Should you go to New York, you may get my diploma and keep it for further orders.

There are various rumors afloat about a split between Gens. Foster and Hunter.[2] It was reported last week that both were on their way to Washington City to see which should command the Expedition. <which is now at Port Royal> It has been denied that there is any difficulty between them but I think that there is something to matter as Foster and his staff arrived on the Spaulding from Port Royal last week and /he/ has since gone with his wife and staff to Fortress Monroe on his way to Washington City.

Gov. Stanly is still in Newbern, awaiting an answer from the War Department in reply to his letter tendering his resignation.

I cannot see for what purpose the Government would send a judge to this State. If a court of admiralty were established here, it would facilitate the disposition of the prizes which are taken off Wilmington but that I fear would cost more than it would be worth.

Write oftener.

Your brother,
John A. Hedrick

---

[1] John J. Cisco, assistant treasurer of New York and a Democrat, was initially given his position by President Franklin Pierce but was retained by the Lincoln administration due to his competence. Carman and Luthin, *Lincoln and the Patronage*, 57.

[2] Maj. Gen. David Hunter (1802-1886), a West Point graduate from Washington, D.C., commanded the Department of the South from March 31 to August 22, 1862, and from January 20 to June 12, 1863. Sifakis, *Who Was Who in the Civil War*, 327; *American National Biography*, s.v. "Hunter, David."

Troops from John G. Foster's XVIII Corps were sent from North Carolina to South Carolina to assist in the attack on Charleston. Hunter wanted these soldiers to become part of his X Corps. General Halleck, President Lincoln, and Secretary of War Stanton ruled that Foster's men were to remain in the XVIII Corps, but while in the Department of the South, they were to be under Hunter's control. Edward A. Miller Jr., *Lincoln's Abolitionist General: The Biography of David Hunter* (Columbia: University of South Carolina Press, 1997), 132-134

SHC
Beaufort, N.C.
Feb. 19th. 1863.

Dear Brother:

Inclosed I send $40, which may go towards paying the University and Mr. Watkins. By next Steamer I will send $20 more. Should you go to New York you may get my Diploma and keep it.

Your letter of the 10th. inst. has been recieved. In my last letter I instructed you to forward me my clothes by Adams Express, if Sec. Chase thinks that he cannot grant me leave of absence. I have about $1680 to deposit.

Mrs. Norcum has received one package of seed, and I, two. She sends her best regards to you and wishes me to say to you that she is very much obliged to you for procuring the seed.

I have no news to write.

Your brother,
John A. Hedrick

———————

SHC
Beaufort, N.C.
Feb. 20th. 1863.

Dear Brother:

By this mail I send a registered letter containing $40.00. I am well and all is quiet. The weather is windy and clear. We have no late news from any place but the Augusta Dinsmore, now off the bar, will probably bring some news from Port Royal.

Gen. Foster left here for Washington City week before last. His business there is not known but it is thought that he went to see whether he or Gen. Hunter would command the Expedition. I have nothing from you later than the 10th.

Your brother,
John A. Hedrick

———————

SHC
Beaufort, N.C.
Feb. 22nd. 1863.

Dear Brother:

Another week has past without any news from the Expedition. Gen. Foster arrived here last Friday from Washington City and proceeded to Newbern or Port Royal—it is hard to tell which but I think that he has gone to Newbern. He came in on the Spaulding and she left for some place about two hours after she came in. Her going out probably gave rise to the report that he had gone to Port Royal. I have not yet learned whether he and Hunter had any /personal/ difficulty or not.

Three young men, about 16 years old, citizens of this place, left here last night during the rain storm, for Dixie. One of them was a son of Dr. Arendell,[1] who is State Senator from this County.

I wrote you two letters last week. One of them (registered) contained forty dollars. I presume that it has not left the Post Office yet. The other, I wrote Friday, under the impression that the Adams Express Steamer was coming in from Port Royal, but she has not arrived up to this time.

I understand that one of the Express Steamers has been seized at New York. Her offence I have not learned. She is due here now.

We have a report that Congress has passed a Conscript Law. It is said that none, who are able to bear arms, are exempt.[2] This law will bring out more traitors in the north than were ever thought of.

Monday morning
Feb. 23rd. 1863.

It is quite cold this morning. I think that there is no doubt that the Augusta Dinsmore is coming in from Port Royal. Of course I cannot get any news from her until she gets in and then I expect that it will be too late to write any, so you will have to depend on the papers for any news that she may bring from Port Royal. To-day there will be a grand inspection of the troops in Newbern in honor of Washington's birthday. A man who came from Newbern yesterday, told me that Gen Foster certainly was there. Gov. Stanly was confined to his house by sickness when I heard from him last. I have not heard whether the Secretary of War has accepted his resignation or not.

Write me as soon as you can whether you have seen Mr. Chase about my leave of absence. If he concluded not to grant it, I wrote you a week ago to forward my clothes by Adams Express.

Write often.

Your brother,
John A. Hedrick

---

[1] Michael F. Arendell (1819-1894), a doctor and member of a prominent Beaufort family, served as state senator from 1850 to 1854, and again from 1860 to 1865. His son, William L. Arendell, was born in 1848. *Cemetery Records of Carteret County*, 148; *Cyclopedia of Eminent and Representative Men of the Carolinas of the Nineteenth Century*, vol. 2. (Madison, Wis.: Brant and Fuller, 1892), 563-565.

[2] President Lincoln signed a bill creating a national draft on March 3, 1863. Men twenty to forty-five were subject to conscription with some exemptions, including high-ranking

government officials. Draftees could hire substitutes or pay three hundred dollars to avoid service. Long, *Day by Day*, 325.

Duke
Beaufort, N.C.
Feb. 26th. 1863.

Dear Brother:

Your letter of the 10th. and 15th. and also Foster's protest have been recieved. The last mentioned document did not reach me till to-day alhough you mention it in your letter of the 10th. which came to hand last week. There is no news of importance afloat. All is quiet in this Army Corps. Gen. Foster is in Newbern and also Gov. Stanly. The latter was sick yesterday. I have not learned definitely whether his resignation has been accepted or not though I think that it has and that he will go back to California any how.[1]

We have N.Y. papers of the 21st. which give the Banking Act as it passed Congress.[2] It is quite a long document and I have not had time to read it.

My official receipts for the present, have been greater than in any previous month. They will amount to about sixty dollars. This includes Salary and Fees.

I wrote you some time ago, what you already knew, that Mr. Harrington had instructed me to send the money, which I hold as Collector, to Mr. Cisco, by the first U.S. Steam Transport, which should leave my port. None have left since the reception of his letter and it is not probable that any will leave soon. I have not determined by what means I will send the money, but I have concluded not to make further application for leave of absence. I can send it by Adams Express and have it insured for 1 1/2 per cent. and I think that this will be as cheap for the Government as any way that I know of.

In a couple of my previous letters I have directed you to send me my clothes by Adams Express, if up seeing Mr. Chase, he thought that he could not grant me leave of absence. In your letter of the 15th. you mention having seen him at his private residence and his having told you to call at his office about my leave. That means that he would prefer me to stay where I am. I think it very good advice. You may therefore let the matter rest where it is and send me my clothes by Adams Express.

I sent you forty dollars in a registered letter last week. It was mailed on the 20th. but probably did not leave here till the 24th. I will send twenty dollars more by the next Adams Express Steamer, which leaves for New York. This will be about the 6th. of next month.

> Write often and fully,
> Your brother,
> John A. Hedrick.

---

[1] Edward Stanly was informed on March 4, 1863, that President Lincoln had accepted his resignation, effective March 1. Stanly left New Bern in March. He traveled to Washington, D.C., where he met with Lincoln in April before going to California. Brown, *Edward Stanly*, 250, 252-253.

[2] The National Bank Act of February 1863 was intended to replace the chaotic system of decentralized state banks and currencies with a system in which banks would be federally chartered and issue national banknotes. McPherson, *Ordeal by Fire*, 204-205.

> *Duke*
> Beaufort, N.C.
> <Feb.> March 1st. 1863.

Dear Brother:

I have not anything to write, which would interest you, and besides I do not feel much like writing; you must therefore excuse the shortness of my letter, and take it as an evidence of the existence of the Sabbath day in this State. This is the most lonesome day that I have experienced lately. In my last letter I instructed you to send me my clothes by Adams Express. I sent you forty dollars on the 20th. ult. and will inclose you twenty dollars more when the next express steamer comes back from Port Royal. In one of my previous letters I directed you to apply this money to paying for my Diploma and clothes. I would have sent the money directly to Mr. Watkins and Dr. Ferris, but I thought that you /could/ do it better than I could. If you should get the Diploma, you will please send me a translation of it, so that should I ever get that important document, I would know how to read it. I am very well and weigh about 130 lbs. Tell Sister Ellen that I will not get $1000 this year and if I follow her advice I will not get married.

> Write oftener,
> Your brother,
> John A. Hedrick.

P.S. Send me another bunch of large envelopes.

Duke
Beaufort, N.C.
March 4th. 1863.

Dear Brother:

Your letter of the 23rd. Ult. has been recieved. I am very glad to learn that there is some prospect of Mr. Goodloe's coming down here as Military Governor of this State.[1] I think that he could do more good as Governor than as Judge. I don't doubt that he would have considerable trouble at first and perhaps till the war is over, but that should not discourage him. I have had trouble even in my little sphere, which does not come much in conflict with other authorities, but that has passed away. I came very of being summoned to headquarters shortly after I arrived here, for a decision, which has since been given by the Secretary of War, Navy and Treasury. I refer to Governor Stanley's authority to grant permits to vessels to go to Newbern and places on the Sounds. Again in the case of the Schr. Governor of Turks Island, which was seized by Capt. Ottinger of the "Cutter," for entering and landing her cargo, which was cleared for New York but put in here in distress. The Captain of the Cutter contended that it could not be landed without special instructions from the Secretary of the Treasury, as the vessel did not have the consular license, which is required of vessels trading with this port. I contended that I had the right to judge whether the Captain of the Governor could pay the duties and land his cargo. The Secretary in his letter releasing the vessel decided in my favor. So far I may consider myself as having been very lucky. My only hope is that my good luck may continue.

Day after to-morrow I expect to go down to a vessel which is stranded between Ocracoke and Hatteras Inlets. She was bound from the West Indies to Baltimore with a cargo of Molasses and Sugar. It is about 30 miles from here and out of my district but as I am the nearest Collector, I will go there and see what I can do. A letter from Dr. Davies[2] of the Hospital at Portsmouth, dated the 23rd. of last month informs me that the Captain had sold the cargo and that it was being removed. I expect that it will be hard to find by the time that I get there.

The weather has been quite cold to-day. It is now about 10 P.M. /I will quit/ and write some more in the morning if I have time. The steamer Fah-Kee came in from Port Royal this evening. I have not learned when she will leave. I will not send the 20 dollars by this steamer but will wait till I hear from the $40 that I sent last month.

Your brother,
John A. Hedrick.

[1] Although President Lincoln considered appointing Daniel R. Goodloe military governor of North Carolina after Stanly's resignation, he did not do so. Harris, *With Charity for All*, 71.

[2] Asst. Surgeon J. M. W. Davies of the Ninth New Jersey Infantry. Mallison, *Civil War on the Outer Banks*, 126; *The Medical and Surgical History of the Civil War*, vol. 6 (Wilmington, N.C.: Broadfoot Publishing, 1991), 682.

Duke
Beaufort, N.C.
March 13, 1863.

Dear Brother:

In my last letter I informed you that I was going to Portsmouth to look after a vessel from the West Indies that had gone ashore with a cargo of sugar and Molasses. Upon my arrival there the sugar and molasses had been sold and removed and the captain had gone north. The vessel went ashore about 4 miles this side of Hatteras Inlet during the early part of last month. I have reported the facts in the case as near as I could ascertain them to the Secretary of the Treasury so that the duties may be collected from the bond for the register of the vessel. The duties would amount to about $900.

I arrived home day before yesterday morning but have been busy since then and therefore have not written to you before now. Upon my arrival here I found your letters of the 26th. & 28th. ult. and yesterday I recieved yours of the 5th. inst. inclosing reciept for my clothes. I have not sent you any money since the $40 which you recieved. If Mr. Goodloe should come down here as Governor of the State, you tell him to have his powers as accurately defined as possible before he leaves Washington. If he be made Dictator in the State, let him have it so stated in his instructions from the Secretary of War. I think that Gov. Stanly would have had much less trouble if his powers had been well defined. He had verbal instructions to consider himself absolute Dictator in the State, while his written instructions only gave him power to use such measures as would protect the loyal inhabitants. Loyalty is very different according to the notions of different individuals.

It would be better to adopt some regulations for the government of the people in State. The people generally I think are easily governed. The regulations should be few and definite. They may be prepared by the War Department or by /the/ Military Governor and submitted by him to the Department. It would be well to get the approval of the Secretary of the Navy to them: because cases often arise in which the Naval Officers are concerned and they do not like to act without authority from their department.

I will write again shortly.

Your brother,
John A. Hedrick

———————

SHC
Beaufort, N.C.
March 15, 1863.

Dear Brother:

I wrote you last Friday and recieved your letter of the 5th. inst. the day before. All was quiet in this Department then but I can't tell how it is now. The train did not come down from Newbern yesterday and there was heavy canonading in that direction commencing night before last and continuing <all> pretty much all day yesterday. Yesterday was the anniversary of the taking of Newbern but it would hardly have taken so much firing to celebrate the event. There are a great many rumors afloat but nothing definite is known. It is very probably that there has been an attack on Newbern.

I don't know where Gov. Stanly is, though I heard last week that he had gone to Washington, N.C. I think that he will return to Sanfrancisco when he leaves the State. The weather is quite spring-like. It is warmer to-day than it has been since last November. We have New York papers of the 9th. inst. I have not seen them but I have heard that they contained nothing of particular interest. I was not here when the last Mail Boat left, and did /not/ send you the additional $20. I will let you know when I send it. My clothes have not arrived but I expect them on the next boat, which will be here to-wards the end of the week. If they suit me, I think that I shall / not/ order any more till I wear them out. The cloth coat that I have looks pretty well with the exception of the lining. My summer coat with new sleeve lining and new buttons will last 6 months longer. I did not wear it much last Summer. I wear flannel shirts to save washing and have a couple of them. What I need worst now, is teeth. I would like to have a good dentist to work on /much/ my mouth for a little while.

I was at church to-day for the first time for the last two months and heard a sermon from the Rev. Mr. Van Antwerpt, Minister of St. Paul's Church at this place. It may have been a good sermon but it did not interest me much. It was badly delivered. I hope that you have become more frequent in your attendance on Divine service. Tell Ellen to pull your ears every

Sunday that you don't go to church. I think that the performances at your church look a little too much like that of the Episcopal Church, and those of the Episcopal Church too much like those of the Catholic Church. You had better go back to the old long faced Presbyterians where you belong. If I hear any news from Newbern this evening, I will write it in the morning before the mail closes. The mail leaves here every morning, Sundays excepted, at 10 A.M. for Newbern, North Carolina. There is no particular time for it to leave going north. I think that we will have some news from Charleston shortly. The Steamer "Ocean Wave" arrived here from Port Royal yesterday and brought news that they were expecting an attack at that place from the Rebels. It would be strange if the Rebels should be the attacking party, after all the trouble and expense that we have been at, preparing to attack them.[1]

> Write often,
> Your brother,
> John A. Hedrick
>
> March 16th. 1863.

The train came down yesterday evening but I don't know whether it came all the way from Newbern or not. It brought the report that the firing heard towards Newbern was by the gunboats shelling a few rebels in the woods near Newbern. I understand that some of the rail-road was torn up.

> Your brother,
> J.A.H.

---

[1] Federal troops began organizing at Port Royal, S.C., in February 1863 for an ultimately unsuccessful attack on Charleston under the command of David Hunter. Barrett, *Civil War in North Carolina*, 150 n.

> *SHC*
> Beaufort, N.C.
> March 22nd. 1863.

Dear Brother:

I recieved your letter containing news of the capture of some of our Generals at Fair Fax C.H. last Thursday.[1] Tell Ellen that I did not take her advice. I would get married, but that I do not think that that will be the case soon. Much to my satisfaction my clothes arrived last week. I am very much pleased with them. I like them better than any suit I ever had before. They fit elegant and look beautiful. Were it necessary, I would not feel ashamed to get married in them. I owe the University the Contingencies for the last half year /Spring 1861/ ($5.) but no longer. Contingencies were paid semi-annually—$5 each time. The weather is quite nice to-day but for the last three days previous we have had nothing but rain, rain, rain. All is quiet in this Department. I wrote you last Sunday that heavy firing was heard the Saturday previous in the direction of Newbern. There was an attack made by a body of Rebels on the Union Regiment stationed on the East side of the Neuse. There was very little damage done on either side. The Rebels lost two guns by their exploding. The Dinsmore is coming in from Port Royal. She will hardly leave before 11 o'clock to-morrow. If she brings any important news from the South, I will try to put it in this letter. The Guide came from Port Royal last week but brought no news of importance. She is going north for repairs.

I understand that the humbug Foster is coming back to North Carolina for the purpose of converting the different companies of N.C. soldiers into a Regiment. I have lately seen a small pamphlet containing a portion of the protest of Foster and also the evidence taken before the Provost Marshal at Newbern in relation to the meeting held at the courthouse in this place on the 6th. of January last, at which those bitter resolutions against Gov. Stanly were passed. This investigation shows up Foster in his true light. Old Congleton swears that the resolutions were sent down from Newbern to him to be passed upon & that they were submitted by him to about a dozen soldiers and sent back to Foster and /that/ they now contain language, which was not in them when he put his signature to them. I do not know who published this pamphlet but if I can get a couple I will send you one. I think it better than any denunciatory letter. It shows the facts and not the feeling in the case. Besides the evidence is from one of Foster's warmest friends. The 51st. Reg. Mass. Vols. are here now. I like them better I did the 43 Massachusetts. The officers are more social.

March 23rd. 1863.

I have heard no news from Port Royal per Augusta Dinsmore.

Your brother,
John A. Hedrick

[1] On March 9, 1863, John S. Mosby's Confederate ranger battalion captured U.S. Brig. Gen. Edwin H. Stoughton at Fairfax Courthouse, Va. James A. Ramage, *Gray Ghost: The Life of Col. John Singleton Mosby* (Lexington: University Press of Kentucky, 1999), 58-76.

SHC
Beaufort, N.C.
March 29th. 1863.

Dear Brother:

I recieved last week your letters of the 16th. and the 21st. inst. I would never have dreamed of hearing of Ice Wood[1] in Washington City. Does he know any thing about his religious antagonist, Adam S. Hedrick?[2] Perhaps you have heard of the controversy that Ice and Adam had at the School House. I understood that Adam overstepped the rules of propriety and interrupted him in the midst of his sermon. I am very sorry to hear that Ice has been put to so great suffering, and I hope that he may get something to do to make a living. I will bet that Ice can split more rails in a day than Uncle Abe can. If you should go to Uncle Abe's with Ice, you can rally the President on Ice's rail-splitting. I have heard that Uncle Abe prides himself very highly on rail-splitting. Old Daniel Ford[3] told me that Ice was the best hand to split rails that he ever employed. I was not surprised to learn that Zeke Kountz[4] was in the Rebel Army but I did not think that Samuel[5] would be. Ice Wood may know something of Father's family and our relations in Salisbury as he was in prison there awhile. Geo. Weiss[6] lives so near the old factory building, which /is/ used as a prison, that he would be apt to visit it occasionally.

The battle at Newbern so far as it went, resulted favorably to our side. There were not many engaged on either side. There were five regiments of Rebels and one regiment of United States forces together /with/ a few gunboats. The darkies on one gunboat got a chance to try their courage and I heard that they did well.[7]

We have no news from any place. The last we heard from Port Royal, all was quiet. A boat came from there yesterday. New York papers of the 24th. have been recieved. I have been directed by the Secretary of the Treasury to make monthly requisitions on the Commissioner of Customs for sums to liquidate the Pay Rolls of the three Revenue Cutters in this State. I do not get any Commissions for cutter disbursements. I expect to get the disbursement of the Light House and Light Boat Salaries in this State. The Collector is entitled to 2 $^1/_2$ per cent on Light House disbursements. I did not send the additional $20.00.

> Your brother,
> John A. Hedrick

Monday March 30th. 1863.

This morning is cloudy and cold. The weather feels as if we should have some snow shortly. There has been no snow here worth naming this winter. The ground has not been covered with snow at any time. All is quiet and I do not see any prospect of any movement of the Army in this State shortly.

I do not know whether Gov. Stanly has left the State yet or not but he was packed up ready to leave last week. He was waiting for a special steamer to convey him to Philadelphia. He expects to visit Washington before he returns to California.

I am well with the exception of a slight cold.

> Write often.
> Your brother,
> John A. Hedrick

---

[1] Isom Wood (b. ca. 1821) was a laborer in Davidson County before the war. Confederate authorities jailed Wood for seventeen months due to his Unionist sentiments before he escaped to the North. Eighth Census, 1860: Davidson County; Isom Wood to Benjamin S. Hedrick, April 7, 1863, Hedrick Papers, Southern Historical Collection.

[2] Adam S. Hedrick (1829-1905), Benjamin and John's brother, was a Davidson County farmer. Although their father purchased a substitute for Adam, he was later conscripted into the Confederate army. Adam served in the Army of Northern Virginia and joined the secret Unionist organization the Heroes of America. Frank Swicegood et al., eds., *Cemetery Records of Davidson County, N.C.*, 8 vols. (Lexington, N.C.: Genealogical Society of Davidson County, 1986-1989) 6:196; Adam S. Hedrick to Benjamin S. Hedrick, June 24, 1865, Hedrick Papers, Duke Special Collections; Manarin and Jordan, *North Carolina Troops*, 11:387.

[3] Daniel H. Ford (1795-1864) was a Davidson County farmer. Swicegood et al., *Cemetery Records of Davidson County, N.C.*, 5:36; Eighth Census, 1860: Davidson County.

[4] Ezekiel Koonts (b. ca. 1833), a Davidson County farmer, enlisted as a private in the Fourteenth Regiment North Carolina Troops in July 1862, and was killed two months later at the Battle of Antietam. Eighth Census, 1860: Davidson County; Manarin and Jordan, *North Carolina Troops*, 5:477-478; John W. Moore, ed., *Roster of North Carolina Troops in the War Between the States*, vol. 1 (Raleigh: Ashe and Gatling, 1882), 539.

[5] Samuel Koonts (b. ca. 1823), a Davidson County farmer, was married and the father of six young children. He served in the Third North Carolina Artillery. Eighth Census, 1860: Davidson County; Janet B. Hewett, ed., *The Roster of Confederate Soldiers*, 16 vols. (Wilmington, N.C.: Broadfoot Publishing, 1995-1996), 9:245.

[6] This is perhaps a reference to George W. Hedrick (b. ca. 1829) of Davidson County. Eighth Census, 1860: Davidson County; Ninth Census, 1870: Davidson County.

[7] On March 13, 1863, Confederate troops under D. H. Hill launched an unsuccessful attack against New Bern. This included a March 14 assault on Union-held Fort Anderson, located across the Neuse River from New Bern. The attack on the fort was repulsed with the aid of gunboats. Barrett, *Civil War in North Carolina*, 151-156.

SHC
Beaufort, N.C.
April 2nd. 1863.

Dear Brother:

I recieved yesterday per the Steamer "Saxon" from New York, your interesting letter of the 26th. ultimo. The Latin preposition "ante" governs the accusative case.

I have not yet done any thing further about depositing the U.S. funds in my hands. I intend to recommend to the Department to allow me to send the money to New York by Adams Express. I think that it will be as cheap and safer than any other way. It will cost 1 $^1/_2$ per cent to have it insured.

There are some rumors afloat in this Department but nothing definite. It was reported here yesterday that Gen. Foster had gone over to Washington and had been cut off from returning to Newbern by batteries placed on the river by the Rebs this side of the former place. The Rebs are said to be 15,000 strong and our forces about 2,000.

The Fah-Kee brings news from Port Royal that the iron-clads had left that place for Charleston when she left Port Royal. If they are out in this gale, they will have a hard time. It has been blowing quite hard for the last three days. March is stealing a little from April to make up for lost time.

I recieved quite a batch of correspondence from the Asst. Secretary of the Treasury yesterday. It seems that there has been some difficulty between the officers of the Cutter "Agassiz" at Newbern and the matter has been refered to me for investigation and a report thereon. I have my hands rather full just now and will not be able to make the investigation before the 10th. inst. It looks like putting a big thing in a little man's hands.

I am well and weigh about 135 pounds.

Write often.

Your brother,
John A. Hedrick

SHC
Beaufort, N.C.
April 5th. 1863.

Dear Brother:

I wrote you last Sunday and Monday, and again during the week, but I think that neith of my letters has left port, as it /has/ been so stormy during the last four days that the Fah Kee could not leave port. Your letter of the 26th. ult. has been recieved. We have no definite news from any place since I wrote you last. There are a great many rumors afloat concerning Gen Foster at Washington, but I do not place much confidence in them. I don't think that any one here knows what is going on at Washington. It is very probable that an attack will be made by the Rebs on some place, but it is hard to tell where. I can't see what they can gain by taking Washington. It looks as if they were making a feint on Washington in order to divert attention from Newbern and that their real object <was> /is/ to take Newbern.[1] I think that they will have a hard time of it if they should attack Newbern. The "Spaulding" has just come in from Port Royal but no one from her has come ashore. It don't think that any thing has been done at Charleston yet. The weather has been too rough for the iron-clads, and I understand that another coat of plating is to be put over their decks before they attempt the attack on Charleston. We have had New York papers of the 30th. ult.

The weather is somewhat better to-day than it has been for some time but it is still quite cold. It snowed a little yesterday. We have had worse weather since the 1st. of April than at any time during the whole Winter. I have just seen a man, who has been over to the Spaulding. He says that she brought no news from Charleston. There was some talk of making an attack on Charleston to-day, but if it was not made to-day, they would have to wait till the next full moon on account of the tides. I think that we will have pretty good weather tomorrow. It is more pleasant this evening than it was this morning. There has been no train drown from Newbern to-day. It is not usual for it come down on Sunday, without something special is on hand.

The Spaulding stopped here about two hours and proceeded on to Fortress Monroe. The "Fah Kee" is expected to leave tomorrow evening. The "Augusta Dinsmore" will arrive here from New York about Tuesday. The Mary Sanford is due from Port Royal. My receipts for last month were not as great as for the month before. I have enough of business to transact now but do not get any thing for a great deal of it. The monthly disbursements for the Cutter service is between $1500 & $2000. I hold $1899.58 U.S. funds, which is derived from Duties on Imports, Tonage Dues and Hospital Money.

Fletcher Harper of Harper Brothers[2] is here. I know that Ice Wood was a Baptist preacher but had no license to preach when I left N.C. in the Fall of 59. He and Adam had a controversy on baptism at the School House some time during the Summer of 1859. Adam thought that the hogs were drowned but that devils were not.

I did not go to church today. I thought that it was /too/ cold to listen 2 hours to the kind of preaching that we have here.

Your brother,
John A. Hedrick

---

[1] On March 30, 1863, Confederates under D. H. Hill laid siege to the Union garrison at Washington, N.C., in part to gather supplies. On the same day, Union general and department commander John G. Foster arrived in Washington and became one of the besieged defenders. On April 14, Foster evaded the Confederates and made his way to New Bern to assemble a force to lift the siege. Foster's column reached Washington on April 19 only to find that the Confederate withdrawal was already well under way. *OR*, ser. 1, 18:211-216.

[2] Fletcher Harper (1806-1877) of New York, along with his three brothers, managed the Harper and Brothers publishing house. *American National Biography*, s.v. "Harper, Fletcher."

SHC
Beaufort, N.C.
April 9th. 1863.

Dear Brother:

I recieved day before yesterday your letter of the 28th. ultimo. The batch of envelopes, no. 2, came to hand in due time and were very acceptible. The "Spaulding" came in this morning from Fortress Monroe, bringing New York papers of the 7th. inst. It seems to think that the attack on Charleston has already /commenced/. I mean the Herald, the paper that I have just been reading. The Herald's correspondent writes from an island nine miles from Charles, which he says is occupied by a New York regiment. His letter is dated the 28th. ult. The Fah-Kee came from Port Royal on the 29th. and knew nothing of this expedition. A tug-boat from Port Royal arrived here about three days ago and brought news that they saw the first gun fired in the attack on Charleston as they passed that place. Operations may have commenced there but I hardly think that much has been accomplished as yet. The Mary Sanford has been due here for the last three days and I think it probable that she is detained by the military authorities at Port Royal to transport troops.

All seems to be quiet here now. I have not heard anything definite from Gen. Foster lately. The light house keeper from Ocracoke N.C. told me this morning that two steamers loaded with troops had entered the Sound at Hatteras Inlet and that more were expected to relieve Gen. Foster at Washington N.C.

There has been some skirmishing around Newbern lately but did not amount to much. The humbug Charles H. Foster is here now. I have not seen him and do not know what his business is.

He was at Portsmouth not long since and told the people that if they did not volunteer, that they would be conscripted before long.

The "Spaulding" brings ammunition and is now discharging a part of her cargo into the storeship "Wm. Badger."

I have not heard anything from Gov. Stanly lately but think that he has gone north before now. You will probably see him in Washington before he returns to California.

Business is very dull in my line and I expect it to be still duller. The President has recently issued a Proclamation and in consequence of that Proclamation all commerce between here and Newbern will be shut off. Heretofore, merchants were permitted to ship goods on the rail Road to Newbern but not by water. Now it will be stopped altogether except as authorized by the President through the Secretary of the Treasury. And no produce can be brought out of the blockaded region except as permitted by the President through the Secretary.[1]

April 10th. 1863.

This morning is beautiful and clear. The weather feels quite springlike. The "Spaulding" is going north to-day but I do not know whether she will take the Mail or not.

All is quiet. We don't hear enough news to make things interesting. The papers of the 7th. do not contain any news from Vicksburg. I am afraid that we will not be successful there. The papers of the 4th. stated that the "cut-off" had been abandoned[2] and that Rebels had repaired the "Indianola."[3]

I see by the papers that Connecticut and Rhode Island have gone Republican.

Write often.
Your brother,
John A. Hedrick

---

[1] Issued March 31, 1863, these regulations made Northern trade with occupied regions of the South illegal, except under the supervision of the Treasury Department. *New York Times*, April 7, 1863.

[2] The "cut-off" refers to an attempt by Grant to bypass the Vicksburg batteries by digging a canal across the bottom of a horseshoe-shaped bend in the Mississippi River. Construction began in January 1863 and continued until March, when high water ended the project. William C. Everhart, *Vicksburg National Military Park, Mississippi*, National Park Service Historical Handbook Series, No. 21 (Washington, D.C., 1954; reprint, 1957), 10, 12.

[3] The *Indianola*, a Union ironclad, was partially sunk and captured by Confederates on the Mississippi River, south of Vicksburg, on February 24, 1863. The Southerners hoped to raise and restore the *Indianola*. On the night of February 26, however, the Confederates saw what they thought was a Union gunboat approaching, and they destroyed the *Indianola* and fled. What they actually saw was a Union vessel hastily disguised to look like a gunboat. Shelby Foote, *The Civil War: A Narrative*, vol. 2, *Fredericksburg to Meridian* (New York: Random House, 1963), 197-201; Long, *Day by Day*, 322, 323-324.

SHC
Beaufort, N.C.
April 12th, 1863.

Dear Brother:

Were it not Sunday I should not write you to-day. For I wrote you a letter, a few days ago, which is now leaving this place on the "Mary Sanford," and it will be several days before another boat leaves. The Mary Sanford brings but little news from Port Royal and that little very uncertain. She reports the monitor, "Kiokup" sunk and the "Nahant" injured in the attack on Charleston. I think that it will take some hard fighting to get into Charleston.

One of the Clerks in the Post-Office at Newbern came down to-day and reports that a boat succeeded in running the blockade between Newbern and Washington last Friday night and brought news that Gen. Foster was in good spirits. An attack was expected to be made on the Rebel battery to-night. Papers of the 8th. have reached Newbern but I have not heard of any so late being here. This post-office clerk's name is Rand and is a brother of the Rand in Johnson & Dow's office, 270 /B-way/ New York.

Gov. Stanly left Newbern last Wednesday. I do not know where he will /go/ first but expect that he will be in Washington City before he goes to California.

What is Mr. Goodloe doing? How are Mr. & Mrs. Pigott? We are having very nice, warm weather.

Your brother,
John A. Hedrick

SHC
Beaufort, N.C.
April 17th. 1863.

Dear Brother:

I recieved your letter of April 7th. a few days ago. I wrote you a short letter last Sunday. Nothing much has taken place here since then. The 9th. New Jersey and the 10th. Connecticut have returned from Port Royal. They arrived here yesterday. They bring no additional news from the attack on Charleston.

Gen. Foster was still hemmed in at Washington N.C. when last heard from. Gen. <Ledlie> /Neglee/[1] arrived here on the "Spaulding" last Tuesday and proceeded to Newbern. Quite a number of expeditions have left Newbern for the relief of Gen. Foster but none sent by land had reached him at the last news. One steamer with supplies for him succeeded in running the blockade last week. Our latest New York papers are the 11th. They contain very little news of importance. There had been some fighting in Tennessee between Van Dorn and one of our generals.[2]

I have just heard that Gen. Foster has made his escape from Washington, N.C. and is now in Newbern. He ran the blockade on the night of the 15th. inst. and was fired into when passing the battery by the Rebels. A ball went through the berth in which he had been lying and took the covers off of the bed. It is lucky for him that he was not in it at the time.

The weather is very pleasant and spring like. We will soon have a plenty of fresh vegetables.

The humbug Foster was here last week. He told Mr. Rumley[3] that he was Lieut. Col. of the 1st. N.C. Regiment. I am disposed to doubt it, because I have heard that a Mr. McChesney[4] formerly a Captain in the 9th. New Jersey was Lieut. Col. of the 1st. N.C.

What is Mr. Goodloe doing about the governorship of North Carolina?

Write often
Your brother,
John A. Hedrick

---

[1]James Hewett Ledlie (1832-1882) and Henry Morris Naglee (1815-1886) were Union brigadier generals. Ledlie served as chief of artillery of the Department of North Carolina from December 1862 to May 1863, and Naglee commanded the Second Division, XVIII Corps, from January to May 1863. Warner, *Generals in Blue*, s.v. "Ledlie, James Hewett," "Naglee, Henry Morris."

[2]Confederates commanded by Earl Van Dorn defeated Union troops at the Battle of Thompson's Station, Tenn., on March 4-5, 1863. The Confederates captured 1,221 prisoners,

including the Federal commander, Col. John C. Coburn. Arthur B. Carter, *The Tarnished Cavalier: Major General Earl Van Dorn, C.S.A.* (Knoxville: University of Tennessee Press, 1999), 167-170.

[3] Either John or James Rumley. John Rumley (b. ca. 1815) was the Carteret County register. He and his family were sent into Confederate lines in June 1863 because of alleged disloyalty. Eighth Census, 1860: Carteret County; Mallison, *Civil War on the Outer Banks*, 126.

[4] Joseph M. McChesney served as captain of Company M, Ninth New Jersey Infantry. He was subsequently commissioned as lieutenant colonel of the First North Carolina Union Regiment on February 20, 1863, and assumed his duties with the regiment on March 24. McChesney was promoted to colonel on September 18, 1863. After transferring to the First North Carolina, he commanded the Sub-districts of the Pamlico and Beaufort in the Department of Virginia and North Carolina. John Y. Foster, *New Jersey and the Rebellion: A History of the Services of the Troops and People of New Jersey in Aid of the Union Cause* (Newark, N.J.: Martin R. Dennis, 1868), 203; Compiled Service Records, Record Group 94; *OR*, ser. 1, 47, pt. 2:625; 18:678.

———————

SHC
Beaufort, N.C.
April 19th. 1863.

Dear Brother:

Your letter of the 11th. inst. was recieved last Friday. I wrote to you on the same day but had not recieved your letter. We have had no additional news from Charleston. When last heard from, the iron-clads had withdrawn after an engagement of about three hours. The amount of damage done to Fort Sumter is not known <that> /but/ it is believed that a breach was made in the walls.[1] Gen. Heckman's[2] brigade has returned from Port Royal and gone to Newbern. I mentioned in my last letter that Gen Foster had made his escape from Washington, N.C. It is reported by the passengers from Newbern to-day, that the Rebels have abandoned their batteries below Washington and that Gen. Foster is in pursuit of them. The "Dudley Buck" arrived last night at Newbern with a Northern Mail, which will be down here to-morrow. The mail never comes down on Sunday.

The "Fah Kee" has been expected in here from New York for the last three days but I heard to-day that the Government had taken her for a transport. I wish that they would get some other boats and let our line alone. The Express Steamers are a great convenience to us. They charge high but still it is better to pay their prices than to be with/out/ them. We have news of a fight in Tennessee between Rosecrans and Van Dorn. The latter is said to have been defeated. New York papers of the 15th. are in town but I have not seen any thing later than the 11th. Capt. Manson,[3] one of the Rebel officers taken at Fort Macon and exchanged last August has resigned his Commission in the Confederate Army and returned home. He arrived here this morning. I do not know what news he brings not for what purpose he comes.

Business has been very dull during the present month. The disturbance at Washington, N.C. has frightened the shippers.

I have seen the Proclamation of the President and the Regulations of the Secretary of the Treasury of March 30th. which closes the seceded States against the ingress or egress of merchandise except as permitted by the President through the Secretary of the Treasury. The Regulations provide that the President shall give notice, in such newspapers as he shall think proper, as to what districts, in what articles and by what persons, this trade shall be carried on, and under what regulations. So far the tendency of the Proclamation is to cut off the trade here and thereby decrease the amount of business for me.

All is quiet here and the weather exceedingly pleasant and beautiful.

> I am your brother,
> John A. Hedrick

> April 20th. 1863.

This morning is calm and a little inclined to be sultry. We have had no news since yesterday. We will probably get some news to-day from Gen Foster's expedition. All is quiet. I am well and weigh about 133 pounds. This is a little less than I weighed during the Winter, but the diminution is not caused by sickness, but perhaps by the warmth of the weather. Garden peas are nearly large enough to eat. Mrs. Norcum has some about an inch and a half long.

> Write often,
> Your brother
> John A. Hedrick

---

[1] Nine Union ironclads attacked Fort Sumter on April 7, 1863. The fleet, under the command of Flag Officer Samuel Du Pont, was heavily damaged by Confederate batteries and retreated. Before withdrawing the Union vessels inflicted serious damage on Fort Sumter. This was quickly repaired, however. Long, *Day by Day*, 335-336.

[2] Brig. Gen. Charles Adam Heckman (1822-1896) held a variety of commands in North Carolina, including the District of Beaufort from May to July of 1863. Boatner, *Civil War Dictionary*, 391-392.

[3] John C. Manson, former Carteret County merchant and captain of "Manson's Battery" (formerly Stephen D. Pool's Battery), resigned March 17, 1863, because of physical infirmity. Wilson, *A Researcher's Journal*, 123, 131; Manarin and Jordan, *North Carolina Troops*, 1:126.

SHC
Beaufort, N.C.
April 26th. 1863.

Dear Brother:

I have not recieved any thing from you later than the 11th. though I expect a letter of to-morrow by the Mail which is in Newbern. The Express Steamers have been taken off and now we get all of our <news via> Mails via Newbern. The "Spaulding" came in to-day from Fortress Monroe bringing New York papers of the 24th. I think that the prospects are brightening. A barque from Port Royal arrived here yesterday, and brings news that the iron-clads had gone back to Charleston. I hope that they may have a fair trial this time and not be signaled off before they have time to accomplish anything. Every thing has settled down into complete quietness in this department, and the troops are talking about going into Summer quarters. The Buffaloes (1st. N.C. Vols.) left here to-day for Washington N.C. where the principal part of their regiment is stationed. They have gone over for regimental drill, and will be back here again (perhaps). The weather is very pleasant. There is not much doing in my line of business. I have been busy during the last few days writing out the evidence in the Webster-Traverse case. It consists of 20 pages foolscap paper. There were two witnesses absent and whose testimonies we did not get.

The Traverse-Cary case has not come off yet. Both of the parties have gone north with the intention as I think, of resigning. If I don't soon get other instructions from the Department at Washington I shall notify them to be present and proceed to take the testimony.

My new regulations from the Treasury Department have not been recieved. I have been expecting them for some time.

I was at Mr. Norcum's last /night/ and found them all well. The peas and other garden stuff is coming on fast.

Write often as it takes a letter so long to come.

Your brother,
John A. Hedrick

P.S. I forwarded yesterday a letter to Mr. Pigott which had been sent to him here from the Dead letter Office.

J.A.H.

April 27th. 1863.

The weather is still beautiful. All is quiet. The "Spaulding" yesterday in port only about two hours and proceeded to Port Royal. She is a smart boat. It takes her about three days to go to Baltimore and back.

Your brother,
John A. Hedrick

SHC
Beaufort, N.C.
April 28th. 1863.

Dear Brother:

Your letters of the 15th. & 18th. were recieved yesterday and that of the 21st. to-day. I wrote you a letter Sunday and added a few lines yesterday. I am glad to learn that the Hedrick family has been increased by the addition of a permanent member, and that he and his mother are doing well.[1] You and sister Ellen keep good time. For as well as I remember it was between the 18th. & 21st. of April 1861 when Jeannie was born.[2] I hope you may do as well during the next two years. You had better call the bab's name, Bill, and then you will have satisfied both of the grandfathers with name sakes. I know of only one Billie Hedrick, and he will hardly /eclipse/ your son's renown. Old Uncle John has a son named Billie.

There is no news whatever to-day. It rained considerably this morning and is cloudy and chilly now. I received to-day the recent Regulations of the Secretary of the Treasury concerning Internal & Coastwise Commercial Intercourse, but do not see that it will add materially to my official emoluments for the present. There may be some future regulations, which these point out, which will add to my pay. My receipts for this month have been less than for any month since last September. Any military operations stop trade. In some instances the vessels are taken by Government for transports and in others, they are afraid to venture.

In a former letter, /I gave/ certain points, which Mr. Goodloe must have defined before he comes here should he be appointed Governor of this State. In the first place he must have clearly defined by the Department sending him here, what things they wish him to do and to what powers here he shall apply for aid in carrying those things /out/. I would advise him to have as little discretionary power as possible. There are here the representatives of the three great Departments at Washington. Gen Foster represents the War Department, R. Ad. Lee,[3] the Navy, and myself, the Treasury. Gen Foster has some thirty thousand men, R. Ad. Lee some dozen gunboats in the waters of North Carolina, commanded by Com. Murray, and I have three Cutters commanded by Capt. Ottinger. My force is a mixture /of/ the naval and civil arm of the government, and its service is principally preventative. Accordingly when I recieve instructions to stop any commercial intercourse unless it be carried on in a particular way, I consider it my duty to seize all goods, wares and merchandise, except supplies belonging to the U.S. transported under military and naval orders, transported contrary my instructions. I suppose that the officers in charge of the other departments are similarly situated. I do not wish Mr. Goodloe /to/ fall into the mistaken idea, that there is no civil law here. For where commerce goes, civil law must follow. Nor must he think that whatever the military authorities do, is right. In emergencies, the Commandant of a Department may do most any thing and be justifiable for his acts; but it is not so in the common routine of business. It is as much his duty to obey the laws of the United States as it is that of any other person.

My regulations, are based on laws of Congress, issued by the Secretary of the Treasury, and accompanied by orders from the Secretary of /the/ Navy, and War.

Mr. Goodloe will have to do with persons principally employed on the water, and therefore he should have a correct understanding with the Navy in the waters of North Carolina. Therefore he should have his instructions countersigned by the Secretary of the Navy. He must have something to fall back on. It would not do to try to force things to be done. The office of military governor is a novel thing in this country and it is exceedingly hard for people to understand the nature of it. Gov. Stanly can give him the information needed better than I can write. Tell him that he need not expect any instructions after he leaves Washington, because as I have been informed by Gov. Stanly, the War Department, were very slow to answer his letters.

Excuse grammatical errors and other mistakes.

Your brother,
John A. Hedrick

---

[1] William Adam Hedrick (1863-1937) was the fifth of Benjamin and Mary Ellen Hedrick's eight children. He would become a physics teacher in Washington, D.C. Vic Kirkman, *The Heritage of Adam Alexander Young* (n.p., 1995), 20.

[2]Jennie Hedrick (1861-1946) became the director of the Washington School for the Correction of Speech Defects. Kirkman, *Heritage of Adam Alexander Young*, 20.

[3]Samuel Phillips Lee (1812-1897) of Virginia, cousin of Robert E. Lee, commanded the Union North Atlantic Blockading Squadron from August 1862 until September 1864, when he was transferred to the Mississippi Squadron. *American National Biography*, s.v. "Lee, Samuel Phillips."

SHC
Beaufort, N.C.
<April> May 3rd. 1863.

Dear Brother:

Your letter of the 24th. ultimo was recieved yesterday. I hardly know what to say in relation to the "utility, and advantage to be derived from" Mr Goodloe coming to North Carolina. All of the citizens to whom I have spoken concerning his coming, have expressed themselves favorable to it. If he be vested with the proper powers, he could undoubtedly do a great deal of good. The great difficulty in the way of a Military Governor, arises from the complicated masses with which he has to deal, and the critical condition in which this part of the State is in. If our army could advance into the interior and leave only small bodies of troops here and there, for police duty and these troops were placed under command of the Governor as a kind of posse comitatus, he might /do/ much good in organizing a government and protecting peaceable citizens. We are now hemmed /in/ here in a strip of country bordering on the Sounds and every thing is under the strictest martial law. Nothing is allowed to go out of this place or Newbern without a permit from the Provost Marshal. If a man buys a pound of coffee or a paper or pins he must go to the Provost and get a permit to take it from the wharf with him. Every one except commissioned officers must have a pass from the Provost Marshal to leave town. Where every thing is so completely in the hands of the military authorities, it is hard for a power having no existence in law, novel in its character, and weak unless supported by the other powers, to come in and do much good. The difficulty does not arise from the citizens. For the most of them are willing to obey almost any regulation. They are generally disposed to be peaceable. If the military and naval authorities should fall out with Mr. Goodloe as they did with Gov. Stanly I think that the citizens would fare better without a governor. The mere fact of a man's having a safeguard from Gov. Stanly would subject him to the enmity of the military and more especially to the naval authorities. I would be glad to see Mr. Goodloe down here, but I do not know what to advise him about coming. He had better consult his own feelings and follow his own judgement in the matter. As he is /a/ military man himself, perhaps he can get along with the military authorities better than Gov. Stanly did. Should he come, he must not expect to get along without trouble. But then he should remember that "Nil sine magno vita labore dedit mortalibus."[1] While I remain in my present office I shall endeavor to aid him all that I can.

I don't think that he need apprehend any danger from his anti-slavery views; for the people here are as much anti-slavery as he is, though in a different way. They wish to get rid of slavery and negroes, and if they can not dispose of the latter any other way, they wish to kill them.

The weather is quite warm to-day. We are having a change in the troops at this place. The 81st. Mass will leave to-morrow. Maj Curlis is to be Provost Marshal. He belongs to the 9th. N.J. and has been Provost before. I have recieved the Regulations of March 31st. 1863, concerning Internal and Coastwise Commercial Intercourse and instructions from the Secretary of the Treasury in relation thereto. As soon as the President opens this district to trade it will give me considerable more work to do. I have stopped merchandise from going to Newbern on the cars. It creates considerable fuss among merchants. I forgot to mention above that we are to be honored with the presence of a Brigadier among us. This we have not had since Gen Parke left, shortly after my arrival. Gen Naglee will make his headquarters in this town.

I think that you deserve great credit for writing to me so promptly during the last month. For some time now you have averaged one /letter/ every three days. My best hope and earnest desire is that you may continue to do so well. I nearly always write to you on every Sunday and once during the week if I have anything to write or recieve any letters from you during the fore part of the week. I want another batch of large envelopes.

Your brother,
John A. Hedrick

---

[1] Life gave nothing to mortal beings without great effort.

SHC
Beaufort, N.C.
<April> May 10th., 1863

Dear:

Your letters of April 27th. and May 2nd. have been recieved. I can not tell you on what days you should mail your letters in order to reach me in the shortest time. Yours of the 2nd. was received on the 7th. which is about as short a time as I ever get letters from Washington. There are no regular days for the steamers to leave New York. Lately they have been reaching Newbern during first part of each week. The "Dudly buck" and the "Ellen S. Terry" from the last two trips have arrived at Newbern about the same time. They usually remain in Newbern one day, so that there is no chance for me to get a letter off on the same boat that brings yours. Your last letter I think came through the Canal by way of Norfolk. That is the shortest route, and when every thing is quiet about as quick as any, though I would not at present advise you to send your letter that way.

All is quiet here now. There were about a dozen Confederates and 40 horses captured near Newport last week. I saw some of the horses as I was going to Newbern but none of the men. The Philadelphia Inquirer of the 4th. has been recieved. I saw a man who had read it. He said that Gen Hooker had crossed the Rappahannock and got in the rear of Lee's Army, and had compelled him to come out of his entrenchments at Fredricksburg.[1] My informant was afraid that it might /not/ be as good as the paper represented and that perhaps the story was gotten up to make the paper sell. The "Albany" is expected in Newbern shortly. We have not had any steamers running between here and New York since the Express steamers were taken off. There is very little doing in the way of shipments under the recent Regulations. They cut every thing off in the way of exports off until the district within the Union lines is declared open to trade. There is nothing here worth naming to ship. It must come from the interior.

The weather is beautiful and pleasant. We have more pleasant weather here than you do in Washington.

> Write often
> Your brother,
> John A. Hedrick

P.S. In my last I requested you to send me another batch of large envelopes.

> Your brother,
> J.A.H.

---

[1] Joseph Hooker led the Army of the Potomac against the Confederate Army of Northern Virginia, crossing the Rappahannock River on April 30, 1863. Robert E. Lee's Confederates subsequently defeated the Federals at the Battle of Chancellorsville. Foote, *Civil War*, 2:261-316.

SHC
Beaufort, N.C.
May 15th., 1863.

Dear Brother:

I have written to the Secretary of the Treasury in relation to commercial intercourse in this State. Section VI of the Regulations of March 31st. is as follows: "Whenever commercial intercourse with any part or section of a state heretofore declared in insurrection is permitted by the Secretary of the Treasury, under the license of the President, in pursuance of said act, approved July 13, 1861, notice thereof and of the conditions under which the same may be conducted shall be published in such papers as the Secretary may think expedient, in order to the general information of parties interested."

Section VII After commercial intercourse with any part or section of an insurrectionary State has been permitted as aforesaid, permits to transport to or from any place therein for use in any other place, shall be granted only by such persons as shall be specially authorized by the Secretary of the Treasury after the date hereof. And no permit shall be granted by any such person to transport to or from, or to purchase or sell in any place or section whatever not within the military lines of the United States army.

Section XIX. Supervising Special Agents of the Treasury Department will be appointed by the Secretary of the Treasury to supervise within designated limits, the execution of these regulations, not inconsistent with them, as may be proper for that purpose, and to change the same from time to time, and temporarily suspend or qualify the authority to grant permits, as the public interests may require, subject to the approval of the Secretary of the Treasury; and all <clearances> permits and clearances authorized under these regulations will be granted only in compliance with such local rules and restrictions as may be approved as above said."

By Section VI, you will perceive that /trade by/ the part or section of the State must first be permitted by the Secretary of the Treasury, and the conditions under which it must be conducted published in such papers as the Secretary may think fit.

I have been authorized to /grant/ the permits under such local rules and restrictions as may from time to time, be made by the Secretary of the Treasury, or by a duly authorized Special Agent of the Treasury Department, subject to his approval.

I have not been informed that any part or section of this State was open to trade nor have I recieved any local rules and restrictions for my government. I cannot see that I am authorized to grant any permits to trade until the Section or part of the State is open to trade. If you have time I would be glad if you would call at the Department and see if they have recieved my letter and ask them whether my views are correct. This cutting off of trade under the recent Proclamation of the President makes a great deal of trouble and very little pay for me. By this Proclamation no place in this State is open to trade except the mere port of Beaufort and there is a dispute as to how far the port extends.

All is quiet here now. We have had nothing from the Army of the Potomac later than 8th. There are rumors that Hooker has advanced but I cannot learn how true those rumors are.

Write soon
Your brother,
John A. Hedrick

May 16th. 1863.

We learned by the passengers from Newbern yesterday that the Richmond Dispatch of the 11th. had been recieved and that it contained the news of the deaths of Stonewall Jackson, Gens. Heath, Patton, and Garnett,[1] and that Gen. Hooker had been heavily reinforced and was driving Lee towards Richmond.

Peck had gone up the James River.[2]

Your brother,
J.A.H.

---

[1] Hedrick's information about these Confederate officers was partially correct. Lt. Gen. Thomas Jonathan "Stonewall" Jackson (1824-1863) was mortally wounded at Chancellorsville. Maj. Gen. Henry Heth (1825-1899) participated in the battle but was not wounded. Brig. Gen. Richard Brook Garnett (1817-1863) was not present at the battle but was killed in July 1863 at Gettysburg. Col. George S. Patton of the Twenty-second Virginia commanded a brigade in operations in West Virginia during the campaign. He was mortally wounded in September 1864 at the Battle of Winchester. Ezra J. Warner, *Generals in Gray: Lives of the Confederate Commanders* (Baton Rouge: Louisiana State University Press, 1959), s.v. "Heth, Henry," "Jackson, Thomas Jonathan," "Garnett, Richard Brooke"; *OR*, ser. 1, 25, pt. 2:650, 716-718, 763; Douglas Southall Freeman, *Lee's Lieutenants: A Study in Command*, vol. 3 (New York: Charles Scribner's Sons, 1944), 581.

[2] Maj. Gen. John James Peck (1821-1878) was commander of Federal forces at Suffolk, Va. Confederate troops under James Longstreet besieged Suffolk from April 11 to May 4, 1863, but eventually withdrew. Warner, *Generals in Blue*, s.v. "Peck, John James"; Boatner, *Civil War Dictionary*, 817.

Beaufort, N.C.
May 19th. 1863.

Dear Brother:

I recieved yesterday your letter of the 7th. inst. Which is the latest. I wrote you last Friday and Saturday and therefore omitted to write Sunday my usual time of writing. We have recieved N.Y. papers of the 14th. Gen Hooker was still on the north side of the Rappahannock. I saw a dispatch from the Secretary of War in which he said that it was the intention of Gen. Hooker to recross the river, but from the news in the papers, I could see no movement in that direction. I hardly know how we stand at present. It seems to me that the losses in the recent battles in men on both sides were very nearly equal. Of course the data from which I form my opinion is very imperfect. The death of Stonewall Jackson however will be severely felt by the Rebs and his loss will be almost equal to a brigade. His place cannot well be filled by any other person. Our loss in general officers seems to have been comparatively small. From the Richmond papers of the 11th. which were recieved last Saturday we were in hopes that Gen Peck would take Richmond by way of <Fredricksburg> /Petersburg/. About that time there must have been great confusion in the Rebel Capitol and little trustworthy news. Our last news from Banks and Porter was encouraging. The fortifications at Grand Gulf had been taken and an immediate attack on Vicksburg was expected.[1]

Nothing of interest has taken place in this department since I wrote last. Quite a number of regiments, whose time of service will expire between now and the 1st. of August, will leave this State within the next two months. I don't know where troops to take their places will come from.

I wrote you in my last letter concerning my interpretation of the Regulations concerning Internal and Coastwise Commercial Intercourse of March 31st. 1863, and requested you if you had time, to call at the Treasury Department and ask the meaning of /the/ sixth seventh and eighth sections of those regulations. I consider that Section six together with the President's Proclamation stops all trade in this State except at the port of Beaufort, until further notice is given by the Secretary of the Treasury.

I would also like to know how much territory was imbraced in the port of Beaufort, which is declared open to trade. Some think that the port of Beaufort includes Morehead City, Carolina City, Newport, and the various creeks and inlets flowing into <the> Beaufort Harbor, while others contend that the town of Beaufort only is included.

I have had much trouble lately in consequence of the indefinite nature of the recent regulations of the Secretary of the Treasury.

Mrs. Norcum has been sick for the last few days. She has had a violent pain in the head. She has a very fine garden of peas, cabbages & c. the result of the seeds recieved from the Patent Office.

This morning is quite pleasant.

> Write often,
> Your brother,
> John A. Hedrick

P.S. The Envelopes, batch No. 4 have been recieved. I sent you last week $20.

> J.A.H.

---

[1] Hedrick seems to be attributing the capture of Grand Gulf, Miss., on May 2, 1863, to Nathaniel P. Banks, who from May to July 1863 conducted a problem-plagued although ultimately successful campaign against Port Hudson, La. The threat posed by Ulysses S. Grant's advancing army early in the Vicksburg campaign was the actual reason for the evacuation of Grand Gulf. Comdr. David Dixon Porter led the Union naval forces in that campaign. Foote, *Civil War*, 2:344-350.

SHC
Beaufort, N.C.
May 24th./62 [*1863*]

Dear Brother:

Your letters of the 10th. and 12th. and also the Chronicle of the 9th. have been recieved. I am not certain that I know any of the men whose names are contained in the Chronicle.[1] I know /two/ Dan Colemans[2] but do not know whether they have any middle names or not. I do not think that the Capt. Parks[3] mentioned by you is my friend David M. Parks.[4] I am very sorry to hear that Sidney T. Wilfong[5] has recieved so great injury in his arm. Should he not be furnished with proper clothing by the hospital, you may let him have what he needs on my account. His father is well off, and he treated me very kindly while I was at Newton.[6] I have never recieved as good board and attention at any other place as I did at Mr. Wilfong's. Sid was quite a boy when I saw him last in the Fall of 1856. I think that he was about 13 years old. I noticed some time ago in the Newbern Progress, the name of Y.M. Wilfong, one of Sid's brothers, and as 3rd. Lieut. and M.L. McCorkle[7] as Captain. Mr. McCorkle married Mr. Wilfong's only daughter.[8] I sent the note for Mr. Jackson to Ocracoke yesterday. I think that I will have an opportunity to forward the one for Mrs. Simmons to her some time shortly. Your friend, Levi Yost[9] of Cabarrus I can not exactly locate. I know Elie Yost, who lives near Father's, very well, and I think that one of his brothers from Cabarus called with<in> him once to see Father.

I have not seen any one who knows Bryan Tyson.[10]

We are having Summer time though it is not very warm. Fresh potatoes, peas, and strawberries are getting plentiful. We have had garden peas occasionally off and on since the 1st. of the month. Fresh fish is a common dish the whole year round.

Every thing is qui/e/t in this Department. A great many of the troops are going home on furfoughs and I see nothing that looks to an intention of active opuerations in this State soon.

We have had New York papers of the 19th. I can see no indications of a forward movement by Gen. Hooker.

The operations out West lately seem to /have/ been very successful.

I would like to have a bunch /of/ envelopes about one third larger those last sent. I think I shall shortly send you some blanks for you to have struck off for me. This thing of getting along in an office like mine without printed forms is a poor way.

I have not heard from the Treasury Department in relation to Section VI for Internal and Coastwise Commercial Intercourse. If this State should be openned to trade, it will make a great deal of more work for me. The operations under them will form a separate account and I shall apply to the Secretary for more help.

My Inspector, Pigott, is not worth five cents, and I have often thought of discharging him and getting some /one/ else to take his place. It is very hard to get men here suitable for the place.

I have been away from town pretty much all day to-day. Mr. Norcum, myself, and another man went aboard a very nice schooner in the harbor this morning, took dinner on board and then went down to Schackleford's beach and gathered a few shells. I get three very nice ones and quite a number of others. We had a nice sail.

Write often,
Your brother,
John A. Hedrick.

May 25. Nothing new this morning.

J.A.H.

[1] While the *Chronicle* article to which Hedrick refers has not been located, the date and names included in this letter suggest that it was a casualty list from the Battle of Chancellorsville.

[2] Pvt. Daniel G. Coleman, a resident of Cabarrus County and a member of Company A, Twentieth Regiment North Carolina Troops, was wounded and captured in the Battle of Chancellorsville. After having his right leg amputated, he died in a Washington, D.C., hospital on May 26, 1863. The second Dan Coleman could be either Daniel R. Coleman, a Cabarrus County resident and a musician in the Twentieth North Carolina, or Daniel M. Coleman, a Cabarrus native and a private in the Sixteenth Regiment North Carolina Troops. Both of these men survived the war. Manarin and Jordan, *North Carolina Troops*, 6:66, 435, 438.

[3] Captain Dabney W. Parks (b. ca. 1831), Company E, Fifty-fourth Regiment North Carolina Troops, was wounded and captured near Fredericksburg, Va., on May 4, 1863. He died in a Washington, D.C., hospital on June 12, 1863, of typhoid fever. Eighth Census, 1860: Wilkes County; Manarin and Jordan, *North Carolina Troops*, 13:287.

[4] David Mc. Parks (1837-1906). Ninth Census, 1870: Rowan County; *Rowan County Cemeteries*, vol. 4 (Salisbury, N.C.: Genealogical Society of Rowan County, n.d.), 97.

[5] Sidney Theodore Wilfong (1844-1905) enlisted in the Twelfth Regiment North Carolina Troops in 1861 at the age of sixteen. He rose to the rank of sergeant before being wounded and captured at the Battle of Chancellorsville. His right arm was amputated in a Washington, D.C., military hospital. Wilfong was subsequently exchanged and discharged from Confederate service. *Catawba County Cemeteries*, 7:9; Manarin and Jordan, *North Carolina Troops*, 5:129.

[6] John Wilfong (1793-1883) of Newton township in Catawba County was a farmer and the father of Sidney T. and Yancey M. Wilfong. *Catawba County Cemeteries*, 7:9; Eighth Census, 1860: Catawba County.

[7] Matthew Locke McCorkle (1817-1899) was captain of Company F, Twenty-third Regiment North Carolina Troops. Prior to the war he had been a lawyer in Catawba County. He resigned from his regiment on or about April 16, 1862, because of poor health and was later a major in the N.C. Senior Reserves. *Catawba County Cemeteries*, 7:11; Manarin and Jordan, *North Carolina Troops*, 7:195.

[8] Martha Jane Wilfong McCorkle (1832-1908). *Catawba County Cemeteries*, 7:11; Eighth Census, 1860: Catawba County.

[9] Levi Yost, a private in the Seventh Regiment North Carolina State Troops, was wounded and captured at the Battle of Chancellorsville. He was exchanged and on November 17, 1864, retired to the Invalid Corps. After the war he lived in Cabarrus County as a farmer. Manarin and Jordan, *North Carolina Troops*, 4:430; Ninth Census, 1870: Cabarrus County.

[10] Bryan Tyson (1830-1909) was a proslavery Unionist. He fled North Carolina to avoid the Confederate draft and the repercussions from his attempt to publish an anti-secession book in Raleigh. Benjamin Hedrick befriended him and helped him obtain a position as an assistant messenger for the Treasury Department. William T. Auman, "Bryan Tyson: Southern Unionist and American Patriot," *North Carolina Historical Review* 62 (July 1985): 257-292.

SHC
Beaufort, N.C.
May 26th. 1863.

Dear Brother:

I recieved yesterday yours of the 18th. and wrote you on the day before. We have had New York papers to the 23rd. The capture of Jackson Miss, was confirmed and a battle near Vicksburg was expected. There had been no movement on the Rappahannock, and I can see indications of one soon. All is quiet here now, with no prospect of any offensive operations shortly. Fortifications are constructing at <Morehead> /Carolina/ City and at other places on the Rail Road between here and Newbern.

One hundred and sixty prisoners were taken last week a short distance above Newbern. Col Jones[1] of our forces was killed in the action. The prisoners were North Carolinians but I have not learned from what part of the State. They have been sent north, together with about forty from the jail in Newbern.[2]

A Supervising Special Agent of the Treasury Department is now in Newbern. He sent me word yesterday that he would be down here to-day but he failed to come. I expect him here to-morrow. I presume that he will be able to answer some of the questions which I wrote you some two weeks ago concerning Internal and Coastwise Commercial Intercourse. There ought to be some arrangement made by which these bankers between this place and Hatteras, can go to Hyde County for corn. They cannot raise any grain worth naming on the sandy beach extending from here to Roanoke Island and have always been in the habit of trading off their fish and oysters to the people of Hyde County for corn. I sent in my report on one of the Cutter cases last week. I appointed yesterday for hearing the other but neither of the parties appeared. Both of the parties have gone north with the intention of not returning. I gave them twenty days notice to appear in, and will proceed /to take testimony/ as /soon as/ I can get the witnesses from Newbern whether they appear or not, unless I should recieve orders to the contrary from the Secretary of the Treasury.

May 27th. 1863.

All is quiet and it looks a little like raining this morning. Troops are going home on almost every boat that leaves. I have heard that the Mass 54th. (colored) was to be sent to this department.[3] If many more soldiers go home, we will need some body to take their places. It looks now as if we would have to act mostly on the defensive during the coming Summer. The time of the two years and the nine months men will soon be out and it will take some time to put the drafted men into a condition to do much fighting.

In your last letter you dont say any thing about Mssrs Yost and Wilfong. How are they and what is to be done with them?

We have been having Mails more regular lately than usual. Quartermaster Biggs, who has charge of transportation, seems to be a very efficient officer. Much more so than Capt Slaght,[4] late Chief Quartermaster in this Department.

If Mr. Goodloe is appointed Judge of North Carolina, is it probable that this will be done soon?

I saw Dr. Page about two weeks ago. He was well. His head quarters are in Newbern.

Write often and all you can.

Your brother,
John A. Hedrick.

---

[1] J. Richter Jones, colonel of the Fifty-eighth Pennsylvania Regiment, was described by a Massachusetts officer as "the best officer in this Department after General Foster." Rowland M. Hall to David P. Hall, May 26, 1863, Julia Ward Stickley Papers, Private Collections, State Archives, Division of Archives and History, Raleigh; William C. Harris, ed., *In the Country of the Enemy: The Civil War Reports of a Massachusetts Corporal* (Gainesville: University Press of Florida, 1999), 174, 177, 179.

[2] This is a reference to an engagement known as Second Gum Swamp. Located between New Bern and Kinston, Gum Swamp was the site of an attack made on May 22, 1863, by about 2000 Union troops against the Fifty-sixth North Carolina, which numbered about 500 men. Approximately 144 members of that regiment were captured, most of whom were sent to New Bern, paroled, and transported to City Point, Va., to be exchanged. Weymouth T. Jordan Jr., " 'Drinking Pulverized Snakes and Lizards': Yankees and Rebels in Battle at Gum Swamp," *North Carolina Historical Review* 71 (April 1994): 219, 227; Manarin and Jordan, *North Carolina Troops*, 592-704 passim.

[3] The Fifty-fourth Massachusetts was sent to the Department of the South rather than to North Carolina. The regiment arrived at the departmental headquarters in Hilton Head, S.C., on June 3, 1863. Russell Duncan, ed., *Blue-Eyed Child of Fortune: The Civil War Letters of Colonel Robert Gould Shaw* (Athens: University of Georgia Press, 1992), 40-41.

[4] Capt. James C. Slaght of New Jersey. Heitman, *Historical Register*, 1:891.

SHC
Beaufort, N.C.,
June 1st. 1863.

Dear Brother:

I have recieved nothing from you later than May 18th. The two last Mails did not bring me any private letters, or papers. New York papers of the 26th. ultimo have been recieved. Things about Vicksburg seemed to be in a favorable position though I do not think that the City had been taken.

All is quiet here. The weather is quite windy. I went sailing yesterday and therefore neglected writing to you at my usual time. This letter however will reach you as soon as one written yesterday.

Mr. Heaton,[1] Supervisory Special Agent of the Treasury Department arrived here day before yesterday but has been sick and confined to his room since then so that I have not had an opportunity to learn what he expects to do about Internal & Coastwise Commercial Intercourse. Every thing here is at a dead stand still awaiting some action by him.

Write often.

Your brother,
John A. Hedrick,
Collector.

---

[1] David Heaton (1823-1870), a former member of the Ohio and Minnesota state senates, was appointed as a special agent for the Treasury Department in 1863. During Reconstruction he played an active role in the North Carolina Republican Party, serving as a delegate to the state's 1868 Constitutional Convention and representing the state in the U.S. Congress. *Who Was Who in America*, vol. 1 (Chicago: A.N. Marquis, 1963), 244.

SHC
Newbern, N.C.
June 4th. 1863.

Dear Brother:

I recieved yesterday yours of the 16th. ultimo. Yours of the 18th. and 25th. were recieved a few days previous. I have been here since yesterday evening and have been pretty busily engaged today in taking the testimony in the Rev-Cutter case 12. I have examined six witnesses and have four more to examine. These however I will examine at Beaufort, N.C

New York papers of the 1st. inst have been recieved. Vicksburg had not been taken. The losses on both sides had been heavy. I have just been round to Dr. Page's. He is well and inquired about your welfare. Mr. Heaton, Sp. Agt. Treasy. Dept. is still sick. Nothing has been done towards opening trade in this State, but it will probably be done about the 1st. of next month.

Mr. Heaton is from St. Anthony Falls, Minnesota and is a native of Ohio. He seems to be a nice man. All is quiet.

> Your brother,
> John A. Hedrick.

[On same sheet of paper as previous letter]

> *SHC*
> Beaufort, N.C.
> June 5th. 1863.

I wrote what is on the previous page last night and expected to have dropped it in the Post Office at Newbern this morning, but forgot to do it till I got into the cars when it was too late.

The "Spalding" arrived at this port from Fortress Monroe this morning bringing N.Y. papers of the 3rd inst. I did not hear any special news from them. Vicksburg had not been taken.

There is nothing new here except that Brig. Genl. Spinola[1] has assumed the duties of Provost Marshal of this town.

Day before yesterday he had the whole town kept in and I believe that he will not let any one leave now without a pass from him. The funniest part of the story happened day before yesterday. The General gave orders not to let any one leave town without his pass, and then left himself so that every one who did not evade the blockade had to remain in town all day. I left that day about 11 $\frac{1}{2}$ A.M. in the Cutter's boat and was not asked for a pass. Others left in the Quartermaster's boat and evaded the blockade in that way.

I cleared the Schr. Joanna Ward from this port to New York before I left but <he> the Captain had to remain here all day. Every thing looked very quiet in Newbern. I have never seen the town so free from drunken officers and soldiers. I did not see a drunk man while I was there. The streets and houses are in a better condition that usual.

> Write often,
> Your brother,
> John A. Hedrick.

June 6th.

This morning is warm and sultry. It is never very hot here. We experience more heat in the morning from sunrise to ten o'clock than during any other part of the day. Mr. Heaton is still unwell but not confined to his bed.

Mr. Norcum's family is well except the baby.

---

[1] Francis Barretto Spinola (1821-1884) of New York commanded a Federal brigade in North Carolina from January to June of 1863. He was later court-martialed and allowed to resign from the army in January 1865. Warner, *Generals in Blue*, s.v. "Spinola, Francis Barretto."

SHC
Beaufort, N.C.
June 7th. 1863.

Dear Brother:

I have had nothing from you later than the 25th. ultimo. Yesterday I added a few lines to a letter written on the two preceeding days and put it in the Post Office. All is quiet here now. New York papers of the 4th. inst. arrived here this morning. I have not seen them but understand that they contain very little more news from Vicksburg than was in the papers of the 3rd. I took a dinner at Mr. Norcum's to-day. Mrs. Norcum /had/ fresh beans, cucumbers, raddishes, letuce, cabbage, potatoes, peas and onions. I expect that we are a little ahead of you in the vegitable line.

I went a short distance into the country this afternoon and got a few dew and straw berries. The season for the former is just commencing and for the latter, about over. I got also some bay flowers which is a species of Magnolia. They are quite fragrant. I have not fallen into love yet. Times are dull and the weather somewhat warm especially the fore part of the day.

Write as often as you can and give me all of the news.

Your brother,
John A. Hedrick.

SHC
Beaufort, N.C.
June 14th. 1863.

Dear Brother:

I sent you a few days ago a drft. on the Asst. Treas. U.S.N.Y. for $40. You will please keep an account of the money I send you and also of the sums paid by you on my account. I sent also a batch of blanks for you to have printed. I guess that you will have to send them by Mail. There is no express here now. It will cost 1 cent an ounce by mail if you have to pay the Postage and nothing if Mr. Hays[1] will frank them. I could send you quite a lot more of blanks to print but I think one batch is enough for the present.

I do not know how Prof. Doherty[2] stood in Newbern. I never saw the man nor heard any one speak of him and I think that he left N.C. before I arrived here.

The Dr. Wheeler,[3] whom you mention in one of your letters, lives in Washington, N.C. and not in Newbern. I am acquainted with him and think him a nice man. He was raised in the State of New York and has been appointed A.Q.M. in the U.S. Service. The man, whom Dr. Wheeler proposed for a candidate for Congress, I am informed is Capt. Ulysses H. Rich.[4] I am not acquainted with Capt. Rich but would judge from an application to ship corn, lately received from him, that he is quite an intelligent and businesslike man. I have never heard the citizens of this place say any thing about holding an election in August for a Member to Congress. Mayor Respess[5] of Washington N.C. told me that Capt Rich was meant in Dr. Wheeler's letter to Mr. Goodloe.

My Inspector in the first place is not overstocked with common sense; in the second he /is/ affected with laziness, and in the third he and one of the Cutter officers has fallen out, and I think that he is a little afraid to go on board of vessels lest he might meet this officer.

Under the new Internal & Coastwise Regulations of the Secretary of the Treasury there will be a great many little offices but I can't tell how they will pay. If I can do any thing for Jesse Wheeler[6] I will let you know.

There is a great deal of talk here about enforcing the draft in this place <this> but I do not think that it will be done.

There are not many vessels coming in now. Every thing is quiet. I have had nothing from you later than the 5th. inst. Papers of the 8th. have been recieved and a steamer is expected in Newbern to-morrow or the next day. There are four mail steamers between Newbern and New York but they run so near together that we don't get a mail more than about once a week.

I hope that Mr. Goodloe may come down as U.S. Judge for North Carolina. I think that he can do more good in that capacity at present than he could as Military Governor. The other officers mentioned by you might do good service.

Write soon & often
Your Brother,
John A. Hedrick.

---

[1] John L. Hayes of New Hampshire was the chief clerk in the U.S. Patent Office. *Scientific American,* June 22, 29, 1861.

[2] William H. Doherty, professor of chemistry and former director of the New Bern Academy, later became inspector of schools for the Department of North Carolina. After the war he served as a sanitary inspector for the Freedmen's Bureau. Benjamin Hedrick, questioning Doherty's loyalty to the Union, declined to support his application for a Treasury Department position in July 1863. *New Bern Progress,* April 5, 1862; *North Carolina Times* (New Bern), March 16, 1864; Watson, *A History of New Bern and Craven County,* 466-467; Benjamin S. Hedrick to William H. Doherty, July 21, 1863, Hedrick Papers, Duke Special Collections.

[3] Capt. W. H. Wheeler (b. ca. 1838) was subsequently quartermaster at Washington, N.C., and later at Morehead City. General Orders for the District of North Carolina, September 15, 1863, Myers House Papers, Brown Library, Washington, N.C.; Edmund J. Cleveland Diary, November 8, 1864, Southern Historical Collection, University of North Carolina Library, Chapel Hill; Eighth Census, 1860: Carteret County.

[4] Ulysses H. Ritch (1819-1866) was a Washington, N.C., shipbuilder and Unionist. After briefly serving as a treasury agent in Washington in early 1864, he was appointed local special treasury agent for New Bern in May 1864. *North Carolina Times* (New Bern), May 18, 1864; David Heaton to Ulysses H. Ritch, 1864, Myers House Papers, Brown Library, Washington, N.C.; Ulysses H. Ritch to Benjamin S. Hedrick, October 17, 1863, Hedrick Papers, Duke Special Collections.

[5] Isaiah Respess, a merchant, was arrested by Confederate authorities in the spring of 1862 for aiding the enemy but was acquitted in court. Later he was briefly imprisoned by Federals under the command of Benjamin F. Butler for allegedly violating trade regulations. *OR,* ser. 2, 2:1547; Isaiah Respess to Mary Respess, December 10, 1863, Mary F. Credle Papers, Southern Historical Collection, University of North Carolina, Chapel Hill.

[6] Jesse Wheeler was an antislavery North Carolinian and prewar friend of Benjamin S. Hedrick. Jesse Wheeler to Benjamin S. Hedrick, August 20, 1859, Hedrick Papers, Duke Special Collections.

SHC
Beaufort, N.C.
June 19th. 1863.

Dear Brother:

We had a northern Mail day before yesterday but I recieved nothing from you. My last letter from you was dated June 5th. and was recieved about ten days ago.

We have had northern papers of the 14th. inst. Vicksburg had not been taken but prospects looked favorable. There is nothing new here except the raising of negro troops. There is a recruiting office in this town for colored soldiers and a few already uniformed.[1] They don't look as dangerous and bloodthirsty as might be expected. There have been near a hundred contrabands enlisted in this town and about seven hundred in Newbern.

Gen Foster has been down in the neighborhood for the last three days but has not been in town.

The weather is quite pleasant to-day. There is not much doing now in the way of shipments from this port. Mr. Heaton, Sup. Sp. Agt. of the Treasy Dept, has not yet recieved the approval of the Secretary of the Treasury to his local rules for carrying on trade in this State. I send inclosed a form for certificate of reciepts of Tonnage Dues, which you will please have printed instead of the form already sent if the latter has not been printed.

Our friend Gen. Spinola is still acting Commandant of this post. Provost Marshal, port Collector &c. He is a very smart man! I hope that Gen. Naglee will come back soon. I am well and weigh about 133 pounds.

> Write oftener
> Your brother
> John A. Hedrick.

---

[1] On May 18, 1863, Union officers arrived in New Bern to begin recruiting African American soldiers. By May 21, their efforts had expanded to Beaufort. This was one of the earliest official attempts to recruit former slaves for the army. Richard Reid, "Raising the African Brigade: Early Black Recruitment in Civil War North Carolina," *North Carolina Historical Review* 70 (July 1993): 266, 278; Descriptive Book, Thirty-fifth Regiment, United States Colored Troops, microfilm, State Archives, Division of Archives and History, Raleigh.

SHC
Beaufort, N.C.
June 21st. 1863.

Dear Brother:

I wrote to /you/ last Friday and inclosed in my letter a blank reciept for tonnage dues, to be printed provided the one previously sent has not been printed.

Yesterday evening I recieved yours of the 12th. making mention of yours of the 10th. which has not reached me. The "Spaulding" has just arrived from Fortress Monroe bringing New York papers of the 18th. I have not read anything later than the 15th. but understand that the papers of the 18th. contain very little additional news. Gen. Lee has been moving northwestward, but I did not understand to what point he had reached.[1]

Mrs. Norcum's youngest child, little Laura, died last night after an illness of about three weeks. Her disease commenced with a bad cold, which changed into the bowel complaint and it was thought that she had <a> slight chills at times. She was about eight months old. Two other children died in this place yesterday and last night. The Climate here is not good for children. It is too moist.

Mr. Heaton thinks that this place agrees with him very well. He says that it is more like Minnesota than any place he was ever at. There are no very sudden changes here and the range of temperature is very small. We are so close to the Gulf Stream that it warms the atmosphere in the winter, and so close to the sea that the seabreezes keep us cool in the Summer. We had only a few spits of snow last Winter—not enough to cover the ground at any one time, and the ice was never more than $1/2$ inch thick.

There is no news in this department. Gen. Spinola is still acting factotum. I did not mean by my previous letters that he had been appointed Provost Marshal of this place, but that since his arrival he had been performing the duties of a Provost. He is Commandant of the district of Beaufort, in the absence of Gens. Naglee and Heckman who have gone north. He's only a temporary commandant and does not belong to this district. Gen. Heckman is expected back soon. I have not heard any thing about making Gen. Wilde,[2] Military Governor of N.C. I saw a letter /to that effect/ from Newbern in one of the N.Y. papers but I did not pay much attention to it, but thought that it, like many of the letters written at the same place, had very little foundation in fact. How is Mr. Goodloe's judgeship progressing? Has Gov. Stanly returned to California? How are Mr. Pigott & lady? Have you named your Major General? You had better call him Frank B. Spinola after the illustrious hero of Blunt's Mills.[3]

The schedule of the Rail Road has changed and the cars now leave Morehead at 8 A.M. and Newbern at 4 P.M.

> Write often,
> Your brother:
> John A. Hedrick.

---

[1] On June 10, 1863, Lee's Army of Northern Virginia began moving northward on a raid into Pennsylvania, which resulted in the Confederate defeat at Gettysburg and subsequent retreat to Virginia. Foote, *Civil War*, 2:428-581.

[2] Edward Augustus Wild (1825-1891) of Massachusetts had been promoted to brigadier general of volunteers in April 1863. He played a leading role in organizing and commanding African American troops in North Carolina and Virginia. Boatner, *Civil War Dictionary*, 919.

[3] See letter of July 5, 1863, in this volume.

SHC
Beaufort, N.C.
June 24th. 1863.

Dear Brother:

I recieved yours of the 10th. day before yesterday—yours of the 12th. having been recieved last Saturday. New York papers of the 19th. have been recieved. Gen. Ewell[1] had left Chambersburg. Vicksburg was still holding out.

Mr. Heaton has adopted temporary rules for carrying /on/ internal traffic. General Foster requests shipments to be made and Mr. Heaton thereupon grants the permits.

The weather is quite warm to-day and there is considerable sickness in town. A great many of the citizens are frightened—some are afraid of being drafted and others of being sent out of the lines. Gen. Spinola is a pretty good rowdy and he has to do some thing to keep up the excitement.

June 25th. 1863,

It is understood here that Gen Spinola has been ordered to Fortress Monroe or Washington N.C. with his Brigade.

New York papers of the 22nd. have been recieved. I have not seen them. Ewell was up about Frederic, Maryland. The fall of Vicksburg was expected daily. All is quiet here. It has been raining to-day, and the weather is quite close. I have not had any thing later from you than the 12th.

I sent you a short time ago a draft on the Asst. Treasurer U.S. New York for forty dollars. This makes one hundred dollars altogether that I have sent you, since my arrival here.

How are all of the folks in Washington? What is Mr. Goodloe doing?

Write often.
Your brother
John A. Hedrick.

---

[1] Lt. Gen. Richard Stoddert Ewell (1817-1872) succeeded to the command of the late "Stonewall" Jackson's II Corps, Army of Northern Virginia, in May 1863. On June 15, 1863, Albert G. Jenkins's cavalry from Ewell's Corps, raided Chambersburg, Pa., but remained in the town only a short time. On June 24, Rodes's Division of Ewell's Corps occupied Chambersburg in force. Donald C. Pfanz, *Richard S. Ewell: A Soldier's Life* (Chapel Hill; University of North Carolina Press, 1998), 273, 292, 297, 505.

SHC
Beaufort, N.C.
June 28th. 1863.

Dear Brother:

I wrote you last Sunday and again on Wednesday the 24th. I have not had any thing from you later than the 12th. Our Mails have been very irregular lately. I am expecting a northern Mail to-morrow evening.

Gens. Foster and Spinola with about all of the 9 months men in this department have left for Fortress Monroe. Gen Spinola left this morning. Gen Heckman is in command of the district of Beaufort. We have had no northern news later than the 23rd. which was brought from Fortress Monroe by a transport. I think that this time something has been done at Vicksburg. If all the channels of supply have been cut off as we have been informed I cannot see how they have held out as long as they have. I have seen the supplies from this place cut off from Newbern a couple of times for a few days, and have noticed what a commotion it makes among the people there although their communication with New York was left open. The weather is quite warm and I am about as lazy as usual.

My Inspector has resigned and I am glad of it. I have nominated Stephen F. Willis as his successor. I think that Mr. Willis will make a very good officer. He was a Douglass Democrat and /is/ an Episcopalean.

I do not know any thing about the Chaplain of the 2nd. N.C. Regiment. Mr. Norcum has been unwell lately. The people here have had the time for taking the oath of allegiance extended to the 30th. inst.

Write often.
Your brother,
John A. Hedrick.

Duke
Beaufort, N.C.
July 1st. 1863.

Dear Brother:

I recieved your letters of June 17th. & 20th. last Monday and wrote to you on Sunday the 28th. ultimo.

We have had New York papers to the 26th. ult. Things looked very scary in Maryland and Pennsylvania. It was thought that Lee and Longstreet had crossed the Potomac up about Frederic, Maryland.[1] Ewell was still in Pennsylvania.

Vicksburg was still holding out and Gen. Grant was represented to be as strong against Johnson as Pemberton against Grant.[2]

There is no news here whatever. Every thing is as calm as a hot summer day can make it. Gen. Spinola has left to the general satisfaction of every body here. Gen. Foster is also temporarily away. Gen Heckman is in command here now and I believe in command of the whole department. I hope that some one will take Gen. Hunter's command in South Carolina that will do more fighting and make less fuss. He and Dupont[3] have been trying to put down each other more than they have the rebellion: I don't like either of them. I do not know any thing about Gen. Gilmore.[4] Foote,[5] who was said some time ago to have been ordered to supercede Dupont, is a good officer.

Business has been a little brisker the last few days than it had been for some time back. I have been quite busy during /the/ last week making out my quarterly returns. I sent some time ago a drft. on Asst. Treas. U.S.N.Y. for $40, which I have not yet heard from, though it is hardly time for me to hear from it. Inclosed I send $10 northern money, which is good, but not current here. Nothing is current here except "green backs." If you can pass it, or make use of it, you will place it to my credit, if not send it back to me.

Write often,
Your brother,
John A. Hedrick.

---

[1] On June 24, 1863, James Longstreet's First Corps and A. P. Hill's Third Corps of Lee's Army of Northern Virginia crossed the Potomac River at Shepherdstown, W.Va., and Williamsport, Md. Foote, *Civil War*, 2:441.

[2] Gen. Joseph E. Johnston was expected to attempt to rescue the Confederate force under John C. Pemberton, which was besieged in Vicksburg by U. S. Grant's army. Johnston, daunted by the inexperience of his troops and Grant's strong position, did not vigorously try to raise the siege. McPherson, *Ordeal by Fire*, 312-317.

[3] Samuel Francis Du Pont (1803-1865), a veteran naval officer from New Jersey, fell into official disfavor after failing to take Charleston and was relieved of command in July 1863. *Dictionary of American Biography*, s.v. "Du Pont, Samuel Francis."

[4] Quincy Adams Gillmore (1825-1863), a regular army engineer officer from Ohio, commanded the Department of the South from June 12, 1863, to May 1, 1864, and from February 9 to June 26, 1865. Sifakis, *Who Was Who in the Civil War*, 249; *American National Biography*, s.v. "Gillmore, Quincy Adams."

[5] Andrew Hull Foote (1806-1863) commanded Union naval forces in the western theater in 1861 and 1862 and suffered a severe wound at Fort Donelson. He was assigned to replace Du Pont as commander of the Atlantic Squadron in June 1863 but died while in transit to the fleet. Boatner, *Civil War Dictionary*, 287.

Duke
Beaufort, N.C.
July 5th. 1863.

Dear Brother:

I recieved last night your letters of the 22nd. 24th. and 26th. ultimo and wrote to you about the middle, on Wednesday, (the 30th.) I believe, of last week. All of the steamers came into Newbern at one time. There are six mail steamers now. They brought New York papers of the 1st inst. I have read them but I can hardly tell what the position of affairs is. I should think that Ewell's tax on York, Pa. would make some of those old Dutch open their eyes.[1] I do not know any thing about our new Commander of the Army of the Potomac.[2] I do not think that I ever saw his name until he was appointed to his new command. The attack on Vicksburg seems to be everlasting, and /on/ Port Hudson about the same. There is no news here of any consequence. Gen. Foster has returned to Newbern. What I meant sometime ago by the hero of Blunt's Mills, was that while Gen. Foster was blockaded at Washington, Gen. Spinola with his brigade was sent from Newbern across the country towards Washington to relieve Gen. Foster. He got along very well until he arrived at Blunt's Mills and found the planks taken up, and saw about 200 rebels with a couple of field pieces stationed on the opposite bank. The rebs peppered his advancing column so strong that he ordered his men to charge on Newbern at double quick. Gen. By Jesus could not stand it any longer. Capt. Belger of Belger's Battery was badly wounded[3] but unfortunately Gen. Spinola came off untouched. Spinola has recieved a great deal of cursing for his gallant conduct in this action. I have been informed that /the/ creek was only about 20 feet wide and that the sills of the bridge were all there, and that by throwing a few poles on them, our forces could have crossed and taken their little guns from the rebs in spite of them.[4]

The weather has been very warm for the last few days.

Yesterday evening (4th.) I /went/ down on Shackleford's beach[5] to see the negro pic-nic. There were about 400 of them there and they seemed to enjoy themselves very well. They had singing, speaking, promenading and cheering for the Union cause and officers, and groaning for the Confederates. There were three societies represented—the Atlantic, the __ Chapel Society, and the Sunday School Benevolent Society. The members of the Atlantic Society had large scarfs with anchors thrown across their shoulder. The others had nothing except their banners with the name & purposes of the society <with> written on them. We came very near of having the pleasure of witnessing a fight just as they were getting ready to come home. It seems that a couple of the negroes had a dispute between them, and one told the other to go away and leave him, and he himself started up the plank to get into the flat, when the other negroe shoved him off into the water. But the water being salt did not lower his temper but rather increased it. So they flew at each other and friends came to the rescue and some white folks hallowed "Let them fight" and others said "that it was no place," that if "any one wished to fight let them go to the battlefield." I for my part thought that it was a beautiful place to fight and got on the prow of the boat so that I could see it all. I sent in my last letter Ten dollars of northern money, which is not current here.

Your brother,
John A. Hedrick.

---

[1] Richard S. Ewell's Confederate forces demanded twenty-eight thousand dollars from merchants and banks in York during their raid into Pennsylvania. Similar fines were levied on other Pennsylvania towns. James M. McPherson, *Battle Cry of Freedom: The Civil War Era* (New York: Oxford University Press, 1988), 649.

[2] George Gordon Meade (1815-1872) was commander of the Army of the Potomac from June 28, 1863, to December 30, 1864, and from January 11 to June 27, 1865. Sifakis, *Who Was Who in the Civil War*, 440-441.

[3] Capt. James Belger commanded Battery F of the First Rhode Island Light Artillery and had earned a reputation as one of the most capable Union officers in the Department of North Carolina. Belger was wounded in the hip and thigh. Janet B. Hewett, ed., *The Roster of Union Soldiers, 1861-1865, Rhode Island and Connecticut* (Wilmington, N.C.: Broadfoot Publishing, 1997), 9; Rowland M. Hall to Caroline M. Hall, December 22, 1862, and April 24, 1863, Stickley Papers, State Archives; *OR*, ser. 1, 18:246.

[4] For Spinola's account of this engagement, see *OR*, ser. 1, 18:245-246.

[5] Shackleford Banks, an Outer Banks island near Beaufort. William S. Powell, *North Carolina Gazetteer* (Chapel Hill: University of North Carolina Press, 1968), 446.

Duke
Beaufort, N.C.
July 12th. 1863.

Dear Brother:

I recieved last night your letters of the 30th. ult. and 2nd. & 3rd. insts. We have had New York papers to the 9th. Vicksburg surrendered on the 4th. of July. Lee's Army was pretty closely pressed, and was retreating through Maryland. The greater portion of it was between Funkstown and Falling Waters. I have just returned from a visit to Cape Lookout Light

House. I found it in a splendid condition. The tower is 175 feet high and every step from the bottom to the top is as clean as a ward room. The Principal Keeper, Capt. Chadwick,[1] was absent, having come to town this morning, and of course was not expecting a visit. There is no news in this Department. I wrote you last Sunday and once during the week.

Write often,
Your brother,
John A. Hedrick.

[1] Gayer Chadwick (b. ca. 1797). Eighth Census, 1860: Carteret County.

Duke
Beaufort, N.C.
July 19th. 1863.

Dear Brother:

I wrote you last Sunday and recieved yours of the 8th. inst. during the week. Business has been rather dull since the commencement of Lee's invasion of Pennsylvania. The weather is quite warm with some prospect of rain soon.

Gen. Foster has left Newbern for Fortress Monroe to take charge of Virginia.[1] We had news yesterday that Charleston, and Port Hudson had been taken. The report of the surrender of the former place was stated as a rumor in the New York papers of the 14th. and the news of the taking of the latter place was in the Richmond papers of the 9th. inst. I should not be surprised if the latter report were true. The former I do not place much confidence in.

The blanks and envelopes have all come to hand, and also one reciept for the blanks. I send you in this letter twenty dollars, which with the amount already sent makes one hundred and thirty dollars.

I do not know where C.H. Foster is now but I think that he is up about Newbern or Washington. The last time I heard of him he was in Newbern with Captain's shoulder straps and said that he had been authorized to raise another regiment of N.C. soldiers.[2] I often see pieces in the New York papers, written from Newbern, which, I know, are from either Foster or Carpenter. These pieces generally contain some truths but they are so mixed with falsehoods, that you must know what is really so from some other source, before you can tell what to believe. I was at Newbern last

Thursday and saw Dr. Page, who said that he expected to go north in about a fortnight and would visit Washington before he returned to North Carolina. Mr. Heaton is still unwell and not able to do much.

Write often,
Your brother,
John A. Hedrick.

---

[1] John G. Foster's Department of North Carolina was enlarged July 15, 1863, to include both occupied North Carolina and Virginia. Boatner, *Civil War Dictionary*, 598-599.

[2] The Second North Carolina Union Regiment never reached full regimental strength. Browning, "Little Souled Mercenaries," 342.

Duke
Beaufort, N.C.
July 22nd. 1863.

Dear Brother:

I recieved yours of the 11st. inst. inclosing a second reciept for printing blanks day before yesterday, and wrote to you Sunday the 19th. inst. We have New York papers for the 17th. There seems to have been very riotous times in the City for several days previous.[1] The excitement, however, had somewhat abated on the evening of the 16th. The news from the west, Charleston and Tennessee was very encouraging. Port Hudson surrendered on the 9th. Rosecrans had driven Bragg down to Atlanta, Ga, and captured quite a number of prisoners from him.[2] The batteries on Morris Island near Charleston had all been taken except two.[3]

In my letter of last Sunday I inclosed twenty dollars.

There is no news of interest in this Department. All is quiet. Gen. Foster left Newbern during the early part of last week for Fortress Monroe. I notice an article in the dispatches from Washington saying that North & South Carolina had been formed into one department and that Gen. Foster had been assigned to the command of it. This must be a mistake. I send inclosed a blank bill of sale for enrolled vessels, from which I wish you to have three quires printed.

July 23rd. 1863,

I recieved last night yours of the 15th saying that you had just recieved a letter from Graham Morrow.[4]

New York papers of the 19th. are in Newbern but I have seen no one here who has one. The riot in New York had been quelled. It was also reported that Beauregard[5] had evacuated Charleston and burnt the place. There is no news here.

John A. Hedrick

---

[1] Urban laborers began rioting in New York against the draft on July 12, 1863. Troops from the Army of the Potomac arrived in the city July 15 and 16 and put down the riot, but only after more than one hundred people were killed. Iver Bernstein, *The New York City Draft Riots: Their Significance for American Society and Politics in the Age of the Civil War* (New York: Oxford University Press, 1990), 3-65.

[2] William S. Rosecrans forced Braxton Bragg's Confederate army to retreat to Chattanooga in the Tullahoma Campaign of late June 1863. During the campaign, the Federals took 1,634 Confederate prisoners. Bragg's army remained in Chattanooga until early September. Current, *Encyclopedia of the Confederacy*, 1:204; Patricia Faust, ed., *Historical Times Illustrated Encyclopedia of the Civil War* (New York: Harper and Row, 1986), 765; Foote, *Civil War*, 2:688.

[3] U.S. troops under Quincy A. Gillmore landed on Morris Island in Charleston harbor on July 10, 1863. Although two assaults on the island's main defenses at Battery Wagner failed, siege operations compelled the Confederates to abandon the island on September 6. Foote, *Civil War*, 2:696-701.

[4] Benjamin Hedrick, after being informed that Morrow had been wounded and captured at Gettysburg, rushed to aid Morrow, reaching him a few days before his death on July 19. Eliza Thompson to Benjamin S. Hedrick, July 24, August 26, 1863, Hedrick Papers, Duke Special Collections.

[5] Confederate general Pierre Gustave Toutant Beauregard (1818-1893) commanded the Department of South Carolina and Georgia from August 1862 to April 1864. He then took command of the Department of North Carolina and Southern Virginia, which he headed until October 1864. Beauregard was then transferred to the western theater. *American National Biography*, s.v. "Beauregard, Pierre Gustave Toutant."

Duke
Beaufort, N.C.
July 26th. 1863.

Dear Brother:

I have recieved no letter from you since I wrote you last, which was about the middle of last week. I sent you a blank bill of sale for enrolled vessels to have printed. We have nothing from New York later than the 23rd. An Expedition under Gen. Foster, who is back again, left Newbern in boats yesterday and some think that it is going to Weldon.[1] A short time ago an expedition cutt off railroad communication between Goldsboro and Weldon.[2] We have no news from Charleston later than the 10th.

Yesterday the 35th. Mass. (Colored) Regiment arrived at Morehead from Boston and proceeded to Newbern.[3] The regiment is over 1000 strong. I don't like to see the negro regiments sent to this State. We have too many negroes here now. I would much rather see a hundred negroes sent from than one into the State. Should you get in a hurry about Tax Commissioners for N.C. I would propose the name of Ulysses H. Ritch of Washington, N.C, as a suitable man for the office. He is the gentleman whom Dr. Wheeler proposed to Mr. Goodloe to run for Congress. Inclosed is $20, making $150 in all.

Your brother,
John A. Hedrick.

---

[1] Union infantry and artillery under the command of John G. Foster sailed to Winton, N.C., to support a cavalry detachment in an attack on the railroad bridge at Weldon. Confederate troops under Brig. Gen. Matt W. Ransom defeated the Union cavalry at Boone's Mill, and the Weldon bridge was spared. Barrett, *Civil War in North Carolina*, 166-170.

[2] Brig. Gen. Edward Elmer Potter led a Federal cavalry raid from New Bern that destroyed considerable property in Greenville, Rocky Mount, and Tarboro between July 19 and 23. Barrett, *Civil War in North Carolina*, 164-166.

[3] Hedrick inaccurately identified the regiment. The Fifty-fifth Massachusetts Infantry (Colored) arrived in New Bern on July 25, 1863, but departed within a week for Folly Island, S.C. Frederick H. Dyer, *A Compendium of the War of the Rebellion*, 2 vols. (Dayton, Ohio: Morningside Press, Broadfoot Publishing, 1994), 2:1266.

Duke
Beaufort, N.C.
Aug. 2nd. 1863.

Dear Brother:

I recieved last Monday yours of the 21st. and last night that of the 25th. ult. We have New York papers of the 29th. The news did not seem very satisfactory to me. The fight on Morris Island was still going on, but slowly. Yesterday the Steamer "Georgianna" with troops for Gen. Gilmore came in and transferred them to the "S.R. Spalding," which left for Charleston about 11 A.M. <yeste> on the same day. The "Georgianna" was out of coal. One day last week the brig "J.W. Hall" with ordnance stores for Charleston arrived here in a leaking condition. Her stores were transferred to a steamer and sent on to their destination. I have not heard any thing definite from Gen. Foster's expedition. It was rumored here yesterday that it had landed at Winton on the Chowan River about 40 miles this side of Weldon. If that be the case it is probable that Weldon will be taken though I do not look for it much.

The military operations in Tennessee and Kentucky I do not exactly understand. The last papers we had before those of the 29th. represented Brag retreating from Chattanooga Tenn. towards Atlanta, Ga. It would now seem that he had got back to the Kentucky River and that he was only 40 miles from Lexington. The Herald of the 29th. has a short dispatch from Cincinnati saying that Morgan and about 30 of his officers and men had been taken and lodged in jaol, but as no mention is made of it in the Washington correspondence nor in the News Articles I hardly knew whether to believe it or not.[1] In my last letter I sent you $20 making in all one hundred and fifty dollars. What has been done about my Diploma? If you have it you will please send /it/ to me either by mail or by Dr. Page should he be in Washington shortly with the intent of returning directly to North Carolina. I would like to see it before I forget all of my Latin. I fear that I shall have to send for a translation to it. I would be very glad to visit New York once more. I think that I could see more of it than I did when I lived there.

The weather has been quite warm for the last few days though not oppressive. I have heard of no trial of the Humbug Foster by courtmartial. I have not seen him for the last three months and do not know where he is, nor what he is doing.

Captain Ulysses H. Ritch, whom I recommended as Tax Commissioner, I have no acquaintance with, but from what I have heard of him I think that he would make a good commissioner. Mr. E.H. Norcum would make a first rate commissioner provided he would have the office. I have not yet spoken to him about it and am a litle afraid that he would not accept the office because the greater portion of his property is up near Edenton and some in Lexington, which would be confiscated by the rebels immediately if he should accept an office under Uncle Abe. I will write you again on this subject. I am well and weigh about 130 pounds.

> Write often,
> John A. Hedrick.

---

[1] John Hunt Morgan (1825-1864), a Confederate cavalry officer from Alabama, was captured by Federal forces in Ohio on July 26, 1863. Morgan escaped from prison in November. *Dictionary of American Biography*, s.v. "Morgan, John Hunt."

SHC
Beaufort, N.C.
August 6th. 1863.

Dear Brother

I wrote to you last on the 2nd. and recieved yours of the 27th. ult. on the 3rd. inst.

What kind of shells does Mrs. Underwood wish for her daughter Alice? And in what way does she wish to use them?

Inclosed I send a strand of native North Carolina beeds for your daughter Alice. In next I will send a strand for Jeannie. These shells are taken from a shoal between this place and Schacleford's banks by scraping them up in long handled pans having the bottoms perforated with holes to allow the sand and water to escape, and leave the shells. I guess there has been $5000 worth of shells sold from that shoal during the last year. A great many are bought up by the soldiers to send home to their friends. Shells are quite plenty here but it takes considerable trouble to get a nice variety of them. Down near the light house there are a great many concks but it takes a considerable hunting to get a lot of perfect ones. Mrs. Underwood would be apt to like small shells—say from the size of a silver dollar down to a pea.

We have had New York papers down to the 1st. inst. Things looked favorable. I think that Gen. Gilmore will take Charleston yet. Meade and Lee had fought a severe battle in a mountain pass between the Shenandoah Valey and Culper Court House.[1] Gen. Herron and the rebel Gen. Johnston were both marching towards Mobile.[2] Commerce was reviving on the Mississippi River.

Monday night Lieut. Pollock[3] of the Unites States Regulars committed suicide by blowing his brains out with a pistol about 9 o'clock. He was about 25 years old and was a graduate of West Point. He has been in the habit of drinking excessively for some time past. I have not learned what was the immediate cause of his killing himself but heard that he was involved in some difficulty connected with official duty. He has for the last eight or ten months been connected with the N.Y. 3rd. Artillery and has been stationed in Fort Macon. He was buried at St. Paul's Church in this place yesterday about 12 M.

All is quiet in /this/ Department so far as I know. I have not heard what the expedition up the Chowan did. There is another expedition fitting out in Newbern ostensibly for Wilmington.

I have not yet done much towards issuing permits to ship goods to the interior. Every thing is in a state of confusion at present and Mr. Heaton is still sick. There has only one copy of the regulations for trade in this department been recieved and it has not been made public. By these regulations the trafficing in naval stores on private account is prohibited until further orders. I presume the government intend to buy up the "Tar, Pitch & Turpentine" for its own use. If they intend to do so they had better go at /it/ pretty soon as these articles are the main dependence to the people around here for subsistence. The land is so poor that they cannot raise enough of grain to support them.

The weather is quite warm and windy to-day.

Write often,
Your brother,
John A. Hedrick.

---

[1] Meade opted not to launch a full-scale assault on Lee's retreating army after Gettysburg, although several skirmishes took place. Boatner, *Civil War Dictionary*, 330.

[2] Maj. Gen. Francis Jay Herron (1837-1902) commanded a Federal division under Grant in the Vicksburg campaign. In July 1863, his division was transferred to the Department of the Gulf. Federal forces did not attack the forts in Mobile Bay until August 1864, and did not assault the town itself until March 1865. Warner, *Generals in Blue*, s.v. "Herron, Francis Jay"; Boatner, *Civil War Dictionary*, 559.

[3] William Pollock of Pennsylvania became a second lieutenant in the First U.S. Artillery in March 1862. He died August 4, 1863. Heitman, *Historical Register*, 1:797.

SHC
Beaufort, N.C.
Aug. 9th. 1863.

Dear Brother:

I wrote you last Sunday and once during the week inclosing a string of shell beads for Alice. In this letter I send one for Jeannie. Haven't you named your general yet. If you don't name him soon we will have to call him General Hedrick. New York papers of the 5th have been recieved. They contain very little news. Preparations for a renewal of the attack on Fort Wagner were progressing favorably. A fight b/etw/een Meade and Lee was expected soon near Culpepper Court House. Vessels on their way to Charleston continue to stop here occasionally. Day before yesterday the Steamer "City of Albany" from Fortress Monroe with a few troops for Charleston put in here and then returned to Fortress Monroe. The "City of Albany" is a new vessel and her copper had worked loose and her boilers had moved so that the captain was afraid to go on with her. I understand that she is owned by the government. Two small gunboats arrived here this morning but I do not know where they are from nor whither they are bound. They look like the "Hunchback" and "Miammi" from Newbern.

There is considerable talk here about N. Carolina going back into the Union. I saw a man last night who had read the Raleigh Standard of the 31st. ult. which contains a strong article from Mr. Davidson of Davidson County. The writer is thought to be John A Gilmore.[1] He tries to prove the rebellion to be a failure and advises the State to take steps to get out of it. For my part I cannot see how the State can get back into the Union until Lee's Army is whipped or driven out of Virginia. Besides I don't place much confidence in what old Holden says, although I know that he has a strong influence over the people of this State. The great loyalty, which is said to exist in some parts of the State, I think, exists in the minds of the news writers rather than in reality. There may be a considerable amount of neutrality and a desire to keep out of the war; but this could hardly be considered loyalty.

It has been some time since we have had a northern mail. I guess though we will be apt to get one tomorrow evening. I have /had/ no letter from you since I wrote you last. The weather is quite warm but there is a pleasant breeze from the sea.

Gen. Foster is in command of North Carolina and that part of Virginia which surrounds Fortress Monroe. His headquarters are at Fortress Monroe. Gen. Palmer[2] is in command at Newbern in the absence of Gen. Foster.

Business is rather dull at present. Nothing has as yet been done towards increasing my Salary. It seems to me that /by/ Sec. 5 of the Act of Congress approved March 12th. 1863 the Secretary of the Treasury might give me a fixed salary. You will find this act in <back of> Treasury Regulations of March 31st. 1863, page 16, a copy of which I send you by to-day's mail. I think that I ought to have at least fifteen hundred dollars a year for what I do.

Foster and Carpenter took dinner at the hotel to-day. I presume there is nothing of Foster's having been court-martialed and ordered to leave the State. Foster has staff officer Capt's shoulder straps.

There is a big Naval courtmartial to take place here next week. Act. Rear Ad. Lee is on his way down here now. He comes in the Minnesota, which however draws too much water to come over the bar. Capts. Lynch, Carr, & Warren[3] and Dr. Bradford[4] are to be court-martialed, the two first and last for drunkenness and neglect of duty, and the third for attempting to commit a rape on Capt. Carr's little daughter, who is about ten years old, and also for putting in double irons, a commissioned officer, a <surgeon on> paymaster on the U.S. Gunboat "Daylight" of which Capt. Warren was in command.

Tell Sister Ellen that I was glad to see her writing in your letter to the Tribune concerning Foster. I would be happy to see some of her composition too. I do not know what she amuses herself at. She certainly does not write many letters. Have you heard from Grandfather[5] lately? I wrote to him about /two/ months ago, but have had no letter from him yet. It has been about 2 $^1/_2$ years since I have had a letter from him and the last that I recieved from him was mixed up with yours so that I never answered it.

Write often.
Your brother,
John A. Hedrick.

---

[1] John Adams Gilmer (1805-1868) was a former U.S. congressman. Hedrick was likely wrong in attributing the letter to Gilmer, who by 1863 had become a supporter of the Confederacy, despite his earlier opposition to secession. *Dictionary of North Carolina Biography*, s.v. "Gilmer, John Adams."

[2] Innis Newton Palmer (1824-1900), a Union general, held various commands in North Carolina, including the District of North Carolina, January 1864-January 1865, and the Department of North Carolina, January-February 1865. Boatner, *Civil War Dictionary*, 616-617.

[3] Comdr. Dominick Lynch, Acting Master Henry P. Carr, and Acting Master Joshua P. Warren. No record of this case has been discovered. Lynch served in the North Atlantic Squadron for the duration of the war; Carr disappears from the *Official Records* after February 1863; and Warren was still on duty as late as February 1864, although no longer in the North Atlantic Squadron. *ORN*, ser. 1, 8:138, 216, 255, 358, 468, 487; 9:609, 703; 15:260.

[4] John S. Bradford of the U.S. Navy's Coast Survey project. Robert J. Schmeller Jr., ed., *Under the Blue Pennant, or Notes of a Naval Officer* (New York: John Wiley and Sons, 1999), 138-139; *New York Herald*, December 30, 1864.

[5] Benjamin Sherwood of Iowa, the maternal grandfather of Benjamin and John Hedrick.

SHC
Beaufort, N.C.
August 16th. 1863.

Dear Brother:

I recieved day before yesterday yours of the 1st. and 4th. insts. And also a batch of blank bills of sale for enrolled vessels.

To-day I am 26 years old. The weather is very warm and we are needing rain. Quite a number of the inhabitants of this place are sick with typhoid fever.

The humbug Foster is still here. He ate at the Hotel yesterday noon. His wife, I understand, is at Morehead City. I do not know what Foster's business is. He wears captain's shoulder straps.

In one of my previous letters I told you about all I know about Capt. Ritch of Washington. I understand that he is a northern man by birth and a ship carpenter by trade. I send herewith a letter written by him inclosing a memorial from certain citizens of Washington asking permission to go to Hyde County for corn. You wished me to recommend, if I could, some lawyer for the office of Tax Commissioner. There are none to be found within the military lines of the Union Army. I have asked Mr. Norcum whether he would accept of the office, but he said that he had enough to do in his store.

Mr. D.W. Whitehurst, whom Mr. Pigott recommends, would make a good commissioner. He is very popular in this county and has represented it in the State Legislature.

Col. J.H. Taylor of this place wants the office and says that he thinks he can give the required surety. He is a very well informed man on all subjects and keeps himself better posted on all subjects than any one in town. He is an excellent man and a graduate of Chapel Hill in its Shakesperean days. He says that if he can get the place he will devote his entire attention to the duties of his office.

I am well.

Your brother,
John A. Hedrick.

SHC
Beaufort, N.C.
August 20th. 1863.

Dear Brother:

I recieved a few days ago yours of the 8th. inst. inclosing reciept of Gideon & Pearson for printing blank bills of sale. I think this the cheapest jobs I have had done there. Some of the previous batch I thought quite high.

The weather is quite cool. We have had no northern news later than the 15th. I saw the New York Journal of Commerce of the 15th. which had very little news in it. The attack on Charleston was expected to take place on the 8th. We however have had news from vessels direct from Charleston as late as the 15th. There had been no attack up to that time.

Mr. Heaton informed me yesterday that he expected to appoint E.W. Carpenter, Special Agent of the Treasury Department at Newbern. His appointment will have to be approved by the Secretary of the Treasury.

The humbug Foster has moved his family to this place and is going to housekeeping. Gen. Peck is in command of this Department[1] and Foster's brother is the General's Chief of Staff.

The turpentine question has not been settled.

> Write often.
> Your brother,
> John A. Hedrick

---

[1] Maj. Gen. John James Peck (1821-1878) was not the department commander but the commander of the District of North Carolina within the Department of Virginia and North Carolina. He served in this position from August 14, 1863, to January 4, 1864, and from February 5 to April 28, 1864. Sifakis, *Who Was Who in the Civil War*, 495.

SHC
Beaufort, N C.
August 23rd. 1863.

Dear Brother:

I wrote you last Sunday and once during the week. The weather is quite pleasant to-day. There is a camp meeting about four miles in the country and quite a number of the town people have gone to it.

There were two deaths in town yesterday. Mrs. Quartermaster Bowen[1] died early yesterday morning and old Mr. Delamar[2] during the day. Their funerals are to be preached this evening. Mrs. Pigott was well acquainted with Mrs. Bowen, having come from Baltimore to this place on the same boat. Mr. Pigott knew Mr. Delamar. Mr. Delamar was sick only two or three days. Mrs. Bowen had had a fever about a month.

A steamer has first arrived from Charleston and it is reported that Sumpter has been battered down. I do not know what foundation there is for the report. I have just learned that the steamer above mentioned is not from Charleston but from Wilmington. She is the "Quaker City" and is in a leaking condition, having come into collision with another steamer off Wilmington, going south. Of course she has no news from Charleston.

Foster and Carpenter are both here to-day.

The two Adamses who were stolen some time ago by the rebels and carried to Richmond and put into the Confederate Army have made their escape and are again at home in Beaufort. They arrived here last Friday. I have not heard them say much about their trip into Dixie, but what I have heard makes the condition of the people about Richmond to be a horrid <condition> one.

> Write often
> Your brother,
> John A. Hedrick.

---

[1] The wife of Capt. J. J. Bowen, an assistant quartermaster in the Department of North Carolina. *OR*, ser. 1, 18:512.

[2] Thomas Delamar (b. ca. 1794) had been a carpenter. Seventh Census, 1850: Carteret County.

> *SHC*
> Beaufort, N.C.
> August 30th. 1863.

Dear Brother:

After the lapse of nearly two weeks we are again in the reciept of a Northern Mail. I recieved last night your letters of the 11th. 15th. 18th. and 22nd. inst. The news of the taking of Fort Sumpter has been contradicted since I wrote last. It is very hard to tell when you have a true story. I thought that the news of the taking of <Charleston>/Sumpter/ came straight enough to be true. I received it from Capt. Ottinger of the Revenue Cutter, who informed me that it came officially from Act. Rear Ad. Dalhgreen[1] to Rear Ad. S.P. Lee. I celebrated the event by taking a glass of wine. Last summer I celebrated the taking of Richmond. Hereafter I believe I will quit celebrating events. It don't do much good and it looks very foolish to rejoice over a thing that never happened.

Foster and Carpenter are still here. They and Mr. Heaton are very thick. Mr. Heaton is going to Washington, D.C. on the first boat going north. Foster speaks of going on too. He says that his employment does not commence until our forces take a particular locality. He is not going to take his wife with him. By to-morrow's Mail I send you the Local Rules & Restrictions prescribed by Mr. Heaton and approved by the Secretary of the Treasury.

Mr. Whitehurst, whom Mr. Pigott wishes appointed Marshall for the district of N.C is a plain, unassuming farmer of the County. He has represented Carteret County in the State Legisature, one, I know and I think two terms. He is a justice of the peace and a man of good judgement.

He writes a fair hand and as I think a is a good business man. He has been afflicted with the Rheumatism a great deal during the last eight months and consequently has been in town very little during that time. There is no doubt about his loyalty.

If the District Attorney must be a lawyer, I do not know where he will be found in this State. Mr. Norcum could turn himself into a lawyer in a short time but he would be unwilling to do so. I have already given you a pretty good idea of Col. Taylor. Should he not get the berth of Tax Commissioner, he might do for District Attorney. He is not a lawyer and rather old to commence the study of it. He is a very fine man and a man of good judgement and a great deal of reading. He is very anxious to get some kind of employment. I now have /him/ as occasional Inspector but this will hardly continue long.

I forgot to tell you in my last two letters that Mrs. Norcum wished me to say to you that she had <driven> turned off her negroes and become abolitionized.[2] She says that she is an everlasting abolitionist and that if you will come down to Beaufort she will give you bread made by her own hands <and>/or/ that of her daughter.

I think that Wm. Adam is a very good name for your general.

We have had a great deal of stormy weather during the last week. It is cloudy and windy now.

---

[1] Rear Adm. John Adolph Dahlgren (1809-1870) was commander of the South Atlantic Blockading Squadron from July 1863 until the end of the war. Boatner, *Civil War Dictionary*, 218.

[2] E. H. Norcum owned eight slaves in 1860. Mrs. Norcum's comment was facetious. She and John A. Hedrick carried on amicable debates on the subject of slavery. Eighth Census, 1860: Carteret County, Slave Schedule.

SHC
Beaufort, N.C.
Sept. 6th. 1863.

Dear Brother:

Your letters of the 25th. and 29th. of last month have been recieved since I wrote you last.

All is quiet in the Department. I was at Newbern yesterday and saw Dr. Page at a distance but did not get to speak to him. I got a Wilmington Journal of the 27th. August. It had nothing of particular interest.

Mr. Heaton left here on the 2nd. inst. for Washington, on board the "S.R. Spalding," which returned to this place this morning. He expected to be gone about three weeks.

Things are getting on a little better than they did some time ago. The sale of Naval Stores is limited to 1 Bll. Turpentine or its equivalent in Tar for each family every two weeks. The Naval Stores purchased and delivered previous to the 25th of July may be shipped upon the payment of 5 per cent on the sworn invoice value. Quite a lot of it has gone out during the last two weeks. Small shipments of Cotton have commenced.

The public meeting in Washington, N.C. which you mention in one of your previous letters was not known to me till I received your letter. I afterward saw a small account of it in the New York Times. I guess there was no great turn out of citizens at it, because no one from the country surrounding Washington is allowed to go into town. I have seen no full report of the proceedings of the meeting. Old man Congleton is now at Washington and I presume that he must have been one of the principal actors in the meeting.

The price of Fish, Oysters, Clams, Eggs, Poultry, Fruits, Vegitables &c. has been and is now regulated by the Provost Marshal /in Newbern/. I do not recollect what the fixed price for oysters is. For Beef, it is 14 cents per pound; Turkeys, $1.25 each; and Chickens 63 cents a pair. If I can get one of these Lists of prices I will send it to you. For a short while last Winter we had the prices of country produce in this place regulated by the Provost Marshal, but it did not work well, and was soon discontinued.

Why don't Mr. Goodloe come to North Carolina as Federal judge. I think that he would make a good judge and perhaps a better one than he would a Military Governor. If we are to have Marshals, Attorneys, and Tax Commissioners, we should have a judge also to tell when they are right.

We have had stormy weather lately, but it has been pleasant and clear to-day.

Write often.
Your brother,
John A. Hedrick.

SHC
Collector's Office,
Beaufort, N.C.
Sunday September 13th. 1863.

Dear Brother:

I wrote you last Sunday and have had nothing from you since then. We have had no mail from the north for more than a week. New York papers, however, have been recieved as late as the 10th. by the U.S. Gunboat, "Maratazas." Our news from Charleston direct is later than that by the papers. A vessel arrived here from Charleston Bar last Thursday or Friday, and reported that the white flag was floating on forts Moultrie and Johnson,[1] when she left, and confirmed the news brought by the Spalding of the taking of Forts Wagner, Greg, and Su/m/pter.[2] The papers of the 10th. say that Gen. Rosecrans has driven the Rebs out of Chattanooga Tennessee.[3] I have heard of no movements by Meade and Lee.

All is quiet in this department. Inclosed is a string of shell beads for Alice Underwood. Give my respects to Mr. Underwood and family and tell him that I received a short time ago a speech delivered by him at Alexandria, Va on the 4th. of July. I was very much pleased with the speech. Tell Mr. Goodloe that we want a judge in North Carolina, and that he is the man for that position.

What has been done about Tax Commissioners. I do not know any one who would make a good District Attorney. Mr. D.W. Whitehurst is /a/ good man and has long been a justice of the peace in this county and has represented the County in the State Legislature but is no lawyer. He is not too old to study law.

Mr. Heaton left here about a week and a half ago, and I presume he is still in Washington City. He can tell you what kind of a man Col. Taylor is.

The weather is a little warm to-day.

> Write often.
> Your brother,
> John A. Hedrick.

---

[1] Forts Moultrie and Johnson, along with Fort Sumter, guarded the main entrance to Charleston harbor. The report of their surrender was incorrect. Foote, *Civil War*, 2:228.

[2] Confederates abandoned Forts Wagner and Gregg on Morris Island, S.C., on September 6, 1863, following an intense artillery bombardment. A Federal assault on Fort Sumter two days later was unsuccessful. Foote, *Civil War*, 2:696-701.

 [3] A flanking maneuver by Rosecrans forced Bragg to abandon Chattanooga. Union troops moved into the city on September 9. Current, *Encyclopedia of the Confederacy*, 1:204; Long, *Day by Day*, 407.

SHC
Beaufort, N.C.
Sept. 14th. 1863.

Dear Brother:

I recieved today your letter of the 2nd. inst. which is the latest. I wrote you yesterday and enclosed a string of beads for Alice Underwood. To-day I send a string for Sister Ellen.

I sent you some time ago the late circular of Mr. Heaton to Traders in the district. You will see from Sec. IX of said circular and paragraph Five of the Appendix, that parties in this State can dispose of one barrel of turpentine or its equivalent in tar every two weeks for the purpose of obtaining family supplies. I hope that Mr. Heaton will settle the Naval Stores question before he returns to North Carolina. I have heard nothing said here in relation to the purchase of Naval Stores by the Navy Department.

All is quiet without further news from Charleston.

Write often.

Your brother,
John A. Hedrick.

SHC
Beaufort, North Carolina,
September 15th. 1863.

Dear Brother:

I have just recieved yours of the 8th. inst. inclosing copy of a letter from Gen. Foster. It seemed very queer to me that the humbug Foster should be ordered to leave the State one week and should be back the next with a captain's commission. I think that it would be well to examine into the authenticity of his commission.

I have just heard some news from Raleigh by E.D. Jones,[1] a citizen of Newbern. He says that some refugees have lately arrived in Newbern, who say that the Georgia Troops have torn down the Raleigh Standard Office, and that the citizens of Raleigh in retaliation sacked the State Journal Office.[2] Mr. Jones says that he is well acquainted with one of the lady refugees. She is direct from Raleigh. Bacon is $1 a pound in Dixie, Meal $5 per bushel and other things in proportion.

We have had no further news from Charleston.

Every thing is quiet here now. Mercantile business is prosperous. Rents have increased about four fold during the last year. Houses are building all along Front Street on the water side for shops. All the little shanties on the back streets have been brought to Front Street for Stores. One story buildings 18 x 24 are renting for from $20 to $50 per month according to the location and rate of finish.

I have just recieved Treasury Adjustment of my Light House Accounts for the quarter ending June 30th. 1863. The Commissioner of the Customs informs me that the commissions on disbursements have been disallowed. There must be some mistake at the Treasury Department about my pay. They certainly cannot expect me to pay off all the Light House Keepers Salaries in this State and get nothing for it. Only about two months ago I received a letter from J.P. Smith, Lt. Ho. Engineer at Philadelphia, informing me that the Lt. H. Board had instructed him to have me to pay the salaries of Light Keepers in this State wherever it was practicable. I subsequently wrote him to send me a list of such of the keepers as he wished me to pay off. I have not yet had any answer from him but have estimated for Hatteras Light without any further instructions. I do not know the names of any of the other keepers. I think that the Secretary of the Treasury believes that I have a fixed Salary and has therefore refused to allow me any commissions. From the 1st. March to the 30th. June I had the liquidation of the Pay Rolls of three Revenue Cutters averaging about $1500 per month. I now pay off two Cutters averaging $1200 per month. It don't seem right that a man should do all this for nothing. My pay should certainly be as great as that of the Act. Asst. Paymasters in the Navy, which is $1300 per annum.

I have written the Com. of Customs to know why the commissions were refused last quarter. They have heretofore been allowed. My commissions on Hospital Disbursements (1 per cent) do not pay for the stationary used. I wrote you yesterday and the day before.

Write often,
Your brother,
John A. Hedrick.

[1] In 1865, Governor Holden appointed E. D. Jones (1814-1880) as one of New Bern's five city commissioners. Watson, *History of New Bern and Craven County*, 438; *Cedar Grove Cemetery*, 37.

[2] Georgia troops passing through Raleigh demolished the office of Holden's newspaper on the night of September 9, 1863. They regarded Holden as a traitor for advocating peace negotiations. Holden's supporters retaliated by destroying the presses of the rival *State Journal* the following day. Barrett, *Civil War in North Carolina*, 195-196; William C. Harris, *William Woods Holden: Firebrand of North Carolina Politics* (Baton Rouge: Louisiana State University Press, 1987), 139-140.

SHC
Beaufort, North Carolina,
Sunday, Sept. 20th. 1863.

Dear Brother:

I recieved last Friday yours of the 11th. inst. giving an account of your first meeting with Mr. Heaton. I expected that you and he would have a kind of spat on meeting, from what he said before leaving here. I am to blame for this altercation, because I read to him a part of your letters giving an account of an interview with Secretary Chase, in which Mr. Chase informed you that Mr. Heaton had control of supplies for the people in this State, and that if he was not able to attend to his duty that he must appoint some<u>one else</u>. I should by no means have read this to him, but I was showing him a slip from a newspaper containing a dispatch from Newbern saying that Mr. Heaton was acting Military Governor of North Carolina, and was reading from a couple of your letters parts refering to Mr. Heaton's business and did not notice this clause until I had read it to him. He got raging and said that he would call on you and Mr. Goodloe as soon as he got to Washington, and see you about running to Mr. Chase with stories written by Mr. Conklin.[1] I tried to pacify him by telling him that I know that you and Mr. Goodloe did not mean to be officious by any means, but it did not seem to do any good. So I had to let him alone in his anger. He is very passionate. This, I think is caused by his ailments. If he were well he would get along much better. He was /sick/ on his arrival here and was confined to his bed at least one half of the time during his stay, yet he accomplished a considerable amount of work during that time.

He promised to write me often when he left, but I have not had any thing from him yet. I have not heard any thing said about an election for

Congressman in this district. The humbug C.H. Foster went north with Mr. Heaton and is back again.

T.H. Vanderhoef[2] Special for Washington is a northern man and was superintendent of contrabands at Washington under Gen. Spinola. I never saw him and know but little about him. He and Dr. Wheeler, Quartermaster at Washington have had a controversy of which I do not know the merits but I heard that Gen. Foster was one of the witnesses and that Vanderhoef had got the worse of the controversy, and was going north.[3] He is one of C.H.F.'s crowd and I judge that he is no great shakes.

E.H. Willis,[4] Special for Plymouth, was raised in this country and was here when he recieved his appointment. He's about fifty years old and a widower. I do not know whether he is a man of property or not but I heard it said that he would never allow himself be seen talking with his brother, who lives here and is only in tolerable circumstances. I would judge from this that he considered himself a little better than his brother. When here he and Foster were together most of the time and I did not take the trouble /to/ get acquainted with him. I was introduced to him one day at Mr. Heaton's.

He has lived at Plymouth a good long while. I can not see who the business men of Beaufort were that were anxious to have Carpenter appointed Special Agent for Newbern. I presume it must have been the humbug Foster. For Mr. Heaton was telling me about the time he appointed Willis for Plymouth that every body thought it was an excellent appointment and I could percieve from his conversation that every body meant Foster and Carpenter.

Should Mr. Daniel P. Bible[5] call on you, you can get a good history of Vanderhoef from him. I gave Mr. Bible a letter of introduction to you. You will find him a very excellent gentleman. He told me that Vanderhoef would never do for Special Agent at Washington N.C. Mr. Bible said when he left here about a week ago that he was going to Washington D.C. and that he would call on you.

I see in the N.Y. Herald of the 12th. that Mr. Underwood has been captured in Virginia and had probably been carried to Richmond. Who has been appointed Fifth Auditor? Mr. Smith, Lt. Ho. Engineer, Philada. Pa. has sent a list of five additional light houses and two light boats to pay off, making in all seven light houses and two lights boats, amounting to about Twenty two hundred dollars per quarter, and yet in my last Treasury Adjustment the Commissioner of Customs informs me that the commissions on lighthouse disbursements had been disallowed. It beats hell and damnation! If they are going to make a paymaster of me they should certainly allow /me/ a paymaster's salary. In the Navy the Act. Asst. Paymasters get $1300 per annum and have only one vessel to attend to while I have two Revenue Cutters, Two Light Boats, and seven Light

Houses to pay off and get about $600. And moreover I have the ordinary duties of the collector of this port to attend to besides. If something is not done during the coming Congress to increase my Salary I shall certainly resign. I can not expose myself and sureties to any loss which might happen for the small amount of six hundred dollars per year. My disbursements for the cutter service now amount to about $1200 per month, and previous to the 1st. of July it had been about $1600 per month. The weather is quite cold to-day.

All is quiet in the Department. News came down from Newbern yesterday to the effect that Longstreet was about 15 miles above that place. With what number of men I did not learn. I should not be supprised if /it/ were so, because the Times of the 14th. says that he had left the neighborhood of the Rappahannock and gone south, perhaps /to/ reinforce Beauregard, at Charleston.[6] We have had no news from Charleston later than the 9th. This was in the papers of the 14th. which you have already seen. The news from Tennessee is glorious for old Burney. Two thousand is a good grab.[7]

Write often.

Your brother,
John A. Hedrick.

---

[1] Heaton's clerk.

[2] T. H. Vanderhoef was a treasury agent and superintendent of contrabands in Washington, N.C. General Orders for the Department of North Carolina, September 15, 1863, Myers House Papers, Brown Library, Washington, N.C.

[3] In court-martial proceedings Captain Wheeler was vindicated on charges of "disloyalty and illicit commerce with the enemy." The court further announced that Vanderhoef, who had proffered the charges, had acted out of "vindictive and untrustworthy motives." General Orders for the Department of North Carolina, September 15, 1863, Myers House Papers, Brown Library, Washington, N.C.

[4] Elijah H. Willis (b. ca. 1816) was a "merchant" and the owner of more than one hundred thousand dollars in real estate. His appointment, along with those of E. W. Carpenter as local special agent at New Bern and T. H. Vanderhoef at Washington, was announced in a "Notice to Traders, Shippers, and Carriers" issued by Treasury Department Supervising Special Agent David Heaton on August 27, 1863. Eighth Census, 1860: Washington County; Myers House Papers, Brown Library, Washington, N.C.

[5] Daniel P. Bible was a merchant from Washington, N.C. George W. Bible to Warren P. Ketchum, January 4, 1863, Myers House Papers, Brown Library, Washington, N.C.

[6] James Longstreet's I Corps, Army of Northern Virginia, passed through North Carolina as it moved via railroad to reinforce Braxton Bragg's forces in Georgia prior to the Battle of Chickamauga. Foote, *Civil War*, 2:709-711.

[7] Federal forces under Ambrose Burnside occupied Knoxville on September 3, 1863, capturing its two-thousand-man garrison. Boatner, *Civil War Dictionary*, 467.

SHC
Beaufort, North Carolina,
Sunday, Sept. 27th. 1863.

Dear Brother:

Since I wrote last I have recieved from you one batch Coombs'[1] speeches and "Are North Carolinians Freemen,"[2] Grandfathers letter, and two letters written by you, one dated the 14th. and the other the 19th. inst.

Mr. Coombs' doctrine looks feasible but I do not believe that it would work as well as he thinks. I do not know how it is in other parts of the State but immediately around here most of the slave owners are still on their plantations and have never taken up arms against the United States. They may have aided the Rebels when they were here, yet <it> I am afraid that it would be hard to prove that.

In making shipments to the interior, the owner of the goods has to swear that "he is in all respects loyal and true to the government of the United States and that <they> /he/ has never given voluntary aid to the rebels in arms nor in any other manner encouraged the rebellion." They take this oath, both rich and poor, without hesitancy. They reason thus. "When the Southern forces were in possession here I would bring my corn, flour, fish and potatoes to market and would sell to any one who would give me the most money. Or if a soldier should come to my house and wish to buy potatoes I would sell them to him, not because he was in the Rebel service but because I must have money."

I was very much amused one day at a poor fellow, who after taking the above mentioned oath remarked that he had been a volunteer in the Rebel Army but he did not care for that—"that he had to go into the army or do worse." You will find more of this class, who have been in the Rebel service than any other. It seems that many of them had to go into the army for a livelyhood. The rich men will not fight when they can get others to fight for them.

This section of the State has been considered quite loyal and hence the confiscation act may not operate as extensively as in other parts. It would not free more than half in this County. Perhaps not so many. The young men are mostly in the rebel service while the old men hold the most slaves.

Capt. Ottinger has the keys of the house in which Mr. Heaton lived and had his office. I do not think that the citizens of North Carolina should be compelled to petition the President for an election for Members of Congress. We have a right to be represented unless it is inexpedient to hold an election in the presence of an Army and when this difficulty is removed neither the President nor any one at Washington has any right to say whether we shall have an election or not.

Mr. Goodloe had about as well give up the expectation of the Military Governorship of North Carolina. Gen. Foster is strongly opposed to any Governor being appointed and as the military governor is appointed by the War Department, the General commanding will be consulted in the matter.

New regulations for the government of trade in insurrectionary districts have been issued—a copy of which I send by this mail.

The price of eggs by order of the Provost Marshal of this place shall exceed 25 cents per dozen until further orders. This is the only article the price of which is regulated here by the Provost.

Your brother,
John A. Hedrick.

---

[1] This probably refers to Leslie Combs (1793-1881), who was a veteran Kentucky Whig politician and leading Unionist. During the Civil War he served as clerk of the Kentucky Court of Appeals. *Appleton's Cyclopedia of American Biography*, s.v. "Coombs [sic], Leslie"; *Biographical Encyclopedia of Kentucky of the Dead and Living Men of the Nineteenth Century* (Cincinnati: J. M. Armstrong, 1878), 79-80; *OR*, ser. 1, 52, pt. 1:136-137.

[2] Benjamin S. Hedrick published a pamphlet entitled *Are North Carolinians Freemen?* in 1857, defending his Free-Soil views. A copy is located in the Hedrick Papers, Duke Special Collections.

Duke
Beaufort, N.C.
Oct. 3rd. 1863.

Dear Brother:

Yours of the 23rd. ult. was recieved a few days ago. All is quiet in the Department. The weather has turned very summerlike. We have had nothing later than the 28th. ultimo. From the news up to that time I thought that Rosecrans had been considerably worsted, ought still able to maintain his position.[1] The work at Charleston seems to progress very slowly.

C.C. Upham,[2] U.S.N. Fleet Paymaster Hampton Roads, Va, was here a few days ago and gave notice that he was authorized to purchase Naval Stores for the Navy. He went from /this place/ to Newbern and should have been back yesterday according to promise but did not come. He did not fix any price but from his conversation I judge that he would not give more than $10, or $12, per Barrel for Turpentine. It is selling in New York for $35, and if the restrictions were removed it would bring $25 here. Some are giving as high as $20 and run the risk of shipping it.

Sales on private account are limited to 1 Bll. in two weeks to each family needing supplies and shipments are confined to that purchased previous to the 25th. July. Both purchases and shipments /on private account/ presume will be stopped in a few days, till the Government obtains a supply.

I have been exceedingly busy for the last two weeks. I have not had time to reckon up what my office is worth to me, but think that during the last month it payed about $75.00. The Commissions on Lt. Ho. Disbursements according to what formerly was allowed, would amount to $57.20 the present quarter. I don't think that any thing is allowed for Cutter disbursements though I can see no good reason why it should not. I am now paying out nearly $1200 /per month/ for the two Cutters in North Carolina. One of them is at Newbern and it costs me about $2. each time I go there to pay the men off. This may be set down as a clear loss.

I will write you, Messrs Chase and Goodloe more fully hereafter.

Your brother,
John A. Hedrick.

---

[1] At the Battle of Chickamauga, September 19-20, 1863, Braxton Bragg's Confederate army routed Union forces under William S. Rosecrans, who was soon relieved of command. Foote, *Civil War*, 2:712-757.

[2] Charles C. Upham. *ORN*, ser. 1, 9:459.

Duke
Beaufort, N.C.
Oct. 5th. 1863.

Dear Brother:

I have had nothing from you later than Sept. 23rd. New York papers of the 1st. inst. were recieved here yesterday. They contain nothing of much importance. It was rumored here yesterday that Raleigh papers had been recieved lately and that they contained news of the capture of 40,000 prisoners by Gen. Rosecrans. I hope it may be so but do not think it probable. The National Intelligencer with the articles from the Raleigh Standard were recieved last week. All is quiet here.

To-day is the time set by Mr. Heaton's letter of the 16th. ult. to be back. I hardly think he will be here so soon, because he will be apt to wish to remain in Ohio until the election is over, which comes off on the 8th. inst.

I collected during last month $830.58 from duties on Imports and about $10,000 from Internal & Coastwise Intercourse. I do not know whether Mr. Chase will allow me any Commissions on the latter or not. If he should, it would make me a right nice business. Heretofore I have paid all of these reciepts over to Mr. Heaton at the close of each week.

Trade has been very brisk during the last week. One day last week I took in over $800 from the 5 per cent on shipments to Newbern. No merchant vessels have arrived in port during the last three days and therefore /there/ will be less shipments for the next three of four days at least.

In your last letter you mention your having given the beads to Alice Underwood but say nothing of her Father's having been captured by the Rebs. I would infer from this silence that the report of his capture was not true.

> Write often,
> Your brother,
> John A. Hedrick.

> *Duke*
> Beaufort, N.C.
> Oct. 7th. 1863.

Dear Brother:

Your letters of the 26th. & 30th. ultimo and also the National Republican was recieved to-day. Sutlers do not carry goods & wares to Washington & Newbern on Govt. Transports and thereby avoid paying the five percent Tax.

In Washington however they have pretty much the entire controle of the trade. The same is the case in Plymouth & other places up the Sounds. In Newbern I think citizens have a pretty fair share of the trade.

The goods that are sent to these blockaded ports are not generally consumed by the troops. In Washington there are more citizens than there ever have been soldiers stationed at that place.

The swindler C.H.F has stuck up posters calling for volunteers in this State. He lives here.

No salary so far as I know has been fixed for the Local Special Agents of the Treasury, Department. Mr. Heaton told Messrs Carpenter & Willis that he did not know whether the Secretary would allow them more than the fees for issuing permits, taking bonds, and administering oaths or not. Carpenter, I understand, is taking in some $30 or $40 per day for permits to fishermen and others.

I have had only one letter from Mr. Heaton since he left. He promised to write me often.

New York papers of the 3rd. inst. have been recieved but I have seen nothing of importance in them. I am glad to hear that Mr. Underwood is all safe and sound.

Give my respects to Mesrs Goodloe & Pigott,

> Write often,
> Your brother,
> John A. Hedrick.

SHC
Collector's Office,
Beaufort, N.C.
Oct. 12th. 1863.

Dear Brother:

Your letter of the 3rd. inst. was recieved yesterday. New York papers of the 8th. inst have reached here but I have seen nothing later than the 6th. I understand however that there is nothing of much importance in the 8th.

I am glad that you concur with me in thinking that the President has not right to order an election for Members of Congress. When the time comes I think that we will be represented but not before.

I have been very busy lately and will be more so for the next month. All is quiet in the Department.

> I am well,
> Write often,
> Your brother,
> John A. Hedrick

SHC
Beaufort, N.C.
Oct. 19th. 1863.

Dear Brother:

I recieved yesterday your letter of the 12th. containing the consoling expression that a "man seldom gets his money when he earns it." Yours of the 10th reached me on Saturday the 17th. I have had so much business to attend to lately that I have had no time to write you any letters.

Mr. Heaton arrived here last Monday having left Washington Saturday previous (10th.) He brings an Assistant by the name of Thomas with him.[1] I think that Mr. Thomas will be of considerable good to the Department. He seems to be a quiet, clever kind of man.

We have had papers of the 16th. containing news of the elections in Pennsylvania and Ohio. Curtin's majority is thought to be about 20000 and Brough's between 50000 and 100000 votes.[2]

The weather is quite pleasant and warm.

Mrs. Norcum wishes /you/ to come down and take Christmas dinner with us. She has an old goose blind in one eye, which she is going to kill for my Christmas dinner prov'd Charleston falls and the old goose don't die before then. If you will come, she says, she will put the big pot in the little one and kill the pig.

The package of wheat was recieved Saturday.

I am well.

Write often,
Your brother,
John A. Hedrick

---

[1] Uriah Thomas was an assistant special agent for the Third Agency of the Treasury Department, which included North Carolina. Niven, *Salmon P. Chase Papers*, 4:241; Uriah Thomas to Warren P. Ketchum, January 27, 1864, Myers House Papers, Brown Library, Washington, N.C.

[2] Andrew Gregg Curtin (1817-1894), Republican governor of Pennsylvania, 1860-1866; John Brough (1811-1865), Republican governor of Ohio, 1863-1865. Boatner, *Civil War Dictionary*, 90, 214.

SHC
Beaufort, N.C.
Oct. 21st. 1863.

Dear Brother:

I have just recieved your letter of the 15th. the Baltimore American and my Diploma. I was very glad to get my Diploma, not because I think that it will ever do me much good but in consideration of the time and money that it cost me. Dr. Ferris made an omission or mistake. He should have attached an English translation to it. This would have been of great service to me in the present state of my Latin. Inclosed is the latest circular on the Turpentine question. The Agent is giving $12.00 a Barrel for Turpentine and $3.50 to $3.75 for Tar.

I have not heard of Mr. Ritch's return. New York papers of the 17th. have been recieved but I have seen nothing later than the 16th. There is very little news afloat.

Write often,
Your brother,
John A. Hedrick.

SHC
Collector's Office,
Beaufort, N.C.
October 25th. 1863

Dear Brother:

Yours of the 19th. inst. was recieved yesterday.

I /have/ just been burnt out of house and home. Last night about two o'clock I /was/ aroused by the cry of "fire." Upon getting up and looking out of my windows I found from the smoke that the fire was in the adjoining building. I made all haste I could & got my <took> trunk, clothing &c out into the street and as it was raining a little I carried them to Mr. Norcum's at which place I expect to stay to-night. It was only about fifteen minutes before the fire reached the hotel in which I stayed. It originated in B.A. Ensley's[1] kitchen and spread to Dr. King's[2] house, which stands against Mr. Taylor's Hotel. The hotel has been kept for the last four months by Messrs Davis[3] & Wright. Capt. Fulford's[4] house was blown up to prevent the fire from spreading.

For the benefit of Mr. Pigott I will give you /the names of/ the houses burnt; viz: Jane Ward's;[5] B.A. Ensley's; Dr. King's; Dr. Martin's[6] Apothecary shop, the Ocean House and Capt. Fulford's house. Mr. Hall's[7] house and Mr. Norcum's store were saved with great difficulty. Also some other houses across the way. My office was not more than thirty yards from Dr. Martin's Drug Store.

As soon as I got my clothing in a place of safety I went to my office and got my money and more valuable papers and put them in a safe place. I then got all my other books and documents in readiness to move should there be any occasion to do so. The wind happened to be favorable and saved me that trouble. I lost in the fire only two pair old shoes, which I left under my bed and did not think /of/ them until the house was in a blaze. It seems that Mr. Ensley's cook has been in the habit of filling the stove full of wood and piling other wood around it so as to have it dry for kindling in the morning, and that the fire originated from this dry wood. It is said that it has caught three times before this.

I understand that N.Y. papers of the 22nd. /are here/ and that the bombardment of Charleston has commenced. Also that there has been some hard fighting between Kilpatrick & Stuart in Virginia.[8]

I was at work last night till about half past twelves and so got only about one and a half hours sleep. I intend to go to bed early tonight.

The weather is quite cold.

> Write often,
> Your brother,
> John A. Hedrick,

---

[1] B. A. Ensley (b. ca. 1825) was a resident of Craven County in 1860, but by 1870, he had relocated to Hyde County. Eighth Census, 1860: Craven County; Ninth Census, 1870: Hyde County.

[2] Dr. Francis Lathrop King (1805-1874). A fellow Beaufort resident wrote approvingly in his diary of Dr. King's "well known hatred of the Yankees." James Rumley diary entry for April 1862 published in the *Beaufort Look Out,* January 14, 1910; *Cemetery Records of Carteret County,* 157; Eighth Census, 1860: Carteret County.

[3] John P. C. Davis (1815-1864) was a merchant and had served as town commissioner, county trustee, and member of the Board of Superintendents of Common Schools of Carteret County. *Cemetery Records of Carteret County,* 151; Eighth Census, 1860: Carteret County; *Beaufort Journal,* June 10, 1857; Minutes of the Carteret County Court of Pleas and Quarter Sessions, February 1861 and February 1862, State Archives, Division of Archives and History, Raleigh.

[4] William Fulford.

[5] Jane Bell Ward (b. ca. 1786-1868). *Cemetery Records of Carteret County,* 165; Eighth Census, 1860: Carteret County; Jesse Ward and Jane Bell, Marriage Bond, March 8, 1825, Carteret County, State Archives, Division of Archives and History, Raleigh.

[6] Dr. Lafayette Martin (1826-1880) was a native of Virginia. *Cemetery Records of Carteret County*, 159; Ninth Census, 1870: Carteret County.

[7] Joseph Hall (b. ca. 1787) was a former town constable in Beaufort. Eighth Census, 1860: Carteret County.

[8] J. E. B. Stuart's Confederate cavalry surprised and routed a Union cavalry division under Brig. Gen. Hugh Judson Kilpatrick at Buckland Mills, Va., on October 19, 1863, capturing two hundred prisoners. Foote, *Civil War*, 2:795-796.

SHC
Beaufort, N.C.
Nov. 1st. 1863.

Dear Brother:

Your letter of the 24th. ultimo was recieved yesterday.

Uriah Thomas, Mr. Heaton's Assistant comes from Minnesota, but I presume he was brought up in Ohio as most of Mr. Chase's appointees were. He was acquainted with Mr. Heaton in Minnesota. He was in the Treasury Department about three months before he came to North Carolina. Mr. Heaton gives me triplicate reciepts for the money deposited with him.

Mr. Bible has returned, and did not visit Washington City when he was north. While north he married Mr. Wiswall's[1] daughter—an old citizen of Washington, N.C. and a very nice old man.

Vanderhoef ran away from Washington, N.C. during Mr. Heaton's absence and a man by the name of Ketchum[2] has been appointed in his place.

The weather has been very changeable during the last few days. During the forming part of last week it was winter cold but Friday and Saturday it was as warm as Summer while to-day it is quite cold. I am still staying at Mr. Norcum's. They have no negroes of their own at home and only one little blind boy about ten years old. An old white woman does most of the cooking and Mrs. Norcum hires her washing done. I don't believe we are as bad off here as the people of Maryland are because we know what to depend upon.

There are not as many troops in this Department as formerly.

No news of importance.

Write often,
Your brother,
John A. Hedrick.

---

[1] Howard Wiswald Sr. (b. ca. 1791) of Washington, N.C. Ninth Census, 1870: Beaufort County.

[2] Warren P. Ketchum served briefly as a local special treasury agent for Washington, N.C., in late 1863 and early 1864. Warren P. Ketchum to John J. Peck, November 28, 1863, and Uriah Thomas to Warren P. Ketchum, January 27, 1864, Myers House Papers, Brown Library, Washington, N.C.

Duke
Beaufort, N.C.
Nov. 8th. 1863.

Dear Brother:

I wrote you last Sunday and recieved your letter of the 28th. ult. last Friday.

All is quiet and I understand that Gen. Butler is in command of N.C. and Virginia.

Mr. Norcum's family was considerably stirred up a few days ago. The Provost Marshall put a lot of negroes in the kitchen when the cooking is done. I do not know but that he will feed us on negroes after awhile. The negroes having more good sense than the Provost, left the next day and now all has become peaceable. It was a mean trick in the Provost to fill a man's cook kitchen with negroes, especially where the white folks do the cooking.

I have not as yet recieved my compensation for services under Internal and Coastwise Intercourse but think that I shall recieve the same as under other provisions of the law, that is 3 per ct. on collections and the fees, &c, See Act July 13, 1861, Section IV last clause, Treas. Regs. Sept, 11th., P. 46. Should this be allowed I will get pretty good pay. During last month I collected $9053 $^{03}/_{100}$ from shipments north and South.

Mr. Heaton tells me that he is offered the position of Third Auditor, but that he does not know whether to accept it or not. Should he do so there will be a nice place for Mr. Goodloe made vacant by his resignation of Supervisory Special Agent.

We have had no war news of interest lately.

Write often
Your brother,
John A. Hedrick

Duke
Beaufort, N.C.
Nov. 11th. 1863.

Dear Brother:

I wrote you Sunday.

There are three large prize steamers in port now. Two, the "Lady Davis" and the "Robt. E. Lee" were taken by the "James Adjer"[1] and I have forgotten the name of the steamer that took the "Anna & Elizabeth."[2] The Robt. E. Lee is a very large steamer and in fact all valuable vessels. They will make excellent blockaders. I expect to go aboard of them some time to-day and if I learn any thing interesting I will write you again.

One of these vessels is said to have one million of dollars in specie on board. Sulphur, Nitre and small arms seems to constitute the principal part of the cargoes. Write often.

Capt. Ottinger has just left for Washington City but I never thought of telling him to call on you.

The weather is quite cold. All well.

Your brother,
John A. Hedrick.

---

[1] The USS *James Adger* captured the Confederate steamer *Lady Davis* (previously known as the *Cornubia*) on November 8, 1863, near New Inlet, N.C. The following day the same Union ship seized the *Robert E. Lee* off Cape Lookout Shoals, N.C. *Civil War Naval Chronology, 1861-1865* (Washington, D C.: Navy Department, 1961), pt. 3:153, pt. 6:294.

[2] The correct name of the captured blockade-runner was the *Ella and Annie*. It was seized by the crew of the USS *Niphon* near Masonboro Inlet, N.C., on November 9, 1863. *Civil War Naval Chronology*, pt. 3:154.

Duke
Beaufort, N.C.
Nov. 16th. 1863.

Dear Brother:

Your letter of the 3rd. inst. was recieved last week. I wrote you a few days ago and said that I expected to visit the prizes during the same day. I did not have time to go aboard them and they left here yesterday morning. There were four in all. The name of the last taken I did not learn. The others were the "Robt. E. Lee," "The Lady Davis" and the "Ella and Anna".

All were fine steamers and the "Robt. E. Lee" and the "Ella and Anna" were said to be beautiful.

You put the same construction on /the latter clause of/ Sec. XIV of Treas. Rgs. of Sept. 11th. that I did, though in connection with the former part of the section the construction given it by Mr. Heaton might be recieved. I hope the Department will take Mr. Heaton's construction and allow me to continue depositing with him. Because it will save me a vast deal of trouble. I have reported my actions to the Secretary and have requested /him/ to indicate to me what disposition he wishes me to make of the money.

We have /had/ quite warm and pleasant weather during the last week, but I think that it will be cold again to-morrow. On the 19th. ult. I wrote the Secretary requesting him to allow me a Deputy and recieved in reply a letter dated Oct. 31st. in which he says "The Department is of opinion that with the services of Mr. Willis as permanent Inspector, and of Mr. Taylor as Occasional Inspector, that the business of your port is not sufficient to warrant the appointment of /an/ additional Deputy at this time." The Inspectors do not aid me any so far as office work is concerned; for they are employed out doors all the while. But if the Department is of opinion that I shall have the 3 per cent on all collections I can get along without any additional Deputy.

> Write often,
> Your brother,
> John A. Hedrick.

P.S. Capt. Ritch is here.

Duke
Beaufort, N.C.
Nov. 23rd. 1863.

Dear Brother:

Yours of the 14th. inst. was recieved last week.

Mr. Norcum says that you must tell Abraham to send Lazarus to Greensboro to intercede for George. I mentioned in my last letter that Capt. Ritch was here. He sends his best respects to you and seems to be very thankful for the kindness extended to him by you in taking him to the different departments in Washington. I think very well of Capt. Ritch. He was first mentioned to me by Mayor Respess of Washington, who himself is rather reckless in business, yet is a man of excellent judgment and truthful where dollars and cents are /not/ concerned. I would not convey by this that Mayor Respess would lie for the purpose of cheating, yet he would see that he had the best of the bargain. You have often seen such men. His loyalty is undoubted. And further he has been tried for his life by the Jeff Davis concern for giving aid and comfort to the U.S. forces. His son was the first man to raise a Union Regiment, while his father was in prison at Richmond. He too is somewhat like his father only more so. He was appointed Lieut. Col. of the 1st. N.C. but resigned to go into trade as soon as his father was released by the rebels. He is a spoilt boy. He attended Medical Lectures at the University while I was there but I never became acquainted with him. He did not graduate.

Deserters continue to come in, though I think the reports published in the N.Y. papers in relation to the number are exaggerated. Last week eight made their escape to the blockade off Wilmington and among the rest one Lieutenant. I did not learn any of their names. Mr. Heaton has not left the Department for Washington, as was expected, but is going to Newbern <next> to-morrow. The regulations require him to keep his office at this place so he will leave it in my charge. If the Secretary will give me a deputy and one clerk I will manage the affairs of the whole department I think with satisfaction. I applied some time ago for a deputy collector, but the Secretary seemed to confound deputy collector with Inspector and did not allow me a deputy collector. In his letter of reply he <has>/says/ that he has recieved my letter applying for an "additional Deputy Collector," whereas I had none before.

I wish to give Colonel Taylor a little more employment than he now has. Vessels have not come in so fast lately as they did some time since, and so I have not been able to keep him employed as Inspector.

I am very respectfully,
Your brother,
John A. Hedrick.

Duke
Beaufort, N.C.
Nov. 29th. 1863.

Dear Brother:

Yours of the 16th. was recieved last week. All is quiet here.

Fifty two prisoners were brought into Newbern yesterday, having been taken about thirteen miles out of Washington. They belonged to Whitford's Regiment.[1] All North Carolinians from about Goldsboro. Deserters continue to come in and join Foster's Regiment. He has some fifty or sixty recruits in this town, but some of them are very hard looking cases. The way, the deserters and refugees are treated, is to put them into prison until they are willing to volunteer in the Union Army. They are clothed and put into camp. Mr. Heaton has moved to Newbern.

I presume he has given up the Auditorship.

Col. Taylor has been appointed Agency Aid by Mr. Heaton. He recieves $3 ^{00}/$_{100}$ per day, which is the same that I was paying him except that there was times when I could not keep /him/ constantly employed. He reports to me, and is under my direction for the present.

What has been done about the Tax Commissioners? I think that these poor devils down here have to pay enough of tax under Internal & Coastwise Intercourse, and under military exactions. In the first place they have to pay a License of $3 ^{00}/$_{100}$ together with some other small charges to Mr. Heaton for an Authority for doing business. Then they have to pay 5 per cent on the sworn invoice value of all goods shipped to the interior from this place. Then 4 cts per lb. on cotton and 5 per cent on other goods shipped north. Then each store has to pay from 50 cents to $2 ^{50}/$_{100}$ per week to the Provost. This tax is said to go to the civil fund, a name given to pickings & stealings generally. Lt Lull[2] was agent for this fund in Newbern.

I had no particular objection to his collecting as much as the military required him to from the people in Newbern to be expended in improving the streets and squares there but I never could see the Justice of collecting money out of people here and at Newport to improve Newbern.

The chickens and geese may be thankful that Gen. Foster did not get a chance to make his expedition.[3] Mr. Norcum left this morning for Chowan County near Edenton to see his father.

It is raining like blazes, the weather is quite warm, I am well,

Your brother,
John A. Hedrick.

Tell Mr. Goodloe that we wish a U.S. court and have no<t> particular need of Tax Commissioners.

---

[1] Union troops surrounded two companies of Maj. John N. Whitford's battalion on November 25, 1863, and captured fifty-two Confederates. *OR*, ser. 1, 29, pt. 1: 661; Manarin and Jordan, *North Carolina Troops*, 1:138.

[2] Fred A. Lull of the Second Massachusetts Heavy Artillery. *OR*, ser. 1, 42, pt. 3:1128.

[3] Benjamin F. Butler replaced John G. Foster as commander of the Department of Virginia and North Carolina on November 11, 1863. Foster was transferred to Tennessee. Sifakis, *Who Was Who in the Civil War*, 226; Barrett, *Civil War in North Carolina*, 177.

Duke
Beaufort, N.C.
Dec. 9th. 1863.

Dear Brother:

I recieved last week your letters of the 23rd. and 28th. ult.

Every thing is quiet in the Department. We have had New York papers of the 5th. inst.

I went to Newbern Saturday and did not return until Monday and hense I did not write my usual Sunday letter, and since my return I have not had time to write you till now.

You can tell Mr. Bird[1] that the Rev. Mr. Van Antwerp of this place has been appointed Post Chaplain here, and that the Rev. Mr. Rouse[2] is Hospital Chaplain in Newbern. He had therefore better apply for the chaplaincy at Washington. I think that there is no chaplain stationed at that place. The military lines at Washington are kept pretty close <at Washington> and very little communication is allowed with the neighboring country, on account of the nearness of the enemy. There are quite a number of persons in town, who are loyal and were men of respectability and influence before the war. I do not know of any place in North Carolina, where there are as many men of wealth who are truly loyal as in Washington.

My reciepts under coastwise intercourse for Nov. was $6716 $^{42}/_{100}$, a slight falling off from October.

Write often
Your brother,
John A. Hedrick

---

[1] The Reverend Thompson Bird of Iowa and Benjamin Hedrick became acquainted following Hedrick's well-publicized 1856 ouster from the University of North Carolina. Andrew Stevens to Benjamin S. Hedrick, February 23, 1860, Hedrick Papers, Southern Historical Collection.

[2] John Hill Rouse was appointed New Bern post chaplain in 1862. Barden, *Letters to the Home Circle*, 43.

Duke
Collector's Office,
Beaufort, N.C.
December 13th. 1863.

Dear Brother:

I wrote one day last week and told you why I did not write last Sunday. I was in Newbern that day & saw Dr. Page, who told me to remember him to you and to tell you that he expected to see you in Washington in the course of a month or two.

He did not go north last Fall when I wrote you he would. Every thing seemed quiet in Newbern. The pickets had been driven in on the previous night but nothing serious happened. Small-pox is quite prevalent in Newbern, especially among the negroes. There were 18 cases black, and 8 white reported on Sunday. The Physician in charge of the small-pox camp, told Dr. Page that there were about 250 cases in said camp. All prisoners having the disease are taken to this camp. Gen Butler has ordered that a tax of 1 per cent shall be paid to the Provosts on all shipments to & from this Department. For the present I am collecting this tax at this place by exacting 6 instead of 5 per cent as heretofore. I do not know what arrangement will be made about it in future. It does not give me much additional trouble.

The General has also ordered all able bodied negro men between the ages of 18 & 45 to be mustered into the U.S. Services, and forbids the employment of such negroes on public works. This order has created quite a stir among the darkies. There are very few of them that really wish to fight.

The weather is very mild to-day—so much so that there is no need of a fire.

Mr. Norcum has not returned from up the sound yet. He wrote home last Wednesday was a week from off Bluff Point, in Albemarle Sound which is not far from his Father's. He said that he had a head wind but thought that he would reach his Father's that evening.

Business has been quite brisk during the last week.

Mr. Dibble, whom you saw in Washington last Summer, has been ordered out of the Department by Gen. Butler. <His crime is having some tobacco marked Goldsboro, and dealing in Confederate money.>

Mayor Respess of Washington, has also been ordered to Fortress Monroe. His crime is having some tobacco marked Goldsboro, and dealing in Confederate money.

Mr. Dibble went to Fortress Monroe to see Gen Butler, but I understand that the General gave him very little satisfaction. The general told him that it was enough for him to know that he wished him to leave the Department.

We have had N.Y. papers of the 9th. I weighed yesterday 132 pounds. All well,

> Write often,
> Your brother,
> John A. Hedrick.

Duke
Beaufort, N.C.
Dec. 21st. 1863,

Dear:

During last week I recieved no letter from you.

All is quiet and business quite brisk. During the last week I collected about Five Thousand dollars, Gen. Butler's 1 per cent included.

It is as cold as ice this morning. The Steamer 'Petrel' leaves this port for New York this evening at 4.P.M.

I recieved the Gospel of Peace some time ago and the Chronicle with the Presidents Message week before last.

The vessel which took Mr. Norcum up to his Father's returned from Plymouth last week but did not stop for Mr. Norcum on his way down. Or rather the Captain says that he did stop about 2 hours some distance from the land when passing old Mr. Norcum's, but I think that he was afraid of the guerrillas & that he did not wait long. Mrs. Norcum is very much put out by the Captain's leaving her husband.

Christmas is nearly here, and may it be a joyful time to you all. I wish I could be with you.

> Write often,
> Your brother,
> John A. Hedrick.

Duke
Beaufort, N.C.
Dec 27th. 1863.

Dear Brother:

I wrote a short letter last Monday and received yours of the 15th inst. Thursday.

I was very sorry to hear that brothers Adam and Jimmie[1] were in the Rebel /Army/. I was not surprised to hear that Jimmie was there. Though I thought that Adam's deafness would excuse him. Gas McLean's name is R.G. McLean, and /I/ presume that the man who wrote you from Point Lookout is sister Mary's old man. It is queer that he did not write more about himself.[2] I do not know any R.G. McLean except Gas.

Mr. Heaton has been confined to his bed from hemarhage of lungs for more than a week till day before yèsterday. Mr. Thomas, his Assistant has gone to Washington. I think very well of Mr. Thomas. I did not know that he was going to Washington so soon or I would have written to you by him. He went on the Spaulding direct to Fortress Monroe and would arrive in Washington City in about 40 hours from the time he left here.

My collections under Internal and Coastwise Intercourse will be greater during the present than during any previous month. Including Gen. Butler's 1 per cent even it will reach near $12000 $^{00}/_{100}$.

During the three months ending Nov. 30th. I collected and paid over to Mr. Heaton $23366 $^{24}/_{100}$, 3 per cent upon which would $700 $^{98}/_{100}$. I have made out my account against the government for this amount but it has not been audited yet.

Capt. Ritch is here now and was in to see me yesterday. He had been sent /for/ by Mr. Heaton to come to Newbern in relation to some difficulty between the Military authorities and the Local Treasury Agent at Washington. It seems that the Commandant at Washington has been directed not to allow any one to come into town from outside the lines. and that this cut off all operations of the Local Agent. I did not learn the whole difficulty, but the result of it is, that the Col. Comdg. sent the Agent and his shop to a little island in the River in front of the town. I have the only position that can rule the military authorities in this Department. By shutting off the supplies it will soon bring them to their senses.

Mrs. Norcum had a letter dated the 15th. inst. from her husband in Chowan. He said that his Father, one of his Uncles and an old negro man were down on the beach when Meizell[3] came to anchor with his schooner and that the old man left immediately for his house to tell him but that Meizell taking the old man to be a guerrilla going for the other guerrillas, he hoisted sail, and away he went. Mr. Norcum said that he was getting better but did not intend to come home in his vessel but wished to send some poultry and other things down in her.

I had a very good dinner Christmas day. I was invited out by Mr. Rieger,[4] a worthy citizen of this place, who had his table loaded with turkey, English rabbit and all the other nice things that the season would afford. After dinner we had as much egg-nog as we could drink. We had two egg-nogs at Mrs. Norcum's, one the evening before and one Christmas morning. Upon the whole I had a very good time. A happy New Years to you all

> Your brother,
> John A. Hedrick.

---

[1] This probably refers to James M. Patton (b. ca. 1832), a Salisbury native and a carpenter by trade, who enlisted as a private in the Fifty-seventh Regiment North Carolina Troops in July 1862. Eighth Census, 1860: Rowan County; Hewett, *Roster of Confederate Soldiers*, 12:202; John A. Hedrick to Benjamin S. Hedrick, August 9, 1875, Hedrick Papers, Southern Historical Collection

[2] After the war Benjamin Hedrick discovered that the man who had written him from a Northern prisoner of war camp, requesting money and claiming to be married to his sister Mary, was in fact not her husband. The Hedrick brothers had never met Mary's husband. R.G. McLean to Benjamin S. Hedrick, December 13, 1863; Mary McLean to Benjamin S. Hedrick, June 12, 1865, Hedrick Papers, Duke Special Collections.

[3] This is perhaps a reference to Jonathan T. Mizell of Carteret County.

[4] Henry Reiger (b. ca. 1821) was a machinist. Eighth Census, 1860: Carteret County.

Benjamin S. Hedrick was John Hedrick's older brother and the recipient of almost all of the letters in this volume. He was dismissed as a professor at Chapel Hill in 1856 for his support of Republican presidential candidate John C. Frémont. He later worked in the U.S. Patent Office in Washington, D.C., and his governmental connections led to John's employment as a revenue collector in Beaufort, North Carolina. Photograph courtesy of the Southern Historical Collection, University of North Carolina Library, Chapel Hill.

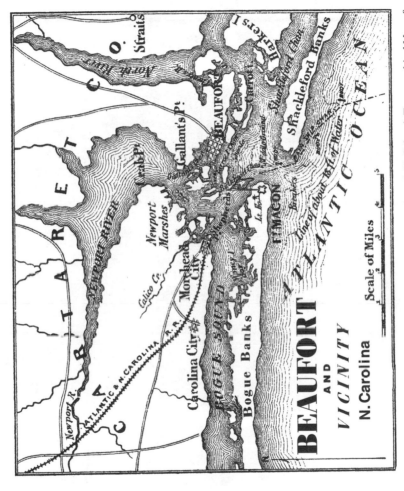

Map of Beaufort and surrounding area based on an inset from J. H. Colton's Topographical Map of North and South Carolina, A Large Portion of Georgia and Part of Adjoining States, published in New York in 1861.

Citizens of Beaufort filled the streets to watch the bombardment of Fort Macon, which guarded the entrance to Beaufort harbor. The Ocean House, in the background, was John A. Hedrick's home from his arrival in Beaufort in June 1862 until the hotel burned on October 24, 1863. In a letter dated June 20, 1862, Hedrick wrote that the Ocean House was the only hotel in town that was open. Of the food there, he said, "The fare is very good but not stylish. We get butter, eggs, clams, soft crabs, oysters, scollops, ham, beef, lamb and pork." Illustration from *Frank Leslie's Illustrated Newspaper*, June 6, 1862, courtesy of the State Archives, Division of Archives and History, Raleigh.

Ambrose E. Burnside led an expedition in eastern North Carolina in early 1862 that established Union control in Beaufort and elsewhere along the coast. He was in charge of the Department of North Carolina when John Hedrick arrived in Beaufort in June 1862 but left the following month to take command of a corps in the Army of the Potomac. Photograph courtesy of the State Archives, Division of Archives and History, Raleigh.

This photograph of the Leecraft House, at 307 Ann Street in Beaufort, was taken in March 1862, the same month Union troops occupied the town and three months before John Hedrick's arrival. Photograph courtesy of the North Carolina Collection, University of North Carolina Library at Chapel Hill.

Salmon P. Chase served in Lincoln's cabinet as secretary of the treasury from March 1861 to June 1864. John Hedrick, as a treasury department revenue collector, worked under Chase. Chase later became chief justice of the U.S. Supreme Court. Photograph from the National Archives, Brady Collection, reproduced from the *Dictionary of American Portraits* (N.Y.: Dover Publications, 1967), 111.

President Lincoln appointed Edward Stanly, a Craven County native living in California, as military governor of North Carolina in April 1862. John Hedrick subsequently accepted an offer to serve as Stanly's private secretary, but before Hedrick could fill this position, Stanly resigned in protest of the Emancipation Proclamation. Illustration courtesy of the State Archives, Division of Archives and History, Raleigh.

Charles Henry Foster was a native of Maine who moved to North Carolina before the Civil War and edited a Murfreesboro newspaper. During the war he recruited North Carolinians into the Union army and ran unsuccessfully for Congress from the occupied portion of the state. John Hedrick held Foster in low regard and consistently referred to him as that "humbug Foster." Photograph courtesy of the Southern Historical Collection, the Library of the University of North Carolina at Chapel Hill.

When Federal troops occupied eastern North Carolina thousands of slaves escaped to find refuge behind the army's lines, including in Beaufort. John Hedrick wrote his brother, "Some call the negroes Firesides, because the Rebs used to say that they were fighting for their firesides, whereas they were fighting for their negroes." Illustration courtesy of the State Archives, Division of Archives and History, Raleigh.

Union general John Gray Foster served in Burnside's expedition in eastern North Carolina. He commanded the Department of North Carolina from July 1862 to July 1863 and the Department of Virginia and North Carolina from July to November 1863. Portrait from *The National Cyclopedia of American Biography*, vol. 10 (N.Y.: James T. White, 1900), 134.

Maj. Gen. Benjamin F. Butler commanded the Department of Virginia and North Carolina, with brief interruptions, from November 1863 to January 1865. Southerners generally despised Butler, calling him "Beast Butler." Hedrick, however, seems to have had no strong feelings about the general one way or the other, despite living and working for a long time within his area of command. Photograph courtesy of the State Archives, Division of Archives and History, Raleigh.

Beaufort became a haven for refugees fleeing from areas of combat. Hedrick frequently noted their presence in his letters and observed that "there must be a great deal of suffering among them." On May 30, 1864, he wrote that the refugees were "dying very fast." Illustration courtesy of the State Archives, Division of Archives and History, Raleigh.

John Hedrick frequently wrote to his brother of naval operations in the area, including the exploits of the CSS *Albemarle*. Built at Edwards Ferry, North Carolina, on the Roanoke River, the ironclad ram threatened Union vessels until sunk by a spar torpedo on October 28, 1864. Hedrick never used the Confederate vessel's proper name, but always called it the "Roanoke Ram." Illustration courtesy of the State Archives, Division of Archives and History, Raleigh.

Fort Fisher was the keystone of the Confederate defenses along the Cape Fear River. John Hedrick wrote his brother on January 16, 1865, that a rumor was spreading that Fort Fisher had fallen, but added, "I think it premature." In fact, Union troops had captured the fort the previous day. Illustration from *Harper's Weekly*, February 4, 1865, courtesy of the North Carolina Collection, University of North Carolina Library at Chapel Hill.

In an addendum to his letter of January 16, 1865, John Hedrick reported to his brother that an unexplained series of explosions had been heard from the direction of Wilmington, and he speculated that the Confederates had blown up Fort Fisher rather than let it fall into Union hands. Federal troops had already captured the fort, however, and the sounds he heard were caused by the accidental detonation of the fort's magazine. Illustration from *Frank Leslie's Illustrated Newspaper*, February 11, 1865, courtesy of the North Carolina Collection, University of North Carolina Library at Chapel Hill.

1864

Dear Brother:

I received no letter from you last week. The weather has been quite cold for the three last days, but is a little more mild now. Yesterday I saw the New York Herald of the 31st. ultimo but found nothing interesting in it. All is quiet here. The negroes celebrated the President's Emancipation Proclamation, New Years day. Mr. Norcum is still absent. I send herein a list of garden seed, which Mrs. Col. Taylor wishes you to have filled from the Patent Office. Mrs. Norcum wishes some seeds also, but has prepared no list. I heard her say last night that she would like to have some egg, and some oyster plant seed. The 4 cts per pound on cotton & 5 per centum on other shipments during last month amounted to $11354 $^{36}/_{100}$. Besides this I collected $1997 $^{53}/_{100}$, the 1 per cent centum ordered by Gen. Butler. Mr. Thomas has not yet returned from Washington. The small-pox is in town.

I am well.

Your brother,
John A. Hedrick,
Collector.

Duke
Custom House,
Beaufort, N.C.
January 10th. 1864.

Dear Brother:

Your letters of the 21st. & the 26th. ultimo were received last Thursday. Our Mails have not been as regular of late as usual. I have seen no N.Y. papers later than the 2nd. inst. There was nothing worthy of note in it, except that Gen. Butler had failed to make an exchange of prisoners with Jeff. Davis. The weather has been exceedingly cold for this latitude during the last 4 days. Last Wednesday it sleeted quite heavy, which is a very unusual thing here. Since then the ground has remained frozen day and night, and in the shade water would freeze in the middle of the day. We have not had any snow this winter.

I do not know yet what the Department at Washington will do about my commissions on collections under Internal and Coastwise Intercourse. I sent on my accounts for commissions at 3 per cent, which is allowed under other provisions of the law, and submitted to the Commissioner of the Customs, an estimate for commissions on the amount deposited to the 30th. Sept. 1863, about a month ago, but have not heard from them since. I collected during last month $11616 $^{66}/_{100}$ under Treasury Regulations, and $1997 $^{53}/_{100}$ under Gen. Butler's order. The former I have deposited with Mr. Heaton, and hold the latter for further orders from the Provost Marshal General of this Department.[1]

Saturday night I cleared a schooner belonging to this port, for St. Kitts, West Indies, and I guess that in about 6 weeks from now she will be back here.

Mr. Norcum has not returned. Mrs. Norcum has the tooth and jaw ache very bad to-night.

Mr. Heaton is still quite poorly but able to be in his office. Mr. Thomas had not returned when left Newbern last Thursday morning but was expected soon.

I am well but have a bad cold.

Write often.

Your brother,
John A. Hedrick

P.S. Tell Mr. Helper that I will compare my receipts for last month with his for the same time.

J.A.H.

---

[1] Col. James Barnet Fry became U.S. provost marshal general on March 17, 1863. Heitman, *Historical Register*, 1:439.

———

Duke
Beaufort, N.C.
Jan. 17th. 1864

Dear Brother:

We received no mail during last week and hence I have no letter from you since I wrote last.

New York papers of the 13th. have reached us, but I have never seen such a dearth of news in any previous papers. There is absolutely no war news and but little doing in Congress.

Every thing is quiet here. Mr. Thomas has arrived from Washington, but I have not seen him. A Mr. Morse,[1] Treasury Agent, arrived yesterday on the S.R. Spaulding, but I have not learned who he is, or what is his business. Business has been very dull during the present month, but is getting better than it was one week ago. The weather has been so bad that vessels could not come down. It is much warmer than it was during the holidays, but the weather is still some what unsettled.

The small-pox, I think, has some what abated, as there are fewer cases reported than there were about three weeks ago. It has prevailed mostly among the contrabands.

There is to be a big ball here next Thursday night. I do not know whether I shall go or not, but think not.

Mr. Norcum has not returned from Chowan. Mrs. Norcum is still complaining of the tooth-ache. I have not heard of the arrival of Mrs. Foster as yet. The refugees continue to come in and join the 2nd. N.C. I think there must be between 300 & 400 in the Regiment. When you write to Mr. Helper again, give him my regards and tell him that I would be happy to receive a letter from him and would return the favor.

Write often.

> Your brother,
> John A. Hedrick

Monday morning Jan. 18th.

About two weeks ago one of your acquaintances and a particular friend [of] Mr. Prof. Kerr called in my office on business. He said that he was in the Nautical Almanac Office, while Kerr[2] was there, and I believe while you were in it. At any rate he said that he was acquainted with you, and inquired about you, Kerr, Graham Morrow & another man whose name I have forgotten. This man is 1st. Lieutenant & Ordnance Officer in the 2nd. Mass. Heavy Artillery and his name is John S. Allanson.[3] He is stationed at Newport between this place & Newbern, and wishes you to write him through me all you know about his old N.C. friends.

It is raining straight down but warm this morning.

> J.A.H.

---

[1] John Flavel Morse (1801-1884), a former Ohio state senator, was a special agent for the Treasury Department from 1862 until 1876. Niven, *Salmon P. Chase Papers*, 1:200.

[2] Washington Carruthers Kerr (1827-1885) worked with Benjamin Hedrick in the office of the *Nautical Almanac* in Cambridge, Mass. Kerr was employed there from 1852 to 1857 and was a professor at Davidson College from 1857 to 1862. Gov. Zebulon B. Vance appointed him state geologist in 1864. *Dictionary of North Carolina Biography*, s.v. "Kerr, Washington Carruthers"; Bassett, *Anti-Slavery Leaders of North Carolina*, 30.

[3] John Sylvanus Allanson (d. 1900) was a first lieutenant in the Second Massachusetts Heavy Artillery from August 22, 1863, to May 2, 1864. Soon thereafter he joined the First New York Engineers. Heitman, *Historical Register*, 1:157.

Duke
Beaufort, N.C.
Jan. 31st. 1864.

Dear Brother:

I received to-day, your letter of the 25th. inst. I wrote you last Tuesday, but it was a very short letter and I am afraid that this will not be much longer.

For the last 12 days the weather has been very mild and pleasant, until this evening, it has clouded up and it has the appearance of raining shortly, and the wind has set in from the northeast quite cold.

Mr. Norcum has not arrived home yet but is expected shortly. The vessel started from Smyrna, a short distance below here, last Monday for him and had two splendid days for sailing, which would probably take her to her destination. Since Wednesday the weather has been calm, and wind ahead for a vessel coming down the sounds.

Business during January was not as good as during December, but I think that I collected $7000 or $8000, during this month. You have asked me several times to give you my opinion of Dr. Tull.[1] The fact is that I know so little about him, I can hardly say that I have any opinion of him. I never saw him but once and then only a few minutes. Last Summer he obtained a permit from me to take a few cases of wine to Newbern for his own use. This is the only business transaction that I have had with him and the only occasion, on which I ever saw. I know that he keeps himself very quiet, and I have heard him spoken of as a thorough Union man. He was placed in charge of abandoned houses in Newbern by Gov. Stanley and was continued in that position by Gen. Foster till the arrival of Mr. Heaton. He and Mr. Heaton had some difficulty about the rents of these houses, but I never knew much of the result of it.

During Mr. Heaton's absence last Summer I was directed to open his letters, and I saw one from Gen. Foster informing Mr. Heaton, that Dr. Tull after paying $3500 $^{00}/_{100}$ on the bridge across the Trent River should hand the balance of the rents to him, Mr. Heaton. Mr. Heaton also told me that he had intended to appoint Dr. Tull, Local Agent for Newbern, had he acted right in regard to the rents.

Mr. Heaton's salary is $2500 $^{00}/_{100}$. At least he told me so last Summer. I do not know what Mr. Thomas gets. Carpenter gets $4 $^{00}/_{100}$ per day, Col. Taylor $3 $^{00}/_{100}$, and Mr. Ketcham $3 $^{00}/_{100}$. Maj. Willis' compensation had not been fixed when I spoken with Mr. Heaton last on the subject.

Feb. 1st. 1864.

This morning is mild and foggy. I have not heard any additional news since last night.

Last Friday 28 reb. Prisoners were brought to the Fort from about Newport. I did not learn to what regiments they belonged.[2] I am boarding in Mr. Norcum's family. We have a very agreeable time.

They are all well.

Write often.

Your brother,
John A. Hedrick

---

[1] John Graham Tull (1816-1870), born in Kinston, was a surgeon who practiced in New Bern until the Union occupation, during which he held several local appointments. He had recently written Benjamin Hedrick requesting help in obtaining a federal job. *Dictionary of North Carolina Biography*, s.v. "Tull, John Graham"; John Graham Tull to Benjamin S. Hedrick, January 8, February 22, 1864, Hedrick Papers, Duke Special Collections.

[2] This may be a reference to prisoners from the Seventh Confederate Cavalry captured in Onslow County on January 27, 1864, by a Union force led by Col. James Jourdan. *OR*, ser. 1, 33:23-24.

Duke
Beaufort, N.C.
Thursday, Feb. 4th. 1864.

Dear Brother:

It is exciting times here now. Day before yesterday the Rebs captured Newport, about 9 miles from Morehead on the Newbern R. Road. Our forces before leaving the place set fire to every thing, both public and private stores. Our loss in men was small—not exceeding 100, killed & prisoners. It is not known in what numbers at Newport the enemy is. Report says from 3000 to 15000.[1] Monday the enemy appeared at

Batchelor's Creek above Newbern and it is thought they are in strong force.[2] They burnt the Gunboat Underwriter.[3] We have had no news from Newbern, since Tuesday noon. There were various reports afloat then. One report was that the Rebs had attacked Fort Totten,[4] which is a little distance out of the town, and between the rivers. Another report was that they had commenced shelling the town.

I think that the Rebs are not far beyond Carolina City because I can see smoke in that direction. It may be that our forces upon evacuating their encampments have set fire to whatever is left.

There is a big fire about Newport and another, in the direction of Havelock.

Yours in haste,
John A. Hedrick

[1] Brig. Gen. James G. Martin's Confederate force drove the Union garrison from Newport Barracks on February 2, 1864. Many of the defenders were new recruits from the Ninth Vermont Infantry. *OR*, ser. 1, 33:81-82, 84-86.

[2] On February 1, 1864, during the early stages of Maj. Gen. George E. Pickett's unsuccessful attempt to take New Bern, Confederate troops crossed Batchelder's Creek, nine miles from New Bern, despite stiff Union opposition. *OR*, ser. 1, 33:93, 95-96; Barrett, *Civil War in North Carolina*, 202-207.

[3] As part of Pickett's drive on New Bern, Confederates under Comdr. John Taylor Wood seized and destroyed the USS *Underwriter* on the Neuse River, February 2, 1864. *Civil War Naval Chronology*, pt. 4:12-13.

[4] Fort Totten was a star-shaped earthen redoubt on the western edge of New Bern, located between the Trent and Neuse Roads. The fort was erected by Union forces soon after New Bern's capture. Pickett's troops made a demonstration but did not assault the fort. Barden, *Letters to the Home Circle*, 64-65; *OR*, ser. 1, 33:54-55.

Duke
Beaufort, N.C.
February 6th. 1864.

Dear Brother:

We have just past through one of the greatest panics that has happened during the war. I mentioned to you in my last letter that the Rebs appeared before Newport Tuesday evening about 4 o'clock, attacked the place and completely routed our forces consisting of the 9th. Vermont and one company of Mix's Cavalry.[1] Our troops before leaving the place set fire to every thing and burnt the Rail Road Bridge and then made a gallant retreat for this place. That night about 9 1/2 o'clock Mr. Hall, a citizen soldier who was going out on picket duty with five others on horseback, stopped at Mr. Norcum's and told me to report at Head Quarters. I accordingly did so. Upon arriving at Troutst House, which is used for barracks and Quarters, I was about going in when I was halted by a little sentinel on the steps, who informed me that I could not pass in. I then inquired for the officer of the day, and was informed that he was away on duty. I then asked for the Commandant of the Post, Capt. Fuller,[2] and was told that he was round at the Market house, attending to putting up a barricade across the street. I asked for the Sargeant in charge, who was brought forth, but he happened unacquainted with me, but he managed to get a person inside who did know me, and I was then admitted. I was informed that Capt Fuller was be in shortly and so took a seat in his room. In about $1/2$ of an hour he made his appearance, a low, husky, thick set fellow, about my height and weighing over 200 lbs, with a nose that looked as if you might wring the whiskey of it. Dr. Ainsworth,[3] surgeon in charge of the Hospital here, another toper, was present. After Capt. Fuller & the Doctor had interchanged views with each other for a few minutes, I introduced myself to him and told him that I had been directed to report at Head-Quarters, and wished to know his pleasure. He replied, "Do /you/ say that you are Collector? I don't know what that is?" I told him, "Yes. I am Collector of the Customs for the Port of Beaufort." He said, "You have something to do with the Custom House and the Entrance and clearance of vessels." I replied "Yes. That is my business." He said "Well you will have to do the best that you can for yourself, but if this place should be attacked, I will have to occupy your office, where you have that flag hoisted every day." Enough to give you an idea of the man.

He was expecting the Rebs in town every minute, and so remained in my office till that night so that I might be on hand should the enemy make an attack. Morning came and brought no Rebs, but still every thing was unsettled. Wednesday night, however, I remained at home.

Thursday evening about 3 o'clock a dispatch came from Newbern and brought news that the Rebs had made two assaults on Fort Totten & had been repulsed each time. During Thursday the merchants were sending their goods aboard vessels in the harbor till about 4 o'clock when Col. Jourdan[4] came from Morehead and told them that he would confiscate any goods sent away after his arrival. At the same time he assured the people that they had no good cause for alarm. We had several times received news that the Rebs were within 8 miles of the town & the military were evidently preparing to evacuate. From my office to the opposite side of the street were a row of hhds filled with sand, another row to Joel Davis' Store, and a third to the water. Hence you may know that I was completely barrelacaded. There was a plank fence across the street near the market and a cord wood fence across the street from Lowenberg's to Davis' Store, forming a kind of bull pen. So much for Fort Folly.

To-day however a hand car came through from Newbern, and brought news that there were no Rebs to be seen between this place and Newbern, that Rail Road had not been torn up, only two bridges destroyed—one by our own forces and that no general attack had been made on Newbern but only some skirmishing near Fort Totten.

Every thing has quieted down and Fort Folly is being removed. The mail closes in a few minutes and so adieu for the present.

Write often.

Your brother,
John A. Hedrick

You will have to supply omissions and make corrections.

---

[1] Col. James Jourdan stated in his report of the fight at Newport Barracks that Mix's cavalry "did good service and were continually harassing the enemy at different points." Col. Simon H. Mix was mortally wounded on June 15, 1864, in an attack on the defenses at Petersburg, Va. *OR*, ser. 1, 33:77; 40, pt. 1:729, 736.

[2] Capt. Nehemiah Fuller of the Second Massachusetts Heavy Artillery was placed in command of Beaufort by Col. James Jourdan on February 1, 1864. *OR*, ser. 1, 33:77, 485.

[3] Frederic Smith Ainsworth, surgeon, U.S. Volunteers, worked at Hammond General Hospital in Beaufort, 1863-1864. *OR*, ser. 2, 5:361; Heitman, *Historical Register*, 1:154.

[4] Col. James Jourdan of the 158th New York Regiment was commander of the Sub-district of Beaufort as of January 31, 1864. Seven companies of his regiment were stationed at Morehead City, while three were at Beaufort. *OR*, ser. 1, 33:77-81, 485, 496.

Duke
Beaufort, N.C.
Feb. 12th. 1864.

Dear Brother:

Yours of the 2nd. inst. was received a few days since.

I do not know how much money Mr. Dibble gave for the Union cause, though I think that five hundred dollars would be nearer the mark than fifty thousand. I recollect having seen a statement in the Newbern Progress about 18 months ago that Mr. Dibble proposed to give \$35 $^{00}/_{100}$ for each volunteer from his native village, a small town in Connecticut. I do not know how much he paid in this way. I saw a statement of his having given a few cases of wines to the hospitals in Newbern, though the price of the same was not given. He gave \$50 towards supporting the families of the 2nd. N.C. and in one other case, I saw it stated that he had given \$100 $^{00}/_{100}$

but for what purpose I have forgotten. Mr. Dibble is a thorough business man, a shrewd Yankee, and pretty liberal but I can't think that all his givings would exceed $5000 $^{00}/_{100}$.

If he should tell me that he had given fifty thousand dollars, I would be disposed to believe him, because I have always found him correct in his dealings with me, yet I would like [to] hear him explain in what way he had given this amount, because he might consider his losses by the fortunes of war, as so much given for the Union cause. I know that he had a lot of turpentine and rosin in Newbern at the time we retook the place, and that our forces took possession of this rosin & turpentine and sent most of it to New York, and that Mr. Dibble had not received his money for it when I last saw him. Dr. Page about 7 weeks ago told me that he had taken a lot of the rosin to fill in around the curvings in the wells around Newbern to make the water good for the soldiers. I have not heard any one here speak of opening the port of Newbern.

I wrote you last Saturday a hurried letter and gave you some account of our fight. It has all passed over now with only the loss of the gunboat Underwriter destroyed by the Rebs just above Newbern, and the railroad bridges at Newport and Havelock destroyed by our own forces. It seems that the Rebs after driving our forces out of Newport did not destroy any thing. I expected to learn that they had so damaged the track that it would take at least 2 weeks to mend it. The cars have been meeting at Newport since Saturday, and by Monday, they will run through regularly.

We have had New York papers of the 8th. inst. but nothing of importance in them.

Mrs. Norcum received intelligence from her husband this morning. He has had a very severe attack of hemorhage of the lungs, and pleurasy but is getting better and would have come home but his physicians did not think it prudent.

We are all in fine spirits.

> Write often.
> Your brother,
> John A. Hedrick

> *Duke*
> Beaufort, N.C.
> Sunday Feb. 14th. 1864.

Dear Brother:

I wrote you last Friday, and have received no letter from you since then.

There is no news afloat. Business has somewhat revived. During January I collected between $9000 & $10000 exclusive of Gen. Butler's 1 per cent.

You asked me some time back how I was paid for collecting Gen. Butler's tax. I have made only one deposit under that head, and then I deducted 3 per cent on the amount deposited from the gross amount. This was for the month of December. I have not heard whether the Genl. objects to this or not. If he does I shall certainly object to collecting his tax for him. I would prefer to have nothing to do with it any way, and it is only by request of Mr. Heaton that I do so. I think it is mixing the Revenue with the Military a little too much. There has been so much confusion since the 1st. of the month that I have been unable to get my returns completed, but they are far enough advanced that I can safely say that I collected $9500 last month. Up to this time I have not had very much to do during February, though during Friday I collected about $1500 $^{00}/_{100}$. My work is done mostly by spells, and depends a great deal on winds and weather.

This last rebel raid I think was intended to obtain supplies. Last week our forces captured seven wagons and a few prisoners from a rebel supply train a short distance out of Washington. Capt. Ulysses H. Ritch is now Local Agent at Washington, in lieu of W.P. Ketchum, who is now engaged in buying naval stores, in place of W.W. McChesney, captured by the Rebs a short distance out of Newbern last Monday was a week ago.

Write often

> Your brother,
> John A. Hedrick

P.S. Mr Phillips of Morehead City, who says that he lived in the old jaol about 18 months ago, informed me a few days ago that Father paid $1200 $^{00}/_{100}$ for a substitute for Brother Adam.

> J.A.H.

————————

> *Duke*
> Custom House,
> Beaufort, N.C.
> February 21st. 1864.

Dear Brother:

I have received no letter from you during last <month> week.

I returned from Newbern yesterday. I saw Dr. Page and he told me as usual that he expected to go north in about ten days. He is looking very well. Mr. Heaton is looking better than I ever saw him. He has but two Assistants, two clerks and one messenger boy to aid him. His assistants get each $5 per day, and his clerks $3 $^{00}/_{100}$.

I mentioned in my last letter that Capt. Ritch had been appointed Local Agent at Washington. I saw the Captain a few minutes on the street in Newbern but as the boat was about to leave for Washington, I had only a few moments to talk to him.

I received Treasury Adjustment of my Disbursements Accounts for the 2nd. qr. 1863, last week. In the settlement I am allowed $62 $^{48}/_{100}$ for Cutter disbursements. I have not examined my pay-rolls but think that that is about 1 per cent. It helps out some. There are two more quarters in last year awaiting adjustment.

There was nothing new in Newbern, when I was there. I went up on Thursday and returned yesterday. I had the dentist to pull 7 roots of teeth for me. This makes my upper a sound jaw. When I go again, I will have 4 pulled from my underjaw, and then I think that I will be done tooth pulling for one while.

Mr Heaton's 2nd. Assistants' name is Blakesley.[1] He has been a member of the State legislature from Northern Ohio.

I have lately received a letter from the Commissioner of Customs, directing me to deposit all moneys received under Internal and Coastwise Intercourse with an Assistant Treasury, or Depositary of the U.S. I showed this letter to Messrs Heaton & Thomas, & told Mr. Heaton that he must write to Mr. Chase and get him to direct me to deposit my collections under Internal and Coastwise Intercourse trade with him. If Mr. Chase does not do this, Mr. Heaton promised to pay me the money back. It is still in Newbern. Mr Thomas said that he mentioned to Mr. Chase when he was in Washington about Christmas, that I was paying this money over to Mr. Heaton and he told him that it was all right.

We have had exceedingly cold weather since last Wednesday. Last Thursday night it snowed about 3 inches deep, and it was so cold that water in my room left in the wash bowl and pitcher froze and broke both while I was in Newbern.

Your brother,
John A. Hedrick

---

[1] Schuyler E. Blakeslee was an Ohio attorney and former state representative. Niven, *Salmon P. Chase Papers*, 1:240.

Duke

Inclosed is $100 $^{00}/_{100}$

Beaufort, N.C.
Feb. 26th. 1864.

Dear Brother:

Your letters of the 12th. and the 16th. inst. have been received. I am glad to learn that you got through the mumps so lightly. There is nothing new in this Department.

The Revenue Steamer "Cayahoga," Capt Gowan, arrived here yesterday from Fernandina Florida via Port Royal and Charleston Bar S.C. She brings news of the repulse of our forces in Florida,[1] and the destruction of the Gunboat "Housatonic" by a rebel torpedo near Charleston.[2]

My business is pretty good though not quite as brisk as it was in December.

There are quite a number of merchant vessels in port and some seven or eight gunboats.

Troops still continue to come in. A few arrived to-day. It is generally thought that there will be some hard fighting in this State during the coming Summer.

This morning I mailed to you the N.C. Times of the 24th. which gives a pretty good account of the fight at Newport. The Times of the 20th. by some means I did not receive but understand that it contains an article in praise of the humbug Foster, saying that he will rise in spite of the efforts of Hedrick, Goodloe & Co. to keep him down. I have been trying to get this number to send you but have not yet succeeded.

Old Mrs. Foster[3] has arrived and has stirred up quite a mess among the women. She says that the negroes have taught the southern ladies all that they know, and that they they /the ladies/ are not as cleanly as they ought to be, & C & C.

I hope that Sister Ellen has got well of her tooth and ear ache long since. Could not you write something and get her to copy it so that I could see how she writes once more?

Write often
John A. Hedrick

Remember the garden seed.

---

[1] Brig. Gen. Joseph Finegan's five thousand Confederates defeated Brig. Gen. Truman Seymour's force of fifty-five hundred near Olustee, Fla., on February 20, 1864. Current, *Encyclopedia of the Confederacy*, 3:1165-1166; Long, *Day by Day*, 466.

[2] The Confederate submarine *H. L. Hunley* sank the USS *Housatonic* near Charleston, S.C., on February 17, 1864. *ORN*, ser. 1, 15:327-338.

[3] This is probably a reference to Caroline Brown Foster (b. ca. 1807), mother of Charles Henry Foster. She was the daughter of the wealthy Benjamin Brown of Vassalboro, Maine. Delaney, "Charles Henry Foster," 349; Seventh Census, 1850: Penobscot County, Maine.

———————

Duke
Beaufort, N.C.
March 1st. 1864.

Dear Brother:

Your letter of the 22nd. ult. was received yesterday. I wrote you last Saturday and inclosed a hundred dollar greenback. I also wrote to Johnnie <yesterday> /Sunday/ and mentioned that the military here were fearful that the Rebs were coming again. The cars came down from Newbern as usual /yesterday/ and brought news of prevalent rumors in Newbern that Longstreet and a large Rebel force were up about Kinston but had not made their appearance near Newbern.

All able bodied citizens, present company excepted, were put under arms yesterday evening, for Provost duty.

I do not know whether the N.C. Volunteers have received their bounties or not but I lately saw posted all over town a circular signed by Lieut. S.A. Carpenter,[1] recruiting officer, containing a letter from the Provost Marshal General to Capt. C.H. Foster, saying that those who enlisted in the 2nd. N.C. previous to Dec. 1st. were entitled to $100 $^{00}/_{100}$ and those who enlisted between the 1st. Dec. and the 1st. March were entitled to a bounty of $300 $^{00}/_{100}$ to be paid by a U.S. Disbursing officer if any have if not then by the first Pay Roll. I do not think that they have been paid off as yet, and I guess that they have not yet received their bounties.

You will find Mr. Dibble a very nice man and one whom I think you would like. The weather is warm and pleasant again.

There is nothing of interest to report at present.

Mr. Norcum has not yet returned from Chowan. Mrs. N. had a letter from him a few days ago saying that he thought he was a little better but had not been out of the house in over a month.

Write often.

Your brother,
John A. Hedrick

———————

[1] Silas A. Carpenter was a lieutenant in the First North Carolina Union Regiment. Compiled Service Records, Record Group 94.

———————

Duke
Beaufort, N.C.
Monday March 7th. 1864.

Dear Brother:

I wrote you a few lines by the prize steamer "Cumberland" which was taken off Mobile some time ago and is now on her way north.[1]

I heard yesterday that Gen. Seymour and all his men had been captured in Florida, but I do not think the report correct because Capt. McGowan of the Revenue Steamer "Cayahoga" came right from Florida a little over a week ago, and said that we had lost about 600 men, and did not mention the capture of Gen. Seymour.[2]

The weather is beautiful but business has been rather dull during the last fortnight, by reason of the rumors that the Rebs were coming down on us. There are several vessels now lying in the stream awaiting the consignees to come for their goods. Every body in Newbern has been mustered into the army and required to drill.

The drill has been left off in this place but all men between the ages of 18 & 45 are enrolled and armed.

There was a mighty confusion among some of these enrolled men last week. Some had broken limbs, others had week eyes, and others had the gravel. I heard them laughing at a fine looking young man, who had the gravel in his left arm, but the doctor said that he was sound in wind, limb and —————.

They are sending the negroes off some where this morning. Perhaps to Morehead City to throw up breastworks. There was another prize steamer brought in last week besides the Cumberland but the Cumberland was so much finer that very little was said about the other vessel, and I did not learn her name or where she was taken.[3] The Cumberland had a lot of plate on board for Jeff. Davis.

I am well.

Write often.

Your brother,
John A. Hedrick

---

[1] The blockade-runner *Cumberland* was captured by the USS *De Soto* on February 5, 1864, near Santa Rosa Island, Fla. *Civil War Naval Chronology*, pt. 4:15.

[2] Union troops suffered 1,861 casualties at the Battle of Olustee. Seymour was not captured. Current, *Encyclopedia of the Confederacy*, 3:1165-1166.

³The other vessel may have been either the *Scotia*, which was captured by the USS *Connecticut* off Cape Fear on March 1, 1864, or the *Don*, which was seized by the USS *Pequot* near Fort Fisher on March 4. *Civil War Naval Chronology*, pt. 4:26, 27.

Duke
Beaufort, N.C.
March 12th. 1864.

Dear Brother,

Your letters of Feb. 27th. and March 2nd. & 5th. were received the two first day before yesterday and the last yesterday.

We had a very hard rainstorm yesterday and day before but it has now cleared up beautifully and it is now beautiful weather.

All is quiet in this department and there is no news of interest. Business has been a little more brisk yesterday and to-day than it had been for the last two weeks.

The garden seed for Mrs. Norcum and Mrs. Col. Taylor reached here day before yesterday. They are very much pleased with them, and send their thanks to you for looking them up.

Mr. Norcum has not returned and I do not know whether he is able to come home or not. When last heard from, which was about a month ago, he had not been able to go out of the house in over six weeks.

Mrs. Norcum is well and mischievous. She says that she is going to write to you and let you know how bad I am getting. I tell her that she is to blame for all of my devilment. Alice and Henry[1] are going to school to Mr. Van Antwerp, Episcopal Minister & Hospital Chaplain.

What has become of your friend Bird, who wished a post chaplaincy. There is no preacher at Washington and I heard a Mr. Morgan when in Newbern N.C. asking for recommendations for said place.

Write often.

Your brother,
John A. Hedrick

---

[1] Alice Norcum (1849-1864) and Henry Norcum (b. ca. 1855). Alice Norcum's tombstone, Old Burying Ground, Beaufort, N.C.; Eighth Census, 1860: Carteret County; John A. Hedrick to Benjamin S. Hedrick, December 3, 1864, Hedrick Papers, Duke Special Collections, in this volume.

Duke
Beaufort, N.C.
March 13th. 1864

Dear Brother:

I wrote you a letter yesterday to go by the Steamer "Petrel" but she did not get off, and as it is Sunday, I thought that I would write again. The weather is quite windy but not cold to-day. I have now on hand a little over Twenty thousand dollars in Green Backs and Twenty one hundred and fifty dollars in Confederate Bonds, and one hundred and ninety seven dollars and eighty one cents in silver. I collected about seven hundred dollars yesterday.

I do not know whether you could obtain a substitute, in case you should be drafted, in North Carolina or not. It seems that pretty nearly all the refugees join the army. You wish to know whether the refugees are kept in the guard house until they are willing to volunteer. I do not know whether they are kept confined till they do volunteer, but I know that they always let them out when they do volunteer. There are a great many things brought to bear upon them to induce them to join the army. Most of them come in a destitute condition. Some of them have their families with them and when they arrive, they have no place to go for shelter and subsistance except it is to the military. They are promised large bounties, a place for their families to live in and an outfit of clothing if they will volunteer. Besides they find friends who have come before them and volunteered, and the army becomes a kind of place of refuge for them and as it were a kind of headquarters for them. When a refugee comes in, it reminds me of my old Davidson College days, when a new fresh came. All the Buffaloes get after him and before he knows what he is about he has joined the regiment. There may be some unfair means used to get these men into the army, but I have not heard of an instance in which it has been practiced.

I think that there is no doubt that the prisoners captured above Newbern some time ago from the 2nd. N.C. were hanged in Kinston.[1]

Mrs. Norcum has promised to write a few lines and I will therefore close.

Your brother,
John A. Hedrick

[*Laura A. Norcum to Benjamin S. Hedrick*]
[*On the same sheet of paper*]

Beaufort March 14th. 1864.

Mr Hedrick

Your brother has not filled this sheet so I told him I would add a few lines to thank you for the seeds so kindly sent. I laid aside all other work and a portion of them are already planted—my peas look beautifully and I can have onions and lettuce next week which were planted last fall, and if you will come down to Beaufort this summer I can feast you on nice vegetables. Mr Norcum has not yet returned his health is too bad and his friends do not think it prudent to come here yet while the weather is so changeable. Your <u>good quiet</u> brother is our Shepherd still and he has us pretty well trained. You would be surprised to see Alice she is quite as tall as I am & quite as full of life as ever I was. (<u>though you know I was not very wild</u>) Whether your brother will be improved by his stay with us I will leave you to judge when you see him, I think myself there is a lurking mischief in him which a stranger would never suspect, beside that <u>new suit</u> fits perfectly, and I think he is getting a little vain, tho' Alice and Jane to blame for that. He likes to go sailing with the ladies and I should not be surprised if he forgets his sister's advice, but I'll promise to have an eye over him, and if he goes astray I'll lead him aright. My love to Mrs. Hedrick, tell her I hope she may never know the privations and vexations which are now the lot of Southern ladies, sometimes I feel as if I could not bear up under them all, but I look forward to a brighter day, not far off I hope.

Very Respectfully
Laura A. Norcum

---

[1] Twenty-two North Carolinians serving in the Union army were tried and hanged for desertion by Confederates in Kinston. They had been captured in early February during Pickett's unsuccessful drive against New Bern. Some had belonged to regular Confederate army units, but the majority had been in home guard units. Compiled Service Records, Record Group 94; Donald E. Collins, "War Crimes or Justice? General George Pickett and the Mass Execution of Deserters in Civil War Kinston, North Carolina," in *The Art of Command in the Civil War*, ed. Steven E. Woodworth (Lincoln: University of Nebraska Press, 1998), 50-83.

Duke
Beaufort, N.C.
March 18th. 1864.

Dear Brother:

Yours of March 10th. was received a few days ago. We have had no news from the north later than the 12th. inst. Every thing is quiet here now.

I was in Newbern yesterday and saw Dr Page, who as usual said that he wished to go to Washington soon but this time he thought he could hardly get off till after <u>crapes</u> were planted. He has 40 acres to plant in vegetables for the U.S. Sanitary Commission.

If it be convenient I would be glad if you stop at the Treas. Department and see if the Commissioner of Customs has received my letter to him of the 27th. Feb. and also whether the matter therein contained has been referred to the Secretary of the Treasury and if so what action has been taken in relation thereto. You will doubtless remember that I some time ago wrote you that the Com. had directed me to deposit the moneys received from coastwise intercourse trade with an Asst. Treas. or Dep. of the U.S., and that Mr. Heaton said that the money was still in Newbern and /that he/ was ready to pay it over to me if the Sec. wished me to make a different disposition of it. Since then Mr. Heaton and the Sec. have had correspondence with each other with regard to the money which the former holds, and the latter in a letter dated March 11th. has instructed the former to report the entire amount held by him in order that if it can be done, the Sec. can draw a draft in favor of some Paymaster for this amount. I would like for the Dept. to know how things are, in order that there may be no conflicting orders. If my letter has not been taken up, I would be glad to have it considered as soon as possible. Mr. Heaton said that he would report yesterday the amount now in his hands. Now if the Sec. should determine that I should make a different disposition of the money collected by me, the draft on Mr. Heaton should be about Fifty thousand /dollars/ less that this amount reported.

We are all well. Mr. Norcum has not returned and we have had nothing from him later than the 11th. ult.

Write soon

Your brother
John A. Hedrick

Duke
Beaufort, N.C.
March 21st. 1864.

Dear Brother:

Your letter date forgotten in which you say that Mr. Goodloe is engaged as one of the principal Editors of the Chronicle was received last Friday morning.[1]

By the last mail I received a letter from the 1st. Auditor acknowledging the receipt of my accounts for January and saying that "no commissions will be allowed on money collected and deposited on account of Commercial Intercourse per Treasury Regulations."

Considering the source from which this comes it would seem to settle the matter so far as the law is concerned yet I can not well see how he can get over the 5th. Section of the Act of Congress dated July 15th. 1861.

It takes them a long while to settle the matter of my compensation.

I wrote you last week to stop and see if the Commissioner of Customs had received my letter of the 27th. ult. and to find out what action had been taken in relation thereto.

Mr. Heaton, has often promised to bring the matter before the Department, but as yet I have not learned of his having done so.

All is quiet in the Department. It is raining quite hard this morning, and if it stops I shall go to Newbern to-day to return to-morrow.

Mr. Heaton has a new Asst. or Clerk every time I go there. He now has seven all told.

I wish the Secretary would let me have a Deputy or Clerk. I have collected as much money as Mr Heaton and all his assistants, yet some time ago when I asked the Secretary to allow me a Deputy he said the Department was of opinion that the business of this port would not allow it.

. Your brother,
John A. Hedrick

---

[1] Daniel Reaves Goodloe was associate editor of the *Daily Morning Chronicle* of Washington, D.C., in 1864 and 1865. *Dictionary of North Carolina Biography*, s.v. "Goodloe, Daniel Reaves."

Duke
Beaufort, N.C.
March 29th. 1864.

Dear Brother:

Your letter of March 20th. was received Saturday, and that of March 19th. inclosing a letter from Sister Ellen reached me yesterday.

The piece in the Tribune concerning the 2nd. N.C. U. Vols. was evidently written by Charles Henry Foster. Upon first reading the sentence, "Belonging to one company of eighty men there are thirty families" & c I thought that Foster was not the author of the article, but the possession seems to refer to the families and not to the writer. Foster is the only man in the Regiment who could write such a piece and he is a line officer, having a commission of Lieut. Col. from General Butler. I do not know by what authority these officers of the N.C. Regs are commissioned but since Gov. Stanly left it has been the practice for the General commanding to give them commissions. Lieut. Col. McChesney of the 1st. N.C. has a commission from Gen. [*John G.*] Foster, so I have been told.

I have made some inquiries about the authorship of the article which you sent me and all seem to agree that Foster wrote it; I do not know any of the facts therein stated to be so. The great suffering therein depicted, I do not believe to exist among the families of the N.C. U. Vols. Rations are issued from the Commissary for the families. There has been no Pay Master around since the Reg. was raised and I guess the writer is correct in saying that they have received no pay nor bounty from the U.S. Should I learn the author of this piece I will let you know what he is.

After the 1st. April the percentage on shipments will be 3 per cent instead of 5 as heretofore.

My letter of Feb. 27 in relation to depositing money with Mr. Heaton was addressed to the Commissioner of the Customs.

We are all well.

Your brother,
John A. Hedrick

Duke
Beaufort, N.C.
April 3rd. 1864.

Dear Brother:

Yours of the 23rd. ult. was received last week

Every thing is quiet here. The Secretary of the Treasury has lowered the percentage fees 2 per cent.

I heard yesterday that the humbug Foster had been reduced to Captain and some said that he had been cashiered altogether.

I see by the N.C. Times of yesterday that Maj Foster has been relieved from duty on Genl. Peck's staff, though for what purpose is not stated.

I sent you /week before/ last week my picture and wish you to send me yours and those of your whole family. You will find my likeness very fresh: for I had it taken in the morning yesterday was a week and sent it in the mail aboard the "Whirlwind" the same evening and the Steamer /sailed/ next morning for New York. The features in this likeness are well taken but you will percieve that the likeness itself is a little blotched.

We have had an awful spell of weather for the last week. I never saw it worse for the season. It has rained and stormed dreadful for nearly two weeks. It is still quite cold.

Mr. Norcum has not returned though he is expected shortly. His family are all well except that they have colds.

There is some talk of an attack to be made on Newbern soon, but I do not know upon what grounds the report is based. You will find an editorial in the Times which I sent you yesterday denying that <the> men had been refused the privelege of the President's Amnesty Proclamation at Newbern.[1]

In the same paper is an order from the Chief Provost Marshal granting one West the exclusive privelege of importing and selling newspapers, periodicals and magazines in this Department.

> Your brother
> John A. Hedrick

---

[1] On December 8, 1863, President Lincoln declared an amnesty, with some exceptions, for those participants in the rebellion who would take an oath of allegiance to the Union. On March 26, 1864, he stated that his earlier offer of amnesty did not include prisoners of war. Long, *Day by Day*, 444, 478.

> *Duke*
> Beaufort, N.C.
> April 7th. 1864.

Dear Brother:

Yours of the 29th. ult. reached me yesterday.

I have not yet received the Secretary's letter in relation to the deposit of moneys.

The weather is still cold but the sun has come out this morning.

The rebs attempted to blow up Cape Lookout Light House Sunday night, and succeed in doing considerable damage to the building. The explosion tore up the floor & nearly two flight of the stairs or about 50 feet, I should judge.[1]

I went down to the light house Monday but could not get up to the top to see whether the lense was broken or not.

The quartermaster sent some lumber and hands down yesterday, to ascertain whether the lense was broken and if not to try to repair the building so as to light the lamp.

I saw a few days ago a notice stuck up by Foster in which he signs himself Late Lt. Col. 2 N.C. Vols. I do not know whether he has been dismissed altogether or not.[2]

There is no war news.

We are all well.

> Your brother
> John A. Hedrick

---

[1] Saboteurs from the Sixty-seventh North Carolina used a keg of powder to damage the Cape Lookout lighthouse severely on April 3, 1864. *OR*, ser. 1, 33:260-261; Walter Clark, ed., *Histories of the Several Regiments and Battalions from North Carolina in the Great War, 1861-'65*, vol. 3 (Raleigh and Goldsboro: State of North Carolina, 1901), 706.

[2] Charles Henry Foster was mustered out of the Second North Carolina Union Regiment on March 25, 1864. Compiled Service Records, Record Group 94, see Walter S. Poor.

> *Duke*
> Beaufort, N.C.
> April 11th. 1864.

Dear Brother:

I have had nothing from you nor any northern mail since I wrote you last.

All is quiet and the weather has again cleared up.

The light house has again been lit, but the repairs are very rough.

Mr. Norcum has not yet returned but is expected soon. I have been exceedingly busy lately.

> Your brother,
> John A. Hedrick

Duke
Beaufort, N.C.
April 16th. 1864.

Dear Brother:

Your letter of the 3rd. inst. was received a few days since. I send herein a copy of the Auditor's letter in relation to my commissions. Yesterday I received a letter from the Commissioner of the Customs, directing me to continue to deposit with the Supervisory Special Agent 3rd. Agency until otherwise directed. Up to the 31st. March I have collected & paid over to him $61964 $^{72}/_{100}$. In the N.C. Times of the 13th. inst. you will find an editorial on Treasury operations in this State, in which the writer gives the amount, which the Supr. Spl. Agt. (who I take to be the author), is ready to turn over for the support of the troops, to be $100,000 $^{00}/_{100}$. Hence it would appear that I have collected more than Mr. Heaton, two Assistants, three clerks and all his Local Agents. I think that the Secretary does wrong in not allowing me more help. I do not like the piece in the Times above referred to. It sounds too much like a puff. But then you used to say that "he that bloweth not his own horn, the same shall not have his horn blown for him."

I have received several Chronicles from you lately, and also a List of Treasury Agents with the amount of compensation paid to each.

Mr. Norcum returned home day before yesterday considerably improved but not entirely well. He gives a rather amusing description of the people in Chowan. He says that they wear coon skin, possum hide, and all kinds of home made caps and raw hide shoes. A horse in his father's neighborhood is worth $2500 $^{00}/_{100}$, making a pair of boots $30 $^{00}/_{100}$. He says that he can tell when he gets into Dixie by the tracks.

The weather is cloudy and dreary. We are all well.

I wrote you a few lines Monday. Write often.

Your brother,
John A. Hedrick

P.S. Where is Jesse Wheeler? I have not heard you mention him lately. I do not know much about his business qualifications but if it were not so difficult to obtain a house, I would advise him to come down here. I could give him work to amount to $50 $^{00}/_{100}$ or $45 $^{00}/_{100}$ per month, and if every /thing/ goes on as it has for the last 8 months he could make more than that. I would like to /have/ some steady trustworthy man, and I think that Mr. Wheeler is such.

J.A.H.

Duke
Beaufort, N.C.
April 18th. 1864.

Dear Brother:

Your letter of April 11th. was received to-day. I wrote you last Saturday the 16th. inst.

The Capt. Steadman, whom you mention as having called up you, was a 2nd. Lieut. in the 81st. N.Y. and is by profession a dentist.[1] I have no personal acquaintance with him. I have often met him at the hotel and passed him on the streets and he was always disposed to speak to and grin at me, but I took it to be his nature to do so. He was acquainted with nearly every body in town, especially the Secesh part of the population. He was sick a long while in the hospital and Mrs. Norcum informs me that he resigned.

I received to-day the Chronicle of the 11th. inst. When you send me papers, you will confer a favor by marking the parts, which you wish me to read.

There is no news.

Your brother,
John A. Hedrick

---

[1] Lt. George W. Steadman served in Company I, Eighty-first New York Infantry. Janet B. Hewett, ed., *The Roster of Union Soldiers, 1861-1865, New York* (Wilmington, N.C.. Broadfoot Publishing, 1998), pt. 5:140.

Duke
Beaufort, N.C.
April 25th. 1864.

Dear Brother:

I wrote you last week on the receipt of yours of the 11th. and have received nothing from you since. We had a small mail yesterday and I received a letter dated April 8th., from Grandfather Sherwood. He and Grandmother were well at the time of writing but had been sick for a long while previous.

We have had very stirring news since I wrote last. The rebels have come down upon Plymouth[1] and taken the whole garrison, and sunk two gunboats, the Miami[2] & Bombshell.[3] The place has been so much cut off since its fall that we have been unable to obtain any definite news from there subsequent to that time, but it is reported that the rebs made an indiscriminate havoc of the negroes and the N.C.U. Vols. There were two companies of N.C. Troops stationed there.[4] The Roanoke Ram,[5] which sunk the two gunboats, seems to have passed the battery prepared to sink her, unobserved.

There are a great many conflicting reports about the ram. Some say that she has been seen in the Neuse a short distance below Newbern, but one of the men from the Cutter stationed about a mile below Newbern, came down Saturday and told me that they had not seen or heard of her in the River. I do not think that she has passed Roanoke Island. There has been a general skedaddling of the women from Newbern. Mr. Heaton's family came down last Thursday. A great many ladies have gone north. I think that the War Department should issue a general order requiring officers wives to stay at home or some where north and not with their husbands.

The weather is a little stormy but pleasant.

We are all well.

The humbug Foster attempted to leave her for the north Saturday but I understand that the Provost Marshal would not let him go.

> Your brother,
> John A. Hedrick

---

[1] Confederates under Brig. Gen. Robert Hoke captured the Union garrison at Plymouth, N.C., commanded by Brig. Gen. Henry C. Wessells, on April 20, 1864. Weymouth T. Jordan Jr. and Gerald W. Thomas, "Massacre at Plymouth: April 20, 1864," *North Carolina Historical Review* 72 (April 1995): 125.

[2] The USS *Miami* fought during the Confederate attack on Plymouth but was not sunk. *Civil War Naval Chronology*, pt. 4:45, 193.

[3] On April 18, 1864, Confederate batteries sank the USS *Bombshell*, an army transport, in Albemarle Sound. Southerners raised the vessel to use in the Confederate navy, only to lose it to Union forces on May 5, 1864. *Civil War Naval Chronology*, pt. 6:206.

[4] Companies B and E, Second North Carolina Union Regiment. Jordan and Thomas, "Massacre at Plymouth," 125.

[5] The CSS *Albemarle*, built at Edwards Ferry, N.C., on the Roanoke River and completed in March 1864, rammed and sank the Union steamer *Southfield* near Plymouth on April 19, 1864. Current, *Encyclopedia of the Confederacy*, 1:22; Robert G. Elliot, *Ironclad of the Roanoke: Gilbert Elliot's Albemarle* (Shippensburg, Penn.: White Mane Publishing Company, 1994), 4-7.

Duke
Beaufort, N.C.
Thursday
April 28th. 1864.

Dear Brother:

I received Monday yours of the 18th. and to-day yours of the 21st. together with the Chronicle of the 14th. & 15th. There is so much news stirring that I hardly know where to begin to relate it. Every thing seems to be in a state of confusion and consternation. The troops have been pretty much all ordered to Fortress Monroe and the rebels have taken Plymouth and come down upon Washington and are expected at Newbern soon. Unless there is some move on Richmond shortly to divert the attention of the enemy from this State, I cannot see how we will be able to hold out much longer. The town is crowded with women and children from Washington and Newbern. To-day three flat loads of Buffalo wives were brought over from Morehead City, having come from Washington via Newbern. The town of Washington had not been evacuated when they left, but it was /thought/ that it would be if the rebs continued the attack much longer. It was reported <yesterday> /to-day/ that there were some Rebel cavalry near Newport, and a reconnaissance was sent out to ascertain their strength, but nothing further has been heard from them.

I never thought that soldiers could be so easily frightened as our troops have been. They seem to be more panic stricken than even the citizens and seem to /be/ ready to run on the first approach of the enemy. Political news and President making does not disturb us much, though Capt Kitch has been talking of holding a convention in Washington for the purpose of appointing a delegate to the Baltimore convention.[1] The Captain is here now and I presume his convention is all knocked into pie. He left Washington some time last week with his books and papers, shortly after the fall of Plymouth.

We can't get any reliable news from Plymouth, nor even from up the Sound. Some say that there is a Monitor up there hunting for the Ram, but I can not find any one who has seen her or knows that she is up there. There is very little doing in the way of granting permits. There are three cargoes of goods mostly for Newbern in port but the consignees are afraid to take them up.

Mr. Norcum did not learn any thing from our folks while in Chowan. He heard from Mrs Norcum's family through his brotherinlaw, who returned from Greensboro about the time he went up there, and who had met James Dusenbury[2] in Greensboro.

We are all well and the weather is pleasant and springlike.

Mrs Norcum has garden peas in bloom.

> Write often,
> Your brother,
> John A. Hedrick

---

[1] The Republican or National Union Party held its national convention in Baltimore on June 7-8, 1864. Morris, *Encyclopedia of American History*, 244; Long, *Day by Day*, 516-517.

[2] James Dusenbury (b. ca. 1821) was a farmer and doctor in Lexington, N.C. Eighth Census, 1860: Davidson County.

Duke
Beaufort, N.C.
May 2nd. 1864.

Dear Brother:

Yours of the 25th. ult. reached me last Saturday.

We have no very recent news. Our forces at last accounts had partly evacuated Washington but it is now thought that the Rebs have left that place and that the Union troops still hold the town.

I think it probable that the Rebs have withdrawn their forces for operations in Virginia. There has been a nightly /skedaddling/ among our citizens and soldiers during the last week, and a great deal of suffering occasioned by it. I understand that three women died last Friday in Morehead City from fatigue and exposure. We have enough of women and children. The N.C. troops have been brought down from Washington and it seems that every one of them has a wife and about a half of a dozen of children.

Genl. Peck has been relieved from the command in North Carolina and Genl. Palmer succeeds him.[1]

Capt. Ritch left here on a schooner last Saturday for Washington on a kind of reconnoitering expedition. If our troops should be entirely withdrawn he was going to try to get his family and some more property away. I am of the opinion that when he gets there he will find no rebs.

Mr. Norcum's family is well. When I say well I mean that no one is confined. Mr Norcum himself is still troubled with a cough and a slight hemorrhage of the lungs, though I think that he is on the mend.

The weather is cloudy this morning and it has rained considerably since yesterday about 4 o'clock.

I don't like to learn that the Tax Commissioners have been appointed without any North Carolinian getting a place. I did think that Capt. Ritch ought to have one of those places. I would not be afraid to bet that he is better qualified for Tax Commissioner in North Carolina than either of the appointees.

I think that you ought to give the humbug Foster credit for appointing North Carolinians to office. I do not know his design in doing so, but he certainly appointed more North Carolinians than all the former appointments put together. Business is rather at a stand point at present. Plymouth is entirely, Washington virtually cut off, and the people in Newbern hesitate to take their goods up. I have just learned from Col. Taylor that Genl Banks has met with a serious disaster up the Red River. It is reported that he lost 3500 men and that 40 of his vessels are above the Rafts, where there is only 4 feet of water.[2]

I am well.

> Your brother,
> John A. Hedrick

---

[1] Maj. Gen. Innis Palmer replaced Maj. Gen. John J. Peck as commander of the District of North Carolina, Department of Virginia and North Carolina, on April 28, 1864. Sifakis, *Who Was Who in the Civil War*, 485, 495.

[2] During the Red River Campaign, Union forces under Maj. Gen. Nathaniel P. Banks were defeated by Maj. Gen. Richard Taylor's Confederates at Mansfield, La., on April 8, 1864, and suffered about twenty-nine hundred casualties. The two armies fought again the following day at Pleasant Hill, La., in a battle that both sides viewed as a defeat. The Union losses at Pleasant Hill numbered approximately fourteen hundred. During the campaign, a Union naval flotilla under Rear Adm. David D. Porter was delayed and placed in danger by low water levels. Dams built near Alexandria, La., allowed the vessels to escape. Current, *Encyclopedia of the Confederacy*, 3:1317.

> *Duke*
> Beaufort, N.C.
> May 6th., 1864.

Dear Brother:

I have had nothing from you since I wrote Monday last.

I can not tell how things are in this Department, because our communication with Newbern has been cut off. The cars did not come down yesterday and the telegraph has been cut between Morehead City and

Newbern. Firing was heard from 2 o'clock yesterday till night in the direction of Newbern and it was reported that Croatan, a small fort about eight miles this side of Newbern had been captured by the enemy.[1] The Cars went up the road yesterday afternoon as far as they thought it would be safe but brought back no definite information.

I have heard no firing this morning and there is no news further from the direction of Newbern.

The citizens are doing Provost Guard duty in this place.

Your brother,
John A. Hedrick

---

[1] Fort Croatan was an isolated post along the Atlantic and North Carolina Railroad. On May 5, 1864, Confederates surrounded the fort and forced the Union garrison to surrender. *OR*, ser. 1, 36, pt. 2:5-6.

Duke
Beaufort, N.C.
May 8th. 1864.

Dear Brother:

The excitement which has prevailed here for the last week, has pretty much passed away. The latest news from Newbern represents that the Rebs have withdrawn from Croatan and it is thought that the whole force has gone to Richmond.

A gun boat from off Wilmington stopped outside of the Bar to-day on her way to Fortress Monroe and reported that one of the Rebel rams came out of New Inlet yesterday but went back in again.

I understand that papers of the 2nd. inst. have been received and that Grant and Lee have been fighting, though the result of the engagement is not known.[1] It is also reported here to-day that Burnside will shortly be in this State with a large force.

We have had some jawing between Lt. Col. Poor[2] of the 2nd. N.C. and Capt. Bartlett, Provost Marshal. The Colonel was absent a few days ago and when he returned, he found his men relieved from guard duty and the citizens with arms doing Provost duty. He considered this a reflection on his men and resented it. The Provost threatened to fire on the Buffaloes, with the citizens but by some means they managed to separate without coming to blows. They are still at loggerheads. For yesterday Capt.

Garrmon /of Schr. J.W. Maitland/ was ashore and inquired where he would find the Colonel and said that the sentinel on the wharf had told him that his pass must be signed by the Colonel instead of the Provost. The citizens are very much rejoiced at being excused from guard duty and give praise to Col. Poor for relieving them. They think it wrong that they should be compelled to take up arms every time the military become a little frightened, and fear that they would be harshly dealt by should they be taken with arms in their hands.

At Plymouth, the citizens were armed and when Genl. Wessels found that he could not hold the place any longer, he told them that they must take care of themselves as best they could. This was done Tuesday night and the place fell about 10 o'clock Wednesday morning. There was a general skedaddling among the citizens for their homes, and /I/ have not heard whether any of them were killed by the Rebs for taking up arms or not. The last intelligence that I have had from there was brought by a man who is now stopping at Mr Norcum's and who made his escape about 3 P.M. the day the place fell.

Mr. Heaton and all his force except two clerks are here now. They came down during the panic last week. He seems to be anxious to return to Newbern and regrets having left there. We are having beautiful weather.

I am well.

Your brother,
John A. Hedrick

---

[1] In the Battle of the Wilderness, May 5-6, 1864, Grant suffered nearly eighteen thousand casualties and Lee eight thousand. Boatner, *Civil War Dictionary*, 919-925.

[2] Lt. Col. Walter S. Poor took command of the Second North Carolina Union Regiment on March 30, 1864, soon after the dismissal of Charles Henry Foster. Poor was placed in command of Beaufort on April 19, 1864. Compiled Service Records, Record Group 94.

Duke
Beaufort, N.C.
May 16th. 1864.

Dear Brother:

I received yours of the 9th. and a few days previous yours of the 5th. inst. We have had nothing from the north later than the 13th. up to which date our losses are represented to be 41,000. There is no news of any fighting going on in this State. We are having beautiful weather.

Garden peas are nearly large enough to eat. Lettuce and raddishes have been abundant for the last month. Four companies of the 2nd. N.C. are here now and about the same number of the 1st. N.C. in the Fort. So you see we are guarded by native troops.

Business has been very dull during the last week. I have hardly collected enough to pay expenses. I still have enough of work to do but am nearer up with my work than I have been for the last eight months.

> Your brother
> John A. Hedrick

> *Duke*
> Beaufort, N.C.
> May 20th. 1864.

Dear Brother:

Nothing of importance except the change of Local Treasury Agent at Newbern has transpired since I wrote last. Every body is anxiously awaiting the result of the fighting in Virginia. At last accounts, which were brought in the papers of the 16th. inst. Grant seemed to have the decided advantage.

Capt. Ritch formerly Local Agent at Washington, has been appointed for Newbern. A change has been contemplated some time and was not made too soon. Business in my line is at a stand still or rather it has taken a backward turn. Large quantities of goods have been reshipped to New York during the last two weeks. The shipments of cotton & other produce from this Port since the fall of Plymouth and Washington has been very small and the inward shipments have not been much larger.

Our town is still filled with women and children from Plymouth & Washington. Quite a number of them are stopping at the hospital and the Baptist and colored Churches are crowded with them. A great many of them are soldiers' wives and their immediate connections. Some of them have doubtless seen better days, though most of them look as if they had been brought up in indigent circumstances. They receive rations from the Commissary and in some cases the Provost Marshal has compelled citizens to take them into their houses. Notwithstanding all this there must necessarily be a great deal of suffering among them.

We have had a great deal of nice Spring weather lately. Fish are plenty in market but I do not like them. They consist principally of Trout, Hog Fish & Sheep's head, all of which smell too strong for me. The trout are not at all like those that we used to catch in the Yadkin River.

Mr Norcum's family and myself are well.

Your /letters/ all down to the 12th. inst. I think, have reached me.

> Write often,
> Your brother
> John A. Hedrick

> *Duke*
> Beaufort, N.C.
> May 27th. 1864.

Dear Brother:

I have heard nothing from you later than the 12th. inst. In fact there has been no Mail since last Saturday. We have had papers, however, of the 21st. which represented things in Virginia to be at stand still.

Every thing here is as dull as night. The children of the N.C. refugees are dying with the measles very fast. One woman has lost three between the ages of 2 & 12 years since day before yesterday. About a dozen have died during the last two days.

I was in Newbern last Sunday and saw Dr. Page, who as usual said that he expected to go north in about 8 days. In my last letter I wrote you that Capt. Ritch had been appointed Local Agent at Newbern. I saw the Captain who seemed to be in pretty good spirits, though he had not heard from his family who are still in Washington, for some time. I saw Capt. Wheeler also. My business has fallen off about three fourths during the present month.

What has become of our friend Pigott? His cousin L.W. Pigott, has moved north but I do not know where he expects to bring up.

Mr Norcum and family are in usual good health. He still has a caugh but upon the whole I think that he has improved considerably since he returned home.

We are having beautiful weather. I am well.

> Your brother,
> John A. Hedrick

Duke
Beaufort, N.C.
May 30th. 1864.

Dear Brother:

I received last Saturday, May the 28th. yours of the 21st. which is /the/ only letter that I have had from you for about ten days. Papers of the 25th. have been received but I have not seen them. I understand that there has not been much fighting lately but a great deal of manoevering by Lee and Grant.

There has not been /any thing/ to disturb our quiet during the last week. The only thing that has caused much excitement in the Department during that time, was the explosion of a Torpedo at Bachelor's Creek Depot, which killed 40 men and wound 17, according to the report given in the Times. The report in the paper calls it "amunition" but the verbal report brought down the next day after it happened called it a torpedo.[1] I guess that our folks did not wish any one to know what the boxes contained, and that the negroes being ignorant of their contents did not handle them as carefully as they should have done.

The Roanoke Ram, has caused no trouble lately and it is reported that she was so badly injured in her last fight with our gunboats in Albemarle Sound that she had to be hauled up for repairs.[2]

Yesterday I walked out into the country a short distance and saw some dirt forts and then Hospital Garden. The forts are not garrisoned and would not amount to much should they be assailed by an enemy. The Garden looks very well and contains about 10 Acres of Potatoes, Corn, Raddishes, Lettuce, Squash, Peas & C. I think that it would be better for the government to send the N.C. refugees to some such plantation and make them work until they could recruit themselves. They are dying very fast. The average deaths is about 6 a day. The negroes too should be put on some place where they could maintain themselves. They are dying off but I think not so rapidly as formerly. Mr. Norcum lost two last week, or rather two died, which had belonged to him.

The different classes of the population have their appropriate names. All who /came/ down with the Union Army are called Yankees. Those who lived here before the war and were opposed to secession and unwilling to go into the rebel army are called Sawed-hoons. The North Carolinians who have joined the Union army are called Buffaloes, while those who are in favor of the dissolution of the Union are called Secesh. Some call the negroes Firesides, because the Rebs used to say that they were fighting for their firesides, whereas they were fighting for their negroes.

The girls have a new way of say Rich man, Poor man, Pedler, Tinker. They now say Secesh, Yankee, Sawed-hoon, Buffaloe.

We are having beautiful weather.

> Write often
> Your brother,
> John A. Hedrick

---

[1] According to the newspaper account, the explosion occurred on the afternoon of May 26 as ammunition was being unloaded from a train. Many of the casualties were from the 132d New York Infantry. *North Carolina Times* (New Bern), May 28, 1864.

[2] On May 5, 1864, the CSS *Albemarle* battled seven Union gunboats in Albemarle Sound but was not severely damaged. The *Albemarle* returned to Plymouth on May 6 and, according to Union observers, did not leave the wharf again until May 24. Elliot, *Ironclad of the Roanoke*, 211, 223, 224.

> *Duke*
> Beaufort, N.C.
> June 3rd. 1864.

Dear Brother:

Yours of May 24th. was received a few days ago.

Every thing is as dull as usual. The sickness among the refugees still continues, though the deaths are not quite as <numerous> /frequent/ as they were a week ago. About an average of five die per day. These poor people have been moved out of town into tents near the Hammack, which is about half a mile from here.[1]

There are rumors of yellow fever in the place, but I think that there is none here.

We have had no news from the seat of war later than the 28th. ult. At that time every thing seemed to be in a very confused state.

We are all well.

> Your brother,
> John A. Hedrick

---

[1] The Hammock is a hill near Beaufort. During the war soldiers used a structure on the hill, called Hammock House, as officers' quarters and the surrounding property as a

campground. Maurice Davis, *History of the Hammock House and Related Trivia* (Beaufort, N.C.: M. Davis, 1984), i, 54.

Duke
Beaufort, N.C.
June 7th. 1864.

Dear Brother:

I have had nothing from you since I wrote last. All is quiet here. We are having quite warm weather. The latest news from Virginia looked encouraging. Grant was reported to within 12 miles of Richmond by road and 8 by direct line. The latest northern papers received are the 4th. inst. I have seen nothing however later than the 2nd. Sherman seemed to be progressing well, and Banks' fleet had succeeded in extricating itself.

The Str. Petrel has just arrived from New York but I do not expect that she will bring any thing later than we have had.

I intend to go to Newbern to-day if I can get off.

We are all well, except Mr. Norcum, who seems to be in low spirits this morning.

Your brother
John A. Hedrick

Duke
Custom House,
Beaufort, N.C.
June 11th. 1864.

Dear Brother:

Your letter of the 3rd. inst. containing your likeness was received three days ago. The picture I think is very good, but I cannot make the same remark about the original that you did about mine, that you look as if you might be in love. Because you look too fat to be in love.

There is nothing of interest to relate in this letter.

The Steamer "Newbern" ran a blockade runner ashore above 5 miles south of the Fort day before yesterday. She was about 600 Tons but was not fully laden. They ran her ashore with a full head of steam on, <shut> closed the valves, and then deserted her. Her boiler bursted about 1 o'clock day before yesterday. It is thought that she may be hauled off on some high tide.[1]

Your brother,
John A. Hedrick

---

[1] On June 9, 1864, the blockade-runner *Pevensey* ran aground near Beaufort while being pursued by the USS *New Berne* and subsequently exploded. The *Pevensey* was carrying food, clothing, and weapons. *Civil War Naval Chronology*, pt. 4:72.

Duke
Beaufort, N.C.
June 18th. 1864.

Dear Brother:

Your letter of the 8th. inst. inclosing your picture for Mrs. Norcum was received about three days ago.

I have seen no northern paper later than the 12th. inst. though I heard yesterday that the 14th. was in town. The news of the 12th. represented things about Richmond in an uncertain state. There seemed to be a disposition on the part of Grant to change his base of operations. It may have been for the purpose of crossing the James River and attacking the enemy on the south side of Richmond. Hunter seems to have made a splendid dash in Western Virginia.[1] The operations under Shearman, according to accounts were progressing favorably.[2]

There has been no fighting in this state since I wrote last.

I have just heard from Plymouth through Wm. Atkinson, who has been in that region trying to get about $4000 $^{00}/_{100}$ left there by him on the surrender of the town. Mr. Atkinson did not go in Plymouth himself, but sent a man in to get his money and endeavor to release his Father who is imprisoned by the Rebs. This man saw his Father but did not succeed in obtaining his release or getting the money. Mr. Atkinson is a citizen of Washington County and has a plantation about eight miles this side of Plymouth on the sound.[3] He came very near of being captured by the Rebs. He went over one night in a small boat and intended to land at his fishery, but thought that he would sail by the place to see if any one was there before he would go ashore. As he was passing he was hailed by a

sentinel on the beach who ordered him to come to. He thought it best
not to obey orders, but to tack ship and lay his course out into the sound
again. The sentinel fired at the boat but did not hit any one. He proceeded
about 4 miles further up the sound where he went ashore, and sent the
boat back to Roanoke Island, thinking that he could /get/ one of his two
boats, which he had concealed in the swamps. The Rebs had cut them up
to prevent conscripts from escaping. In fact they had destroyed all the
boats that they could find on the Sound. So he was left on the enemy's
coast without any boat. And besides the Rebs were expecting him to visit
home and were keeping a sharp lookout for him. A lot of negroes a short
time before had escaped from Plymouth and the Rebs had placed a heavy
picket on a certain creek between where he landed and Plymouth, so that
he could not get into the place. He succeeded after a while in getting an
old boat in which he came off to the gunboats. He then got them to set
him ashore up in Bertie County above Plymouth, and managed to
communicate with his Father. He tells a very amusing account of his trip.
Mrs. Norcum sends her regards to you and thinks that you need not be
uneasy about me while I have such a good Mother (herself) to look after
me.
  We are all well.

Write often,
John A. Hedrick

----

[1] Maj. Gen. David Hunter took command of Union troops in the Shenandoah Valley on
May 19, 1864, and began a campaign of destruction. Hunter withdrew to West Virginia,
however, after encountering Jubal Early's Confederates at Lynchburg, Va., on June 17-18.
Charles C. Osborne, *Jubal: The Life and Times of General Jubal A. Early, CSA* (Chapel Hill:
Algonquin Books, 1992), 247-259.

[2] Maj. Gen. William T. Sherman was moving against Gen. Joseph E. Johnston's army in north
Georgia toward Atlanta.

[3] William Atkinson Sr. (b. ca. 1813) and William Atkinson Jr. (b. ca. 1837) lived in the same
household at or near Mackeys Ferry in 1860. Eighth Census, 1860: Washington County.

Duke
Newbern, N.C.
June 25th. 1864.

Dear Brother:

  I received a few days ago your letter containing Charlie's[1] picture.
Charlie looks very much like himself, only a little more full over his eyes

than usual. We have had New York papers to the 20th. which deny the taking of Petersburg reported in the papers of the 18th. It seems very hard for them to confine themselves to the truth.

About a week ago an expedition fitted out from this place for Kinston and returned yesterday with Col. Folk and 50 prisoners.[2] At the same time another expedition left Beaufort for New Inlet by water and returned yesterday but I did not learn their success.[3] They killed one of their Sergeants through a mistake.

The weather yesterday when I left Beaufort was quite pleasant, but I found it extremely hot before I arrived here. Mr. Norcum and family are all well. Mr. Heaton left Beaufort day before yesterday on the Str. Idaho for Fortress Munro on his way to Washington City. I did not ask him to call to see you this time, because the other time he neglected to visit you without sufficient reason.

I have not as yet been to see Dr Page, but I presume that he is still here. He is always ready to go north but never goes. He is Superintendent of N.C. Refugees. I think that the refugees are not dying as fast as they were some time ago. At Beaufort they have an encampment of over 100 tents a short distance out of town. At this place they are similarly provided for but I do not know how many tents they have.

I am well and weighed yesterday 128 pounds.

Write often,
Your brother,
John A. Hedrick

---

[1] Charles J. Hedrick (1855-1922) was the second of Benjamin and Mary Ellen Hedrick's eight children. He became a patent attorney in Washington, D.C. Kirkman, *Heritage of Adam Alexander Young*, 20.

[2] The expedition was commanded by Col. Peter J. Claasen of the 132d New York and consisted of two infantry regiments and a detachment of cavalry and artillery, 832 men in all. Among the prisoners taken was Col. George Nathaniel Folk (1831-1896) of the Sixty-fifth North Carolina (Sixth North Carolina Cavalry). He was held from June 22 to December 15, 1864, before being exchanged. Folk had been a lawyer and a state representative from Watauga County before the war. *OR*, ser. 1, 40, pt. 1:814, 816, pt. 2:420; Manarin and Jordan, *North Carolina Troops*, 2:457; *Dictionary of North Carolina Biography*, s.v. "Folk, George Nathaniel."

[3] This expedition, led by Col. James Jourdan and directed against the Wilmington and Weldon Railroad, took place June 20-25, 1864. Fifteen hundred men left Morehead City and reached Jacksonville before encountering a large Confederate force, which caused them to abort the mission. *OR*, ser. 1, 40, pt. 1:817-819.

Duke
Beaufort, N.C.
July 2nd. 1864.

Dear Brother:

Your letter enclosing Johnnie's[1] likeness was received a few days ago. You are very much mistaken in thinking that I have very little to do. I have to work from 5 A.M. till 9 P.M. and then can't keep business up as I would like.

I will go to Newbern to-day. The Cutter "A.V. Brown" has been ordered to New York and I wish to pay the crew off for the month of June before she leaves. The Cutter "Antietam" takes her place.

I intend to come back this evening. Papers to the 27th. have been received but I have not seen them.

We are all well.

Your brother,
John A. Hedrick

---

[1] John Thompson Hedrick (1853-1923) was Benjamin and Mary Ellen Hedrick's oldest child. He was ordained as a Jesuit priest in 1878. Kirkman, *Heritage of Adam Alexander Young*, 20.

Duke
Custom House,
Beaufort, N.C.
July 4th. 1864.

Dear Brother:

Your letter of June 26th. was received last Saturday.

I send herein an invitation to a celebration at the Fort[1] to-day, but it is so rainy that I will not be able to go.

We have had New York papers to the 29th. ult. Every thing around Richmond seemed to be at a stand.

Sherman had been considerably worsted in Georgia.[2]

The Buffalo women seem to be doing better than they did some ago but are still in a bad condition.

Mr. Norcum and family are well. I saw Dr. Page at a distance in Newbern Saturday.

Write often!

Your brother,
John A. Hedrick

---

[1] Fort Macon.

[2] Joseph E. Johnston's Confederate army defeated Sherman's forces at the Battle of Kennesaw Mountain on June 27, 1864. Sherman suffered three thousand casualties to Johnston's one thousand. Current, *Encyclopedia of the Confederacy*, 2:885-886.

Duke
Beaufort, N.C.
July 10th. 1864.

Dear Brother:

Yours of the 30th. ult. was received last week.

I have just received the National Intelligencer[1] of the 2nd. July containing the Tariff act passed June 30th. 1864. Section 28 reads as follows: "That in all cases where officers of the customs or other salaried officers of the United States shall be, or shall have been, appointed by the Secretary of the Treasury, to carry into effect the licenses, rules and regulations provided for by the fifth section of the act of the thirteenth of July, eighteen hundred and sixty one, entitled "An act further to provide for the collection of duties on imports, and for other purposes," such officer of the United States shall be entitled to receive one thousand dollars per annum for his services, under the act aforesaid, in addition to his salary or compensation under any other law; Provided, that the aggregate compensation of any such officer shall not exceed the sum of five thousand dollars in any one year." For officers of the customs, whose salaries are fixed by law, this section would evidently give them one thousand dollars additional provided this did not increase their pay to over five thousand dollars per annum, but in my case, where the old salary is almost nothing and the fees & percentage every thing, I do not think it at all fair that I should have only one thousand dollars for my services under the Rules and Regulations for Internal and Coastwise Commercial Intercouse. Inspector Willis thinks that by this Section I would be entitled to $1250 and fees, and commissions on all deposits. I do not think that I could properly be called a salaried officer, though I have a salary. I am therefore of the opinion that I do not come under the provisions of the before mentioned section. If I do come under I assume that I will be poorly paid for my services unless the Department will take Mr Will's interpretation.

The weather has been quite warm for the last few days.

New York papers of the 6th. have reached here but I have seen nothing later than the 4th. I understand that Grant had demanded the unconditional surrender of surrender of Petersburg, but that no reply had been received at last accounts. Every body here seems rejoiced over the destruction of the Alabama.[2]

With all the rain, /the/ 1st. N.C. celebrated the 4th. at the Fort and had a ball, but I did not go. I wrote you that day while it was pouring down rain but neglected to put the letter in the office until a couple of days after. Mr. Heaton has not yet returned. What induced Secretary Chase to resign? I have not yet seen his resignation and no one here seems to know why he resigned.[3] I presume you have seen the resolution of Congress, declaring the act of Congress in relation to abandoned property approved March 12th. 1863 to be inoperative on account of having been signed after the adjournment of Congress. The present Congress will have to pass an enabling act.

There is no Department news to write.

> Write often,
> Your brother,
> John A. Hedrick

---

[1] A Washington, D.C., newspaper. See William E. Ames, *A History of the National Intelligencer* (Chapel Hill: University of North Carolina Press, 1972).

[2] The USS *Kearsarge*, under Capt. John A. Winslow, sank the Confederate commerce raider CSS *Alabama*, commanded by Capt. Raphael Semmes, off Cherbourg, France, on June 19, 1864. *ORN*, ser. 1, 3:59.

[3] As the culmination to a lengthy antagonism, President Lincoln accepted Salmon P. Chase's resignation as secretary of the treasury on June 30, 1864. Sifakis, *Who Was Who in the Civil War*, 117-118.

Duke
Beaufort, N.C.
July 16th. 1864.

Dear Brother:

Your letter of the 6th. inst. was received a few days ago.

All is quiet here but the news from the north is not good. We have rumors that Washington City and all it were captured. I do not think this probably, but it is certain that the Rebs have been making a raid into Maryland.[1] I am well but tired after a hard week's work.

The Scr. "Petrel" has just arrived from New York and /I/ presume that we will get papers of the 13th. The "Carolina" arrived from Port Royal this morning and leaves for New York early to-morrow morning, so I must close my letter to get /it/ in the Mail to-night. Mr. Norcum and family are well.

Write often,
Your brother,
John A. Hedrick

---

[1] On July 4-5, 1864, Lt. Gen. Jubal Early's Confederate force of fourteen thousand moved into Maryland, and on July 11, reached the outskirts of Washington, D.C. Rather than risk an assault on the formidable defenses of the capital, Early withdrew on July 12 and moved south of the Potomac on July 13 and 14. Osborne, *Jubal*, 265; Current, *Encyclopedia of the Confederacy*, 2:504.

Duke
Beaufort, N.C.
July 22nd. 1864.

Dear Brother:

Your letter of the 13th. inst. reached me yesterday evening. It had been missent to Boston, and is the only one that I have had from you for some time.

I have seen New York papers of the 18th. & it is rumored to-night that the 20th. is here, and that it contains news of a riot in N.Y. I think however that here is no such paper here and that it is not probable that there is any riot in New York.

We have also a report from Newbern that there is a large force of Rebels about Kinston and that an attack on Newbern is expected. There is some talk about evacuating Newbern. I do not know any foundation for this report.

Mr. Heaton has arrived and as usual has his head full of undecided plans. He says that a new set of regulations are coming out, and on that account has suspended exporting merchandise for the present.

Mr. Thomas is very badly crippled up with the Rhumatism, and is gone north. I am very sorry for it, for he was a very good man.

All well.

> Your brother,
> John A. Hedrick

[*John A. Hedrick to Mary Ellen Hedrick*]

> *Duke*
> Beaufort, N.C.
> July 27th. 1864.

Dear Sister:

Bennie's[1] letter of the 17th. inst. written on the eve of his departure for New York, was received a few days ago. We have Northern papers to the 20th. inst. but nothing of much interest from the armies.

Our pickets were driven in at Bachelor's Creek, which is about 8 miles above Newbern, day before yesterday, but no engagement took place.

There are various rumors as to the number of Rebs above Newbern & of the probability of their attacking the place. I think that there are not many and that there is no present danger of an attack.

Refugees, however, who come in from about Plymouth, say that they have been ordered to report with 5 days' rations at Tarboro, which would seem to indicate some movement on foot.

We are having hot weather after several quite cold days.

> Your brother,
> John A. Hedrick

M.E. Hedrick

---

[1] Benjamin S. Hedrick.

[John A. Hedrick to Mary Ellen Hedrick]

Duke
Beaufort, N.C.
August 1st. 1864.

Dear Sister:

I wrote you a short letter last week, acknowledging the receipt of Bennie's dated the 17th. ult. which is the last I have had from him. I have received from him however The Boston Daily Advertiser of the 20th. ult. mailed in Cambridge.

Northern papers of the 27th. of July have reached her but I have not read them. I understand that the Rebs are making another raid into Maryland.[1] The force is reported 80000 strong.

I did not learn any thing from Grant. Sherman had fought a hard battle near Atlanta, Ga. in which he captured 6000 in killed, wounded & prisoners.[2]

Every thing here is as quiet as can be. There is no goods arriving from the north, and it is rumored that a prohibition has been placed on the shipment of goods from New York to this place.

I am well.

Your brother,
John A. Hedrick

---

[1] Confederate cavalry commanded by Brig. Gen. John McCausland from Lt. Gen. Jubal Early's army launched a raid into Maryland and Pennsylvania on July 29, 1864. On July 30, McCausland demanded $500,000 in currency or $100,000 in gold from the people of Chambersburg, Pa., as compensation for the destruction caused by Maj. Gen. David Hunter's Union army in Virginia. When the townspeople could not produce that amount, the Confederates burned the town. Long, *Day by Day*, 548.

[2] There were a number of battles in the Atlanta campaign in the days immediately preceding this letter. The Battles of Peachtree Creek, July 20; Atlanta, July 22; and Ezra Church, July 28, were all Union victories. Long, *Day by Day*, 542, 543, 547.

[*John A. Hedrick to Mary Ellen Hedrick*]

Duke
Beaufort, N.C.
Aug 7th. 1864.

Dear Sister:

I have written you three letters since I received Bennie's letter of the 17th. ult. but have had none from you or Bennie since then.

There is neither news nor rumors in this place to-day. We have had no Northern papers later than the 30th. ult. Mr. Norcum's family and myself are well. I weigh 125 lbs which is my usual summer weight.

My salary alone is $1250, and I wish to know whether you would advise me to get married now, provided every thing else is suitable and agreeable, or should I wait till I get $2500 per annum, or thereabouts, to make up for the difference in the value of the dollar.

We are anxiously waiting the forthcoming of the new Treasury Regulations.

Write often

Your brother,
John A. Hedrick

Mary E. Hedrick

Duke
Beaufort, N.C.
August 11th. 1864.

Dear Brother:

Your two letters of the 1st. and 3rd. inst. reached me, the former three & the latter two days ago.

There is no departmental news to write. Nothing has disturbed our peace during the last month.

I fear that Grant is not succeeding very well. We have papers to the 8th. They contained very little of interest from the armies. There is an outside rumor however to the effect that Sherman has fought a hard battle in which he lost 4000 and the enemy 10000 men.

Business has been at pretty much a stand still for the last month, yet I collected a single fee of $1837 $^{91}/_{100}$ to-day. This is the largest I have ever received. My receipts to-day will exceed $2000 $^{00}/_{100}$.

There is considerable sickness in town. Mrs. & Mr. Norcum are complaining to-day, but not confined to their beds.

> Write often,
> Your brother
> John A. Hedrick

> *Duke*
> Custom House,
> Beaufort, N.C.
> August 19th. 1864.

Dear Brother:

Your letters of the 7th. & 11th. insts. the former inclosing Alice's[1] & Johnnie's pictures were received a few days ago. I have not been able as yet to procure you a substitute. I would like to know whether the substitute could be mustered into one of the N.C. Regiments here or would it be necessary for him to be sent on to Washington to take your place should you be drafted in one of the District Regiments.

These refugees do not seem much disposed to join the army. Most of them have come into our lines to keep out of the Rebel Army, and not to fight for their country.

We are all well. I weigh less than I have for a long time, but I attribute the decrease to the hot weather. My weight is 119 lbs. There is a great deal of sickness in town, and it seems to be confined mostly to young ladies and girls.

> Write often,
> John A. Hedrick

---

[1] Alice Hedrick (1858-1952) was Benjamin and Mary Ellen Hedrick's oldest daughter. She married Harry Olcott of Virginia. Kirkman, *Heritage of Adam Alexander Young*, 20.

Duke
Beaufort, N.C.
Aug. 26th. 1864.

Dear Brother:

Your letter of the 18th. inclosing Wm. Adams' pictures was received day before yesterday and Sister Ellen's letter the day before that. Tell Sister Ellen I will not wait so long about writing to her next time and that I thought that I had answered her letter last winter.

There is no news to write.

We have N.Y. papers to the 22nd. We are all in excellent health and have a plenty of hot weather. The Steamer "Carolina" will leave here for New York to-day.

I will write again soon.

Write often,
Your brother
John A. Hedrick

Duke
Beaufort, N.C.
August 29th. 1864.

Dear Brother:

I wrote you by the Steamer Carolina, last Friday, the 26th. inst. and have had nothing from you since that date.

We have New York papers to the 26th. I have read very little of them but from the number of quotations in the news article I would judge that there was not much news.

We had a rumor here Saturday that the Tallahassee had run into Wilmington Friday evening and that our gunboats exchanged several shots with her, without however doing any damage. I am inclined to believe the report of her having run into Wilmington.[1]

Every thing in military matters seems quiet in this State.

There is some stir among merchants concerning Genl. Orders No. 31, Dist. of N.C. requiring wet groceries to be sold at 30 per cent, and dry groceries and other merchandise to be sold at 25 per cent advance on the New York cost. This rule works very unequally on different classes of goods, because it costs more than 30 per cent to bring some goods to this place.

The order is the same for all points in N.C. And besides goods have advanced 50 per cent in New York during the last six months, yet the seller would be obliged to take 25 or 30 per cent on cost, and could not replace his stock for what he would get. There are very few goods coming to this Port now.

The duties on Exports will exceed those on Imports during this month considerably; whereas I used /to/ collect about three times as much on the latter as the former.

Mr. Norcum intended to leave here for his Father's in Chowan County <this evening> to-morrow morning, but the cars ran off of the track coming down about 7 miles this side of Newbern this evening, and as they <cars> will not go up to-morrow and the boats leave Newbern for Roanoke Island, Tuesdays, Thursdays and Sundays, he will not get off before Thursday. His family is well except Henry, who is complaining this evening.

I think that I shall try to come on to Washington some time during October or November.

Mr. Norcum has promised to go with me to see Uncle Abe. If he should conclude to go with me, I wish to take him to New York and show him the sights. He has never been there.

Write often

Your brother,
John A. Hedrick

---

[1] The CSS *Tallahassee* departed Wilmington on August 6, 1864, to begin a cruise that would include the capture or destruction of more than thirty ships. On August 25, the *Tallahassee* returned, under fire from Union vessels, to Wilmington harbor. *Civil War Naval Chronology,* pt. 4:98, 108.

Duke
Beaufort, N.C.
September 4th. 1864,

Dear Brother:

I received last week a letter from you but I /have/ forgotten the date and have not time to refer to it. I was in Newbern yesterday and saw Dr. Page. He showed me some extracts from a letter from C.H. Foster to President Lincoln, taken from the Easton (Me.) Argus of Aug. 11th. 1864. He "<u>demands</u>," "<u>yes Sir</u>," "<u>demands</u>" an investigation into the cause of his ignominious dismal. The Doctor said that if he could have gotten the paper he would have sent it to you. Foster & Carpenter are both in Newbern. Foster told the Doctor that Genl. Butler told him (Foster) that he had a bitter enemy in Washington City.[1]

The negroes are in a great turmoil in this place and Newbern. Genl. Butler has sent for a lot of them to work on the canal up the James River; and the soldiers are hunting up every male contraband able to work, who is not now employed by government.

We have northern papers of the 31st. ult. Baltimore evening papers of that day contain the nomination of the Chicago convention. I expected that Genl. McClellan would be the Democratic Candidate for Presidency.[2]

We are all well.

Your brother,
John A. Hedrick.

Benj S. Hedrick,
Washington,
D.C.

---

[1] Maj. Gen. Benjamin F. Butler wrote Secretary of War Stanton on March 12, 1864, asking permission to replace Charles H. Foster in the Second North Carolina Union Regiment. In the letter Butler referred to Foster's "seeming want of efficiency" and "his fickleness of purpose." Delaney, "Foster and the Unionists," 364; *Private and Official Correspondence of Gen. Benjamin F. Butler During the Period of the Civil War,* 5 vols. (Norwood, Mass.: Plimpton Press, 1917), 3:520.

[2] The Democrats, meeting in Chicago, nominated George B. McClellan for president on August 29, 1864. Morris, *Encyclopedia of American History,* 244.

Duke
Beaufort, N.C.
Sept. 12, 1864,

Dear Brother:

Your letter of Sept. 1st. was received about 4 days ago.

I think that I should have had a letter from you Saturday night, but the Rebs burnt up the mail boat, the Fawn, in the canal.[1] We had a mail however by the Escort from Fortress Monroe through Hatteras Inlet but I got nothing whatever, and this very rarely occurs. I understand Maj Janney[2] Judge Advocate of N.C. and Maj Graves[3] 1st. N.C. were captured.

I have no help at present, but I intend to get Mr. Chadwick, who is now on a trip to New York, and who has occasionally assisted me in my office. I have been doing a very good business during last week. I took in $2800, in one night. By the way, I have been issuing most of my permits in the night, because the train came down in the evening and went back early in the morning, and unless I did this the shippers would have to lay over 2 nights and a day. They have now changed again, and, /I/ will resume my old hours.

We are all well.

Your brother,
John A. Hedrick.

---

[1] Confederates burned the *Fawn*, a U.S. steamer carrying mail, at Currituck Bridge, Va., on the Albemarle and Chesapeake Canal, September 9, 1864. The raiders killed or wounded seven people aboard the vessel and captured twenty-nine prisoners. *OR*, ser. 1, 42, pt.1:956-957; *Civil War Naval Chronology*, pt. 4:111; *ORN*, ser. 1, 10:457-458.

[2] Maj. E. S. Jenney, judge advocate, was captured aboard the *Fawn* but released at Elizabeth City by September 15. General Orders, No. 22, Court-martial Proceedings, February 29, 1864, in W. L. Pohoresky, *Newport, North Carolina, During the Civil War: The True Story* (n.p.: William L. Pohoresky, 1978), 73; *ORN*, ser. 1, 10:457.

[3] Maj. Charles C. Graves, commander of the First North Carolina Union Regiment, was taken prisoner aboard the *Fawn* but was soon exchanged. He returned to his regiment in December 1864. *OR*, ser. 1, 33:485, 1057; Compiled Service Records, Record Group 94.

[*John A. Hedrick to Mary Ellen Hedrick*]

Duke
Beaufort, N.C.
Sept. 19th. 1864,

Dear Sister:

Your very interesting letter of advice dated August 14th. 1864, was received in due time. I have nearly recovered from the castigation given me for not answering your previous letter. I will try and not be so remiss in the future.

By the way, if I mistake not, I might call upon you for an answer to a letter written by me to you during the Fall of 1856. But I will proceed to answer some of the questions propounded in your last letter. 1st. I think that it would be quite impossible for a woman to answer the query, which I put to you, without asking a dozen others. 2nd. I am not in earnest. 3rd. I have no selection made. 4th. Supposing the selection made, I would wish her to be pretty smart, and rich. 5th. I am not deeply in love, and don't know how it would feel to be so. I am very much obliged to you for inviting me to bring Mrs. J.A.H. on to visit you, and for your kind wishes in my behalf, in case the choice was made. Your advice is entirely satisfactory and I will try to profit by it.

You say that I tell you nothing about the ladies, the fun &c. I do not because I have never come to that part of the game. And besides as no one knows better than yourself, I am no ladies' man, and have no gift for pleasing them.

There are a great many young ladies here, but some how or other I have objections to them all. Most of them rub snuff, a practice which I consider abominable. Some are too young and some too old, while others think themselves too good for me. People here are not very social, and I am not inclined to push myself into company where I am not entirely welcome. I have been invited to only 6 houses since my arrival, and have visited only those places. I don't believe that this lack of courtesy rises from any ill will that they bear towards me, because I find that they treat each other in the same way.

There is very little local news afloat. There is a very bad fever raging in Newbern. It has been reported to be Yellow fever, but I am confident that it is not Yellow fever. Though it is said to have some of the symptoms of that disease. Several persons have been cut off by it very suddenly.[1]

Bennie's letter of the 6th. reached me last week. It is the only one that I have received from him for over two weeks. I think that some of his letters must have been captured by the Rebs on the steamer Fawn coming through the canal. He says that he has written to me every week. I have gained some in weight lately. I weigh now 120 pounds.

The people here are generally well. Write often and long letters.

Your affectionate brother,
John A. Hedrick.

---

[1] A yellow fever epidemic began in New Bern in September 1864, or perhaps earlier, and continued to November. About 700 civilians and 303 soldiers died. The disease spread to Beaufort, where 76 civilians and 15 soldiers died. Thomas J. Farnham and Francis P. King, " 'The March of the Destroyer': The New Bern Yellow Fever Epidemic of 1864," *North Carolina Historical Review* 73 (October 1996): 437-447, 469-471; *Medical and Surgical History*, 6:681.

Duke
Beaufort, N. C.
Sept. 20th. 1864,

Dear Brother:

Your letter of the 15th. was received to-day, and that of the 6th. some time about the middle of last week. These are the only letters that I have had from you for over two weeks. I wrote Sister Ellen yesterday. I have been getting Chronicles occasionally from you. I received the 13th. & 14th. to-day.

We have New York papers to the 17th. There seems to be nothing important in a military way.

I notice in the papers of the 15th. that a draft has been ordered in all the States for the 19th. inst.

I also notice in the Republican of the 7th a circular from the Provost Marshal General, in which he says that "Persons not fit for military duty and not liable to draft, from age or other causes, have expressed a desire to be personally represented in the Army." From this it would seem that persons liable to the draft would not be excused by having a representative substitute. How think you about this?

We have no particular news here. Every thing seems to be getting on quietly. I find that there is more sickness among the merchant marine than usual. I have 8 in hospital now, which is a greater [*number*] than have ever been in at any previous time. The receipts for Internal Intercourse for this month is on the increase, especially on outward shipments. Genl. Butler has fixed the amount of inward shipments at $100000 per month. This is to include the town of Beaufort. The average shipments have been about one hundred and fifty thousand per month.

If he continues his limitation, we will have to live on oysters and clams. Mr. Norcum is well and says that he is much obliged to you for your invitation, and will avail himself of your offer if he should visit Washington.

We are all well.

Your brother,
John A. Hedrick

Duke
Beaufort, N.C.
September 26th. 1864,

Dear Brother:

I have had nothing from you since I wrote about the middle of last week. We have received papers to the 20th. inst. but I have been unable to get one. The news seems to be very favorable. Sheridan is represented to have killed, wounded and captured 5000 of Early's men.[1] It is also stated that Grant has retaken a part of the cattle captured by Lee but what number I could not learn. The sickness in Newbern continues unabated. The people are dying very fast. I heard Saturday that the Doctors had given it up as Yellow fever, but I have heard none of them say so, and as we have some of the same kind of cases here, which Dr. Rice[2] in charge of the Hospital assured me was not contagious or infectious, I will have to have further proof before I am sure that it is yellow fever. Dr. Page came from Newbern Thursday, and said that it was Malignant Billious Fever.

There is no local war news. I am well and have gained 5 pounds of flesh in the last two weeks. I have been very busy during this month and will be more so for the next two weeks. There have been three deaths in this place from the fever now prevailing in this department. A young man by the name of Phelps died night before last. He was sick about three days.

The weather has turned a little cool and we have had a very good rain during the last three days, and it is probable we will have fewer cases of fever.

Write often and long letters.

> Your brother,
> John A. Hedrick,
> Collector.

---

[1] Philip H. Sheridan's Union force of forty thousand defeated Jubal Early's army of twelve thousand at the Third Battle of Winchester, Va., September 19, 1864. The Confederates suffered 3,921 casualties. Long, *Day by Day*, 571.

[2] Nathan Payson Rice, surgeon, U.S. Volunteers, was in charge of Beaufort's hospital. Heitman, *Historical Register*, 1:827; *Medical and Surgical History of the Civil War*, 6:963.

> *Duke*
> Beaufort, N.C.
> Oct. 2nd. 1864

Dear Brother:

Your letters of the 19th. and 25th. ult. were received in due time.

The sickness here and at Newbern is about as it was when I wrote last. It is not fully determined whether to call it Yellow fever or not. I think that there have been some cases of Yellow Fever. About 300 have died in Newbern since it commenced.

Col. Taylor lost his youngest child, 6 years old, last Tuesday morning. She died with the croup. Seven persons died in this place the same day.

There are quite a number of sick with different complaints here now. All of Heaton's Clerks are sick except one.

I am in first rate health and have my hands full of <u>work</u>.

Your brother,
John A. Hedrick

Duke
Beaufort, N.C.
Oct. 5th. 1864

Dear Brother:

I wrote you last Sunday after the receipt of yours of the 25th. ult.

The fever continues unabated. People are dying very fast in Newbern. There are a great many cases of sickness here but I do not think that all of them are Yellow Fever. Mr. Conklin, one of Mr. Heaton's Clerks died day before yesterday morning. Mr. Heaton, his wife, son and nephew are sick in this place.

James /W/ Bryan,[1] his wife,[2] Maj Lawson,[3] chief Prov. Marshal of N.C. Col Stone,[4] Dr. Wilson,[5] John F. Jones,[6] and a host of others have died in Newbern. I presume you knew Mr. Bryan. He was a lawyer of considerable reputation. Col. Carrow,[7] who was in Washington with Capt Rich, is sick.

I saw Dr. Page Monday. He said that Dr. Hand,[8] Med. Director, wrote him Sunday that it was perfectfully awful in Newbern. That the dead house was full and that they were still dying. All well.

In haste, Your brother,
John A. Hedrick.

---

[1] James West Bryan (1805-1864) was a state senator from Carteret County in 1835-1836 and a delegate to the 1835 state constitutional convention. *Dictionary of North Carolina Biography*, s.v. "Bryan, James West."

[2] Ann Mary Washington Bryan (1814-1864). *Dictionary of North Carolina Biography*, s.v. "Bryan, James West."

[3] Maj. Henry T. Lawson of the Second Massachusetts Heavy Artillery died October 2, 1864. Heitman, *Historical Register*, 2:120; *Roll of Honor*, vol. 10 (1866; reprint, Baltimore: Genealogical Publishing, 1994), 163.

[4] Lt. Col. Henry M. Stone was commander at Fort Macon earlier in 1864. *OR*, ser. 1, 33:485, 1058.

[5] A Dr. Wilson, U.S. Army surgeon, died on September 24, 1864, and was buried in New Bern. *Roll of Honor*, 10:169.

[6] John F. Jones (b. ca. 1806) operated a hotel in New Bern. Eighth Census, 1860: Craven County.

[7] Samuel T. Carrow was a colonel in the Beaufort County militia, who, according to militia records, had "gone to [the] enemy." *OR*, ser. 2, 2:1548; Roster of the Militia of N. Carolina, Adjutant General's Papers, State Archives, Division of Archives and History, Raleigh.

[8] Daniel Wilden Hand, a surgeon, was medical director of the Military District of North Carolina. He was brevetted lieutenant colonel on November 1, 1864, for his efforts during the yellow fever epidemic in New Bern. Heitman, *Historical Register*, 1:497. For Dr. Hand's report on yellow fever in New Bern and Beaufort, see *Medical and Surgical History of the Civil War*, 6:679-682.

Duke
Custom House,
Beaufort, N.C.
October 8th. 1864,

Dear Brother:

I have written you two letters this week but as the Str. Carolina is going out to-day I thought that I would write again. The Yellow Fever is still raging in this place and Newbern. It is estimated that about a thousand have died in Newbern with it. There have been a good many cases of it here but most of them have been persons who have come from Newbern. The weather has been very dry for the last month and I think that we would have a great deal of sickness even if we had no Yellow Fever, and a great many deaths which are charged to the Yellow Fever may have been from other diseases. Quite a number have had the black vomit before they died.

Col. Amory,[1] Comdg. this District, his wife, F.W. Hamilton, of the firm of W.C. Hamilton &Co. of Newbern, Wm. P. Marshal of this place, Misses Dill[2] and Morse,[3] and several others have died in this place since I wrote last. Dr. Bellangie,[4] Surgeon in charge of Mansfield Hospital, Morehead City died day before yesterday. I think that there are between 80 & 100 cases of sickness in this place.

We have had nothing latter than the 1st. inst.

Write often.
John A. Hedrick.

---

[1] Col. Thomas J. C. Amory (b. ca. 1830) of the Seventeenth Massachusetts Infantry was commander of the Sub-district of Beaufort, August 1-14, 1863, and June 27 to October 7, 1864. He died October 8, 1864. Boatner, *Civil War Dictionary*, 12-13; Dyer, *Compendium of the War of the Rebellion*, 1:393.

[2]Vienna [Vianna] Dill (b. 1848), daughter of S. L. and Elizabeth Dill, died October 6, 1864. *Cemetery Records of Carteret County*, 151; Eighth Census, 1860: Carteret County.

[3]In a later letter, Hedrick mentions the death of "one of Dave Morse's daughters." According to 1860 census records, D. W. Morse (b. ca. 1812), a mechanic, had four daughters and a son, David, age ten. While no record of the death of one of the Morse daughters has been located, a David W. Morse (b. 1851) died of yellow fever on October 16, 1864. John A. Hedrick to Benjamin S. Hedrick, November 5, 1864, Hedrick Papers, Duke Special Collections, in this volume; Eighth Census, 1860: Carteret County; *Cemetery Records of Carteret County*, 168.

[4]James B. Bellangee, surgeon, U.S. Volunteers, died October 6, 1864. Heitman, *Historical Register*, 1:208.

Duke
Beaufort, N.C.
Oct. 13th. 1864,

Dear Brother:

Your letter of the 2nd. inst. was received yesterday. Your previous letter was dated the 25th. ult. I can easily account for the delay of your letters. There are so many routes for them to come. They are first sent to the N.Y.D.P.O. and then if there is a steamer bound to this place or Newbern, they come straight through; if not they are sent to Fortress Monroe where they wait till a steamer does come. Although the papers state that no Washington mail was destroyed on the Fawn, I am of the opinion that some of your letters were destroyed on her. I know that some of my N.Y. Tribunes during that time are missing.

We had a heavy white frost Sunday night, but the Yellow Fever still continues. Seven people died in this place night before last, and I have not heard any reports this morning. In Newbern the deaths are much fewer than they were two weeks ago, but I think that this is owing to there being so few there now. All who could have left the place.

The weather now is pleasantly cool. We had a nice rain last night, and it looks as if it would rain some more today. We have had a very long dry spell. The wells are nearly all dry. There has been no equinoctial gale here.

Col. Heaton and his family are getting better though neither he nor his assistants will resume work in the next ten days. There is not much doing in the way of shipments, either outward or inward, but I still have my hands full making up my quarterly returns.

The Rebs destroyed the Croatoan Light House last Tuesday was a week.[1]

Papers to the 5th. have been received though I have seen nothing later than the 3rd. All is quiet here in military affairs. Admiral Farrigut is expected to relieve Lee soon.[2]

Mr. Norcum's family are well except Mrs. Norcum, who has been complaining a little for the last two days.

My health is good.

> Write often,
> John A. Hedrick.

---

[1] On the night of October 4, 1864, Confederates blew up the lighthouse located at the confluence of the Albemarle and Croatan Sounds. *ORN*, ser. 1, 10:529-530.

[2] Rear Adm. David Dixon Porter replaced Samuel P. Lee as commander of the North Atlantic Blockading Squadron on October 12, 1864. Poor health prevented Rear Adm. David G. Farragut from taking the position. Long, *Day by Day*, 583.

> *Duke*
> Beaufort, N.C.
> Oct. 14th. 1864,

Dear Brother:

Your letter of the 6th. inst. reached me yesterday. I wrote you yesterday morning but as the Albany is going out to-day I thought that I would let you know that we were all well. I think that the Yellow Fever in this place is somewhat abating. I did not hear of any deaths here yesterday and there were only two the day before. The weather is beautiful and pleasant. It was cold enough for frost last night though I did not notice any this morning.

Young Mr. Blakeslee son of the Asst. Special Agent Treas. Dept. is very low and will probably die to-day. Capt. Treadway's son is also sick but not thought dangerously. I am still gaining in flesh. I weighed 122 yesterday.

I received yesterday New York papers of the 10th. inst.

Mr. Bible went north a few days ago and said that he would visit you. If he should call, tell him that his Schr. the Kerne was lost at sea last week, and also one of the men. The rest were picked up by a Gunboat.

> Your brother,
> John A. Hedrick.

Duke
Beaufort, N.C.
October 18th. 1864,

Dear Brother:

Your letter of the 9th. inst reached me to-day, and also a Chronicle the date of which I did not notice. I would be very glad to receive the Chronicle as you propose, and I will send you the Times in return for it as soon as it resumes publication. The editor has gone north on a visit and stopped the paper during the continuance of the Yellow Fever. We have had several frosts, but the Yellow Fever does not seem to improve much. Dr. Babbit, Surgeon, 1st. N.C.U. Vols died yesterday evening with it, and Dr. Steadman, who was in Washington trying to get the Mail contract, is quite low with it. Mr. Blakeslee's son died last week, and Henry C. Jones,[1] a lawyer from Newbern died Sunday.

The disease is said to be on the increase in Newbern especially among the negro camps.

I am still in good health and hope to escape the fever. I returned yesterday from a sail in the Cutter to the Steamer Aphrodite wrecked about 15 miles north of Cape Lookout. We left here Saturday 12 M. & returned yesterday Monday about 3 P.M. I went more to get a little recreation than any thing else.

Mr. Norcum's family is well except Alice, who is complaining of sick head-ache. Col. Taylor sends his compliments to you and says that if you will get him a good fat office without much to do, he will furnish you with a wife should yours die. That is he expects his present wife will outlive him and he will will you the widow. She is under 30 and he is over 62. (By the way she is in a rather corpulent condition at present.)

Ask Sister Ellen whether she has answered all of my letters.

Write often,
Your Brother,
John A. Hedrick.

---

[1] Henry C. Jones (b. ca. 1828). Eighth Census, 1860: Craven County.

Duke
Beaufort, N.C.
October 20th. 1864,

Dear Brother:

Yours of the 12th. inst. was received to-day. We have had several white frosts but I cannot see much alteration in the Yellow Fever. There are fewer cases in Newbern than there were a couple of weeks ago.

There is no military news to write. Mrs. Norcum celabrated the 17 anniversary of her marriage with a baked chicken & a raisin pudding.

We are all well except Joe, who has some fever to-day, but is not much sick.

Col. Taylor is getting somewhat tired of boarding vessels and says that he wishes Uncle Abe to give him a consulship.

> Write often,
> Your brother,
> John A. Hedrick.

Duke
Beaufort, N.C.
October 22nd. 1864,

Dear Brother:

I have not time to write but as the steamer Petrol leaves in the morning and the mail closes in a few minutes I thought I would let you know that all is right.

The weather is clear and cold. There is no war news.

There were two deaths in this place last night and a few are sick but I think the Yellow Fever is abating.

> Your brother,
> John A. Hedrick

Duke
Beaufort, N.C.
October 25th. 1864

Dear Brother:

I send herewith a petition from Col. James H. Taylor, praying Mr. Lincoln, for an appointment to some office which will enable him to live consistent with his social position.

I have previously given you about as complete account of Col. Taylor as I think necessary. You know from what I have said the kind of man <which> he is. The Colonel says that he is a distant relation of Mr. Goodloe. He says that one of his ancestors was named Goodloe Harper. I wish you and Mr. Goodloe would do your best to get the Colonel into a good consulate because I believe that he deserves it.

We are all well. Mrs. Norcum has just received a letter from her Sister Cornelia, dated in August. Everything bears a gloomy aspect in Lexington. All the young men are in the army.

Your brother,
John A. Hedrick.

Duke
Beaufort, N.C.
Oct. 28th. 1864,

Dear Brother:

Your letter of the 16th. inst. inclosing Helper's, and that of the 18th. have been received, the former yesterday and the latter to-day.

Every thing is quiet in this State. Genl. Palmer and suit arrived here from the North yesterday.

The sickness in Newbern is said to have pretty much stopped, but it is worse here now than it was when I wrote last. There were seven buried yesterday. The weather is quite cool but I think we have had no frost during the last week.

We have New York papers to the 24th. inst. Sheridan's fight with Early is given in the 20th. and 21st. & 22nd.[1]

Mr. Helper writes me a very short letter & gives me no news nor any thing relating to his business.

We are all in good health except slight colds.

Write often,
Your brother,
John A. Hedrick.

---

[1] This is a reference to the Battle of Cedar Creek, Va., October 19, 1864. The Confederates enjoyed success early in the day but were soundly defeated in a late afternoon Union counterattack. Long, *Day by Day*, 585.

Duke
Beaufort, N.C.
Nov. 2nd. 1864,

Dear Brother:

Your letter of the 25th. ult. in which you mention your having been at Mr. & Mrs. Underwood's and say that you had not received a letter from me for more than a week, came to hand day before yesterday. I have been writing about twice a week for the last month. The mails are very irregular now.

Mr. Norcum's family and myself are in first rate health.

I have no particular news to write though there are some rumors afloat. There was an expedition sent up the Roanoke River last week to destroy the Ram, and it was reported to-day by passengers from Roanoke Island that it had accomplished its object and <destroyed> captured Plymouth.[1] The first part of the story I think is correct, but the last is probably premature. Genl. Palmer and Staff arrived here last week.

Give my best regards to Messrs Pigott & Goodloe,

Write often,
Your brother,
John A. Hedrick.

---

[1] On October 28, 1864, Union raiders led by Lt. William B. Cushing used a torpedo to sink the CSS *Albemarle* in the Roanoke River at Plymouth. On October 31, a Union flotilla subdued the Confederate batteries at Plymouth, and the town returned to Northern hands. Elliot, *Ironclad of the Roanoke*, ch. 15.; *ORN*, ser. 1, 11:11, 12-15.

Duke
Beaufort, N.C.
Nov. 5th. 1864,

Dear Brother:

I wrote you day before yesterday and told you that the expedition up Roanoke River was reported to have destroyed the Ram and retaken Plymouth, and that I thought the first part of the story was correct but that the latter was probably premature. Parties have since arrived from Roanoke Island, and say that those who returned from the expedition reported at Roanoke Island that the Ram had been blown up by a torpedo, and that Plymouth was occupied by the Union forces. After the Ram was destroyed I guess they did not meet with much opposition.

We have had quite a storm from the southwest during the last 24 hours and it is now very cold for the season. Overcoats and gloves come in place to-day. The health of the town is much better. If you see Mr. Pigott you can tell him that the following old citizens of this place have died since the fever commenced, viz:

John P.C. Davis, Mrs. Horatio Willis,[1] Mrs. Isaac Ramsey,[2] Mr. Geo. W. Morse,[3] Capt. Sam Howland,[4] Miss Vienna Dill, one of Dave Morse's daughters and Capt. Thomas' maiden sister[5] whose Christian name I have forgotten. Also J.S. Pender[6] who was in Washington last summer.

I presume that I will get my commissions on Lt. Ho. Disbursements as it has been allowed on my last estimate.

Write often

Your brother
John A. Hedrick.

---

[1] Abigail Hancock Willis (b. ca. 1808) died on October 12, 1864. Eighth Census, 1860: Carteret County; *Cemetery Records of Carteret County*, 165; Marriage Bond of Horatio H. Willis and Abigail Hancock, November 29, 1832, Carteret County, State Archives, Division of Archives and History, Raleigh.

[2] Charity Jones Ramsey (b. 1811) died on October 9, 1864. *Cemetery Records of Carteret County*, 161; Marriage Bond of Isaac Ramsey and Charity F. Jones, November 27, 1833, Carteret County, State Archives, Division of Archives and History, Raleigh.

[3] G. W. Morse (b. ca. 1820) was a mechanic in Beaufort. Eighth Census, 1860: Carteret County.

[4] This is possibly a reference to Samuel Howland (b. ca. 1820), a fisherman from Smyrna, a community in Carteret County, northeast of Beaufort. Eighth Census, 1860: Carteret County.

⁵This is possibly a reference to Nancy Thomas (b. 1799) who died on October 14, 1864. *Cemetery Records of Carteret County*, 164.

⁶Josiah Solomon Pender (b. 1819) led the capture of Fort Macon on April 11, 1861. He was dismissed from the Confederate military in December 1861 for being absent without leave due to his wife's eventually fatal illness. Pender then served as a blockade-runner until his death on October 25, 1864. *Cemetery Records of Carteret County*, 160; *Dictionary of North Carolina Biography*, s.v. "Pender, Josiah Solomon."

Duke
Beaufort, N.C.
Nov. 9th. 1864,

Dear Brother:

I have had nothing from you later than the 25th. ult. In fact we have had no mails in the last 10 days. Papers however of the 4th. have been received but I have seen nothing later than the 3rd. This had nothing in it of much importance besides the sinking of the Ram Albemarle, which was rather an old tale to us.

Since the taking of Plymouth the Rebs have evacuated Washington.

There seems to be considerable activity in the way of blockade running. Our vessels have captured 13 in the last 10 days. It is reported that the Tallahassee was off here day before yesterday, and was chased first by the Gunboat Lilian who mistook her for a blockade runner, but hauled off when she found out that She was a Prizateer, then by the Osceola under similar circumstances and with like result, and lastly by the Montgomery who followed her up and fired into her but with what resulted has not been heard. All well.

Your brother
John A. Hedrick.

Duke
Beaufort, N.C.
4 P.M. Nov. 12th. 1864,

Dear Brother:

I received to-day your letters of the 28th October and the 1st. November. Also two batches of Chronicles.

I have just learned that Uncle Abe has carried, New York, Pennsylvania, Delaware, Maryland, Ohio, Iowa, Illinois, Michigan, Wisconsin, Indiana and Minnesota by pretty good majorities.[1]

I was taken sick yesterday evening about 4 o'clock. I was first taking with purging which was followed by vomiting. with a slight pain in my stomach. I have had no fever and no chill worth naming, though my teeth chattered as I was going home about 5 1/2 o'clock. This morning I took a dose of salts, which has operated twice, and my bowels feel easy now, though they are still loose. I slept very well last night and have been able to attend to my business to-day. Mr. Norcum's whole family were taken in the same way and also the cook. I think that we must have eaten or drank something poisonous. This morning when awake I felt a pain across the top of my head and the rest are affected in the same way. Alice seems to be the worst off at present. She complains of violent pains through her head. Mrs. Norcum, Anna[2] & the cook have pretty much recovered. Mr. Norcum still complains but he is much better and has been in his store all day, though not able to do much business.

The gunboat Mercidita sails soon and the mail is about to close. So good bye for this time.

Your brother
John A. Hedrick.

---

[1] In defeating Democrat George B. McClellan in the 1864 presidential election, Lincoln carried every state except Kentucky, New Jersey, and Delaware, and won 212 electoral votes to his opponent's 21. Allan Nevins, *The War for the Union*, vol. 4, *The Organized War to Victory, 1864-1865* (New York: Charles Scribner's Sons, 1971), 140.

[2] Ann Norcum (b. ca. 1858). Eighth Census, 1860: Carteret County.

Duke
Beaufort, N.C.
Monday, Nov. 14th. 1864,

Dear Brother:

I wrote you Saturday that we were all sick. We have all recovered and are now as well as ever.

The weather is quite cold this morning. There is no news of interest to write. My visit this year to Washington I think extremely doubtful.

Business not very brisk at present. The sickness has very much abated in this place.

The long expected fleet from Hampton Roads to take Wilmington has not yet made its appearance.

Every body seems well pleased with the result of the late election except Mrs. Norcum, who has slavery on the brain so strong that she could not be satisfied with anything opposing the peculiar institution.

> Write often
> Your brother,
> John A. Hedrick.

> *Duke*
> Beaufort, N.C.
> Nov. 22nd. 1864,

Dear Brother:

Your letter of the 9th. and Johnny's letter were received a few days ago. Johnnie writes a very good letter, and it contains no nonsense, as was expected by you.

Our folks are becoming somewhat pacified again, that is Mrs. Norcum and Alice. They have been mad with me ever since I received Helper's[1] letter, and have hardly spoken to me since then. Last night Mrs. N. condescended to write me the inclosed note, and this morning, she was so far molified as to speak to me as I came through the house. She is at times what she subscribes herself. She had gotten a permit to send John Skinner,[2] one of Mr. Norcum's cousins a few goods, and had omitted to put the bolt of sheeting in the bill. After I had gone to my office in the evening she wrote me the note. When I asked whether she wished to read Helper's letter she said no, that he was a man she wished in hell, and that she believed we were all tared with the same stick, (You, myself and Helper.). I can make her rave at any time I wish. I sometimes do it for amusement but then I don't think it right, while I am living in the same house.

Genl. Palmer is in command of North Carolina.

I have received the Chronicles down to the 13th. inst.

There is no war news to write. We have northern papers of the 17th. The Yellow Fever I think has stopped as I have not heard of any new cases. Mr. D.H.L. Bell[3] arrived here on the Carolina Sunday. He said that he called on you in Washington.

> Write often
> Your brother
> John A. Hedrick

[1] Hinton Rowan Helper.

[2] John Skinner (b. ca. 1821) was a farmer living near Hertford, N.C. Eighth Census, 1860: Perquimans County.

[3] D. H. L. Bell (b. ca. 1823) was a farmer and turpentine maker from Shepherdsville, N.C. He was a census taker for much of Carteret County in the 1860 federal census. Eighth Census, 1860: Carteret County.

Duke
Beaufort, N.C.
Nov. 25th. 1864,

Dear Brother:

Your letter of the 13th. inst. containing Sister Ellen's photographs reached me about three days ago, and another under date of the 17th came to hand yesterday. The Chronicles have been received to the 18th. inclusive.

Yesterday was Thanksgiving day but I did not get any turkey. I closed my office against the public but worked in doors all day. The weather is quite cold and has been so for the last three days. I am now writing with my old thick buckskin gloves on. My fire went out last night, and I have not had another made yet.

There is no local news to write. The Yellow Fever has entirely ceased at this place, but I notice in the N.Y. papers that J.R.C. Mood who lived here during the Summer and left here about two weeks ago died in Baltimore on his way to New York. He had been sick before he left but had pretty much recovered. It seems that removal to a colder climate operates badly on those having the Yellow Fever. There have been several convalescent persons who died on their way north.

I am in excellent health.

Write often and long letters.
Your brother,
John A. Hedrick.

Duke
Beaufort, N.C.
Nov. 30th. 1864,

Dear Brother:

Your letters of the 20th. & 23rd. were received Saturday and yesterday.

It seems that you have to give more for turkey than we do. We are not allowed to give more than $1.50 a piece.

We are all well except Alice, who has diphtheria very bad.

The weather is quite pleasant and not near so cold as it was last week. I was in Newbern yesterday and saw Dr. Page. He had an attack of the Yellow Fever but has entirely recovered and is looking very well.

New York papers of the 26th. have been received. The news from Sherman seems favorable.[1]

There is no departmental news to write.

Write often
Your brother
John A. Hedrick.

---

[1] Sherman's army left Atlanta, beginning the march to the sea, on November 15, 1864. They reached Savannah on December 10 and occupied the city on December 21. Long, *Day by Day*, 597, 608, 613.

Duke
Beaufort, N.C.
Dec. 3rd. 1864

Dear Brother:

Alice Norcum died to-day at 11:15 A.M. of Diptheria Rest all well. The mail closes immidiately.

Your brother
John A. Hedrick

Duke
Beaufort, N.C.
December 9th. 1864,

Dear Brother:

I have received yours of the 1st. inst. which is the latest. We have New York papers of the 4th.

We are all well and the weather is quite cold this morning.

There seems to be no local news to write. An expedition[1] has left Newbern for some place up the country, perhaps to cut the Rail Road near Goldsboro. I still have an abundance of work to do and the Department has given me the disbursements for expenditures under the Coastwise Intercourse Regulations. This will be a pretty large undertaking.

I am glad to see my labors appreciated at Washington though Hcaton did not recognise them in his report to the Secretary last spring.

Write often
Your brother
John A. Hedrick.

---

[1] An expedition left for Kinston on December 9, 1864, but was unable to ford the Neuse River because of high water. *OR*, 42, pt. 3:1014.

Duke
Beaufort, N.C.
December 17th. 1864,

Dear Brother:

Your long letter was received a few days ago and yesterday the Chronicles of the 7th. & 8th. came to hand, one of them containing a small package of something which I do not know what is.

The Harbor is full of coal schooners and gunboats and Monitors. Three Monitors came in day before yesterday. Admiral Porter is here, and some say Genl. Butler also.

I understand that the Kinston and Roanoke expeditions have returned without accomplishing much. We lost one Gunboat & a Tug up the Roanoke.[1]

Every thing seems to be astir in this Department but very little has been done yet.

I weigh 127 lbs.— a gain of 12 lbs. in 2 months,

Write often
Your brother,
John A. Hedrick.

---

[1] The USS *Otsego* and the tugboat *Bazely* were sunk by torpedoes near Jamesville, N.C., on December 9 and 10, respectively. They were part of an unsuccessful expedition to capture Rainbow Bluff and a ram believed to be under construction at Halifax. *ORN*, ser. 1, 11:160-161; *Civil War Naval Chronology*, pt. 4: 144.

Duke
Beaufort, N.C.
7 P.M. Dec. 25th. 1864,

Dear Brother:

Your letter of the 10th. inst., which I believe was the last received, giving directions for using Chlorae of Potash, which came in a batch of Chronicles, came to hand last week. I have received two batches of Chronicles since I have had a letter from you. The latest Chronicle is the 14th.

New York papers of the 21st. have been brought to this place, but I have seen nothing later than the 17th. which is the date of the latest mail matter received. The news from Genl. Thomas[1] was very good, but Sherman's reported capture of Savannah was not confirmed.

Fort McAllister however had been taken.[2] The most important thing now of foot in this State is the expedition against Wilmington. The ball opened yesterday at about 2 A.M. by the explosion of a powder <pow> boat, which was set off near Fort Fisher for the purpose of dismounting the guns. The Gunboat Keystone State came up this morning and I understand that the experiment was a failure. There are various rumors afloat to-day relative to bombardment of Fort Fisher. One is that the Fort has been taken and another that our boats had silenced the Fort but had not taken it. We have heard heavy firing all day in the direction of Wilmington, and it is still kept up to-night but not so fast as during the day. I would therefore conclude that the Fort had not been captured.[3] The weather has been very calm to-day. Genl. Butler left here yesterday morning, and Admiral Porter had preceded him about three days. The transports left here with troops in company with Admiral Porter, but I believe all returned Thursday & Friday on account of the storm. They left again yesterday morning. Col. Taylor said that there were about 10,000 negro Soldiers in the expedition.[4] The Iron-clads did not return with the Transports but I understand that they all weathered the storm.

Christmas has come & is nearly gone. We had a very fine turkey for dinner, but as it was Sunday we could not have much fun. Every thing passed off very quietly in town and to-night you would /not/ know that it was Christmas.

Johnnie wrote to me for some fire-arms and swords for Christmas and as this is a poor place to obtain those articles I had intended to send him money to get them for himself in Washington but I have not had time. I therefore inclose /him/ a $2 ^{00}/$_{100}$ Greenback as a Christmas present. I send also $2 ^{00}/$_{100}$ /each/ for Charlie, Alice, Jeannie & Wm. Adam.

Outward shipments have been quite brisk during this month, though the inward shipments are rather on the decline. I hope by the next time I write I may have the pleasure of informing you that Wilmington is in possession of the United States forces. I do not well know what effect the capture of Wilmington will have on this port, though I think that so long as the Coastwise Regulations are continued in force the business of this <place> office will be increased thereby.

Mr. Norcum's family is as well as usual. It is getting near bed time, so I must bid you good night.

A merry Christmas to you all,

Write often,
Your brother,
John A. Hedrick.

---

[1] Union forces under Maj. Gen. George H. Thomas defeated Gen. John Bell Hood's Army of Tennessee at the Battle of Nashville, December 15-16, 1864. Boatner, *Civil War Dictionary*, 579-582.

[2] Fort McAllister, located on the Ogeechee River near Savannah, Ga., fell to Union forces on December 13, 1864. This enabled Sherman's army to rendezvous with the Union fleet. Long, *Day by Day*, 609-610.

[3] In this attempt to take Fort Fisher, which was planned as a prelude to the capture of Wilmington, Maj. Gen. Benjamin F. Butler commanded an army of about sixty-five hundred and Rear Adm. David D. Porter a fleet of fifty ships. Butler suggested beginning the attack by detonating a powder-filled ship near the fort. At 1:40 A.M. on December 24, the *Louisiana*, packed with explosives, blew up close to the stronghold with little effect. Later in the morning the navy bombarded the fort but again without inflicting serious damage. When Butler, whose army had landed north of the fort, discovered this fact and that a Confederate army was to

his rear in Wilmington, he called for a retreat. The campaign would be resumed in January 1865. Barrett, *Civil War in North Carolina*, 262-271.

[4]The 1st, 4th, 5th, 6th, 27th, 30th, 37th, 39th, and 107th U.S. Colored Infantry Regiments participated in the Fort Fisher campaign. Dyer, *Compendium of the War of the Rebellion*, 1:823.

1865

Duke
Beaufort, N.C.
Jan. 2nd. 1865,

Dear Brother:

Your letter of the 23rd. is the last received.

We are all well except that I have occasional spells of Rheumatism. It takes me mostly by night and spoils my rest. I have had it in my left hip for about two weeks. It is not very painful but comes on me usually if I do not take enough exercise the previous day, about 3 o'clock in the morning. Constant mental labor seems to bring it on. To-day I have been very busy, and I can feel it now, although I did take a good walk this evening. When at Newbern last week, I asked Dr. Page what was good for it, & he told me that he was troubled with it in his shoulder, and that the best thing that he could do for it was to iron it out with a hot sad iron. On my return I did not try ironing but I did what was next to it, I roasted the hide off my rump at a nice hot coal fire. This gave me relief for a few days, but the remedy does not seem to be lasting. I had a little touch of the pain last night, and to-night I think that I shall have it still worse.

Col. Taylor's wife presented him with a New Year's present yesterday morning in the shape of a boy. He was immediately named James Henry after his Father.

I am sorry to hear that Mr. Helper is not doing as well as he would wish. The expedition to Wilmington so far has proved a failure. It seems to have gone off half cocked. There was certainly a want of concert of action. It is reported that the attack will be renewed in a few days. Quite a number of the vessels returned to this place and are lying outside of the bar. Chronicles continue to come.

Write often,
Your brother
John A. Hedrick.

Duke
Beaufort, N.C.
Jan. 7th. 1865,

Dear Brother:

I received yesterday Sister Ellen's letter of the 28th. ult. and yours of the 1st. inst. and also Chronicles to the 31st. ult.

We are all as well as usual with the exception of having Chicken Pox, Sore Eyes & Rheumatism. Mr. Norcum's children all have had the Chicken Pox but are now pretty much well of it. I commenced breaking out with it a couple of days ago and I think that it is now in the height of its glory. At least I hope so. My eyes are considerably inflamed but I apprehend no danger from them.

The Rheumatism gave me another sharp call last night, but I managed to kick it out of the bed. The weather is continually changing and hence the attacks of Rheumatism.

Prof. W.C. Kerr is State Geologist. Brother Triplett[1] is on the south Iredell Circuit. Randolph Thomas[2] of this place is Secretary of State of North Carolina. There has been no further move on Wilmington. Quite a number of the Gunboats still lie off the bar.

Your brother
John A. Hedrick

---

[1] Thomas L. Triplett (b. ca. 1831), a minister, was married to John Hedrick's sister Martha (b. ca. 1835). Ninth Census, 1870: Rowan County.

[2] Charles Randolph Thomas (1827-1891), a Beaufort native, was North Carolina's secretary of state from January to August 1865. *Dictionary of North Carolina Biography*, s.v. "Thomas, Charles Randolph"; Cheney, *North Carolina Government*, 181, 193.

Duke
Beaufort, N.C.
Jan. 16th. 1865,

Dear Brother:

Yours of the 8th. was received to-day. Also Chronicles from the 1st. to the 6th. inst.

We have New York papers to the 13th. but they contain very little news.

The expedition left here for Wilmington last week, and was landed about 10000 strong on Saturday. A combined land and naval attack was fixed for Sunday. There is a rumor in town this evening that Fort Fisher has been taken, but I think it premature.[1]

I have not been troubled with the Rheumatism in several days.

The Tax Commissioners have arrived but I have not seen them.

Dr. Page was in to-day but I only had time to shake hands with him. Every thing is going pretty well now.

Write often,
John A. Hedrick.

(Over)

Tuesday morning.
Jan. 17th. 1865,

Dear Brother:

Last night about 2 o'clock three very heavy explosions were heard in the direction of Wilmington. As we do not know of any powder having been sent there, it is thought that the Rebs have blown up Fort Fisher.[2]

I would be glad if you would send me your accounts against me. I wish to pay what I owe while money is plenty.

Your brother,
John A. Hedrick.

---

[1] On January 13, 1865, Rear Adm. David D. Porter's Union fleet began a bombardment of Fort Fisher, while a force of eight thousand, commanded by Maj. Gen. Alfred H. Terry, landed north of the fort in preparation for an attack on the Confederate fortress. By the evening of January 15, the fort was in Union hands. *ORN*, ser. 1, 11:432-435; *OR*, ser. 1, 46, pt. 1:396-399.

[2] A magazine at Fort Fisher accidentally exploded on January 16. A court of inquiry found that the explosion may have been caused by drunken Union troops celebrating the capture of the fort and plundering the magazine area. The accident caused approximately 130 casualties. *OR*, ser. 1, 46, pt. 1:401, 430-431.

Duke
Beaufort, N.C.
Jan. 24th. 1865,

Dear Brother:

I have had nothing from you since I wrote last.

I am well with the exception of a pretty large boil on my left temple, which swells my eye nearly shut. I have not been troubled with the Rheumatism in some time. I roast my feet and back at the fire every night and I think that this has cured me.

The news from Wilmington is very good. We have taken two blockade runners since the fall of the Forts.[1]

I guess that Genl. Butler has been convinced by this time that the forts could be taken by an assault.

In haste,
Your brother
John A. Hedrick

---

[1] Rear Adm. David D. Porter capitalized on the blockade-runners' unawareness of the recent fall of the Confederate forts at the mouth of the Cape Fear River. By maintaining the usual signal lights and lying in wait, the Union navy captured the *Stag* and the *Charlotte* on January 20, 1865. *Civil War Naval Chronology*, pt. 5:18, 21.

Duke
Beaufort, N.C.
Jany 30th. 1865,

Dear Brother:

Yours of the 15th. inst. was received last week.

There has been very little going on in a military way here during last week. The weather has been exceedingly cold for this latitude during the last 4 days. Gen. Grant was in town yesterday but I did not see him.[1] He went all round town on foot. We can't find out who commands us. Some say Foster and others Palmer.[2]

My receipts from Commercial Intercourse during last month were a little over $10000 $^{00}/_{100}$. Besides I collected $3712 $^{00}/_{100}$ Military Tax, on which I received $112 $^{00}/_{100}$ commissions. I have entirely recovered from all my afflictions.

I was in Newbern Saturday night. I saw Dr. Page's brother but not the Doctor. Norcum has been confined to his house during the greater part of last week, Complaint, cold.

Your brother,
John A. Hedrick.

---

[1] Lt. Gen. U. S. Grant and Brig. Gen. I. N. Palmer met in Beaufort. Grant had come from City Point, Va., while Palmer had traveled by train from New Bern. *North Carolina Times* (New Bern), February 3, 1865; *OR*, ser. 1, 46, pt. 2:267.

[2] The Department of Virginia and North Carolina was divided on January 31, 1865. Brig. Gen. I. N. Palmer headed the re-created Department of North Carolina until February 9, when Maj. Gen. J. M. Schofield took command. Palmer had been commander of the District of North Carolina, within the Department of Virginia and North Carolina, since April 28, 1864. Dyer, *Compendium of the War of the Rebellion*, 1:357, 390, 392.

Duke
Beaufort, N.C.
Feby 4th. 1865,

Dear Brother:

Your letter of the 22nd. ult. containing a statement of our accounts was received a few days ago. I have our old accounts and as soon as I can look them up I will send you a statement of my indebtedness to you together with the money due.

There is no news of importance in this department. We are expecting a large number of troops but they seem a long time in reaching us. There are no gunboats here now, and it is understood that the Naval Store house will be removed to Smithville.[1]

Receipts have been quite brisk lately. Day before yesterday I collected $3600 $^{00}/_{100}$. There are more merchant schooners here than usual. We have had a long spell of very cold weather but it is mild again. All well.

Your brother,
John A. Hedrick.

(over)

P.S. There may be some attempt in Congress to move the Custom House to Morehead City. I think this premature though I expect Morehead sometime will be the principal depot on this harbor. The great objection now is that the town is about ³/₄ of a mile from this place after going over would have to walk that distance. Besides the Post Officc and all the other public buildings are here.

Your brother,
John A. Hedrick

---

[1] Smithville was the name of the town in Brunswick County now known as Southport. During the Civil War, the Confederate stronghold Fort Caswell was located on Oak Island, off Smithville. On January 16, 1865, the fort's defenders blew up the fortification and withdrew, and soon thereafter, the Union navy occupied what remained of the fort. Powell, *Gazetteer*, 466; *OR*, ser. 1, 46, pt. 1:401; Robert E. Roberts, *Encyclopedia of Historic Forts: The Military, Pioneer, and Trading Posts of the United States* (New York: Macmillan, 1988), 611.

Duke
Beaufort, N.C.
Feb. 5th. 1865,

Sir:

I have before me yours of the 19th. Nov, 1862, and January 22nd. 1865, from which our accounts would stands as follows;

Balance due you Nov. 19th. 1862,	$211.91
Amount of subsequent payments by you	$139.35
	$351.26
Less amount of remittance by me	$250.00
Bal. due you	$101.26

I send herein one hundred and twenty-five dollars, ($125 ⁰⁰/₁₀₀), which you /will/ please accept for the above amount and your trouble.

I did not expend any thing for you on account of the refugees.

The weather is mild but changeable. This morning it was as warm as a Spring day, at noon it was cloudy with the appearance of rain or snow, and this evening it is clear with a moderately cold north west wind.

No news from the north later than the 27th. ult. has been received. The mails must be stopped by the ice. I heard that the Chesapeake was frozen so that communication had been stopped with that place and Old Point. The Canal in this State has been frozen over for some time.

I have just had a talk with Mr. Cordell Act. Lt. Ho. Inspector for this district, who returned from the mouth of Cape Fear River yesterday. He says the beach around Fort Fisher is covered with shot & shell. Out of some seventy odd guns on the Fort only one or two escaped unhurt. They still have occasional skirmishes with the Rebs, and /the/ only way to keep them away is to send a regiment of negro troops against them. The Rebs can't stand a charge of negro troops. There are 5 light draft Gunboats and one monitor in the mouth of the River, and the larger vessels outside of the bar. The depth of water on the bar at low water is 8 feet, and the tide rises about 4 feet, but /you/ cannot depend upon more than 11 feet of water. When the wind is S.E. there is a very heavy sea on the bar, so that a vessel is in danger of striking even with 8 feet draught. The Steamer in which Mr. Cordell came up struck drawing less than 8 feet, coming out. There are about 7000 troops in and around Fort Fisher.

They are repairing the Forts as fast as possible. Our gunboats in the River lie about 2 miles below Fort Anderson, which is some 10 miles below Wilmington. Mr. Cordell thinks that it will /not/ be hard to take this Fort by sending 1000 men from Smithville to the rear of the Fort while the gunboats attack it in the Front.[1]

I saw Jas. H. Taylor Jr. to-day for the first time. He is quite a large boy of his age. The Colonel says that he grows from the time he leaves in the morning till he returns at night, perceptibly.

By the way how does the Colonel's consulship prosper?

When you write to Helper again tell him that if he is getting tired of his office, we will soon have some more collectorships to fill, which may suit him better. I think that he ought to be appointed Collector of Charleston, S.C. when we take the place.

Our expected troops have not arrived. I am in first rate health and a good Suit of Clothes, Cost $75. $^{00}/_{100}$

Your brother,
John A. Hedrick.

---

[1] Fort Anderson was constructed on the site of old Brunswick Town on the Cape Fear River. Union forces besieged the fort for a month before driving out the Confederate defenders with an intense bombardment on February 17-19, 1865. The fall of Fort Anderson opened the way for Union troops to occupy Wilmington. Roberts, *Encyclopedia of Historic Forts*, 607-608.

Duke
Beaufort, N.C.
February 13th. 1865,

Dear Brother:

I received last week your letter of the 31st. ultimo and two batches of Chronicles.

We are all well with the exception of colds.

I did the largest business last month I ever did. Treasury receipts were over $13000 $^{00}/_{100}$.

As yet there has not been much done during this month in the way of shipments. Military movements always interfere with trade.

The weather is very cold. The thermometer in my office with a fire all last night stands this morning at 29°.

Col. Taylor wrote to you last week.

Your brother,
John A. Hedrick

Duke
Beaufort, N.C.
Feb. 19th. 1865,

Dear Brother:

Yours of the 7th. & the 11th. insts. were received last week. You seem to be in first rate humor. I am glad to find you so well pleased.

There is nothing of especial interest to write. The troops continue to arrive and the prospect bids fair for a movement up the country soon. Genl. Schofield is now in command of the Department of North Carolina but has not yet arrived at this place.

Genls Mayhear, Carter and several other new generals have gone up to Newbern.[1] Most of the troops are from Tennessee. The railroad from Morehead to Newbern is almost exclusively taken up by government freight.

We have news to-day that Sherman has taken Columbia, S.C.[2]

I have taken Col. Taylor into my office temporarily. The exposure was too great for him crossing the water and standing on decks of vessels all day.

Your brother,
John A. Hedrick.

[1] Brigadier Generals Thomas Francis Meagher (1823-1867) and Samuel Powhatan Carter (1819-1891) commanded Federal divisions that were soon to reinforce Maj. Gen. William T. Sherman. Warner, *Generals in Blue*, s.v. "Carter, Samuel Powhatan," "Meagher, Thomas Francis"; Boatner, *Civil War Dictionary*, 199-200.

[2] Sherman's army entered Columbia, S.C., on February 17, 1865. See Marion B. Lucas, *Sherman and the Burning of Columbia* (College Station: Texas A&M University Press, 1976).

Duke
Beaufort, N.C.
Feby 27th. 1865,

Dear Brother:

Your letter of the 19th. inst. was received last week.

All is going on swimmingly in this department. We have Wilmington and it was reported yesterday that Charleston was in our possession.[1]

Should the Department see fit I would be happy to be transferred to Wilmington with the condition that Col Taylor be my successor here.

If I can spare the time I think I will go to Wilmington in a few days, to look after the percentage on cargo of goods landed at Smithville in distress.

I have very little time to write and you must therefore excuse short letters.

Your brother
John A. Hedrick.

---

[1] Union troops entered Charleston, S.C., on February 18, and Wilmington, N.C., on February 22. Long, *Day by Day*, 640, 642.

Duke
Beaufort, N.C.
March 4th. 1865,

Dear Brother:

We are all well. Every thing seems to be prosperous in this Department.

The Harbor is again full of Gunboats, which are no longer needed at Wilmington.

There are various rumors as to a battle having been fought near Charlotte but nothing definite is known in relation to it.

About seven hundred refugees have arrived from Charleston.

I wish I could be with you to-day.

The weather is again warm but cloudy.

> Write often
> John A. Hedrick.

> *Duke*
> Beaufort, N.C.
> March 10th. 1865,

Sir:

Your letter of the 4th. was received yesterday.

Mr. Helper has not yet made his appearance.

Our forces have passed Kinston, and have had considerable fighting between that place and Goldsboro.[1] Those from Wilmington have left their base and have proceed to the interior but to what point is not known. It is presumed that all of our troops will form a junction about Goldsboro.

I was at Newbern day before yesterday and found pretty nearly all of the camps vacated. There are no soldiers from Carolina City to Newbern except a few darkies. The 1st. N.C. holds the Fort, this place and Carolina City and the 5th. R.I., out 400 men, are stationed in Newbern and the surrounding forts.

The young lady who was arrested for blockade running is Miss Emeline Pigott[2] of Calico Creek, near Morehead, and the stored closed belongs to Lowenberg & Bro. The Store has been reopened but Miss Pigott is still in jaol.

Col. Taylor is still in my office, but makes a rather poor clerk. It is very hard to hammer any thing into his head.

I am first rate health.

> Your brother
> John A. Hedrick.

---

[1] On March 8-10, 1865, at the Battle of Wise's Forks, also known as the Battle of Kinston, Confederates under Braxton Bragg slowed, but could not stop, the Union advance on Goldsboro. *OR*, ser. 1, 47, pt. 1:977-979, 1078-1079.

[2] Emeline Jamison Pigott (1836-1919), daughter of Levi W. and Eliza Pigott, was a Confederate spy who took food and supplies to Southern soldiers. She was arrested and imprisoned in New Bern for nearly a month. Her case never went to trial, and she was

released. Ruth Barbour, "Exploits of Emeline," in Kell, *North Carolina's Coastal Carteret County During the Civil War,* 121-123; Levi Woodbury Pigott Papers, State Archives; Edmund J. Cleveland Diary, February 9, 1865, Southern Historical Collection.

Duke
Beaufort, N.C.
March 12th. 1865,

Dear Brother:

Your letter of the 12th. inst. reached me yesterday You wish to know about a certain meeting, which purports to have been held in Craven County on the 18th. ult. I was not aware that any such a meeting had been held until I saw an article in the Newbern Times, denying that Heaton was editor of the Times, and giving a short extract from the resolutions contained in the World. This is all that I know about the meeting.

Mr. Heaton may not be the editor of the Times but he writes the greater part of he editorials for all that. I think that trade could be thrown open to the public with interest to the government. There is a law of Congress against it. I do not however see any fairness in authorizing parties to purchase one private account although they agree to account to the government for a certain portion of the profits. This is done by the Department at Washington and I do not pretend to call their action in question.

The weather is fine and the news is that Sherman is in Goldsboro.

Your brother
John A. Hedrick.

Duke
Beaufort, N.C.
March 18th. 1865,

Dear Brother:

I have received Chronicles to the 10th. and letters date not remembered.
The weather has been a little blustery during the last two days.
It is reported this morning that Sherman has taken Raleigh but nothing for certain is known of its capture.[1]
All is very quiet here now in the way of business. This is always the case when any military movements are on foot.

The Harbor is still full of vessels. Sherman has made this place his base of supplies.

We have had New York papers to the 13th.

Write often

Your brother
John A. Hedrick

---

[1] Sherman's troops did not enter Raleigh until April 13. Long, *Day by Day*, 675.

Duke
Beaufort, N.C.
March 25th. 1865,

Dear Brother:

Yours of the 15th. inst. came to hand yesterday.

I send herein one of your likenesses, which you sent me last Summer. The other, perhaps you will remember, you directed me to give to Mrs. Norcum, and I did so. The head of your last likeness, I think fully as good as that of your first, but the last seems somewhat sunken in the chest as if you were comsumpted.

We have New York papers to the 19th. inst. but they contain very little news.

The military operations in North Carolina are still progressing favorably. Kinston and Goldsboro are both in our possession.[1]

Of course the rumors here are very vague, and it is hard to tell what is going on. Enough is known however to be sure that all is right so far. I send you to-day yesterday's Times, which I think gives as good an account of the progress of our Army to Goldsboro as any that I can give you. I think it very doubtful<l> about Lee's being in command of the Rebel forces above Goldsboro. The weather is a little cold this morning but fine and clear.

The Steamer Carolina arrived in Port yesterday with a case of Smallpox on board,

Your brother
John A. Hedrick.

[1] Union troops entered Kinston on March 14, and Goldsboro on March 21. *OR*, ser. 1, 47, pt. 1:912-913.

Duke
Beaufort, N.C.
March 31, 1865,

Dear Brother:

Yours of the 21st. inst. was received day before yesterday.

Morehead City Depot until within the last month has been the place of discharge for this Port. It is now entirely taken up by transports and other government laden vessels, and hence merchant vessels have to discharge into lighters in the stream. It is very unfortunate for this place that there is not more water. You cannot come into Beaufort with more than 5 feet draught. Morehead is about 2 miles from this place with Newport River intervening. There are however a great many small baren islands, and sand spits between here & there. The people of Beaufort have the advantage of 3 per cent on goods shipped here. Beaufort is exempt while Morehead is subject to the 3 per cent Treasury fees.

I have not as yet seen or heard of any refugee arriving here with whom I was acquainted before the war.

About 500 negroes mostly women and children were sent here yesterday and day before from Wilmington having followed Sherman from South Carolina and Georgia.

The weather is quite blustery this morning. Genl. Sherman left here last Sunday for Fortress Monroe.[1] I have not heard of his return yet. His army is resting at Goldsboro.

Your brother
John A. Hedrick.

---

[1] Sherman traveled to City Point, Va., to meet with Grant. He returned to Goldsboro on March 30. *OR*, ser. 1, 47, pt. 3:32-33, 65.

Duke
Beaufort, N.C.
April 5th. 1865,

Dear Brother:

Your letter of the 28th. ult. was received yesterday.

I would be very glad to see you and if you can spare the time I think that you could not do better than by coming. If I had time I would like to visit Washington, but I do not see any chance of doing so soon, though Sherman is changing his base of supplies to Norfolk, and this may give me less to do.

Peter Lawson[1] Esq. of Boston has been appointed purchasing Agent for the Treasury and I have been directed by the Secretary to take charge of the articles purchased till ready for shipment. The operations have not yet commenced. Mr. Helper called in here last week on his way to Wilmington. He went on the Cutter Forward in company with Heaton & two or three other men. Mr. Helper spoke to me about a certain association which was being formed and wished me to take part in it. He said that he would see further in relation to it in his return from Wilmington. I do not admire secret associations, though there is one, which I intend joining if I can get admitted. Every thing is quiet here now, though Sherman is expected to move soon. Refugees and negroes still continue to come in.

The weather is quite warm. We have N.Y. Papers of the 1st.

Your brother,
John A. Hedrick.

---

[1] The local newspaper described Lawson as an "agent for the purchase of cotton." *Old North State* (Beaufort), January 21, 1865.

Duke
Beaufort, N.C.
April 11th. 1865.

Dear Brother:

Your letters of the 1st. and the 5th. insts. came to hand to-day.

We have New York papers to the 8th. inst. and glorious news from Gen. Grant's Army.

Sherman's Army was to have moved last Sunday, and I think that it has, as quite a number of half sick and worn out soldiers have been sent to this place during the last two days. To-day the military authorities took charge of two stores and three bowling alleys for hospital purposes. Three churches had previously been taken and several private houses. The refugee negroes are quite a nuisance here now. I think that nearly a thousand have come to this place during the last two weeks. Their condition is wretched indeed. They are nearly naked and look as if they were half starved. They lie about on the ground in the sun and seem to have lost all energy. Some, I have been told, have followed the Army from South Carolina, and cannot speak English.

I was walking around the borders of the town this morning and was hailed by a white woman with a child in her arms, who seemed very much frightened, and told me that a negroe man lying on the other side of the road had been there for the last two days sick, and was now broken out with smallpox. I did not take the trouble to examine into his case but reported the facts to the Post Surgeon, who promised to have him removed to the Small Pox hospital. There have been quite a number of cases of Small Pox in this place lately and I have been informed that it was very prevalent in New York and Brooklyn during the last Winter. Two cases have been brought to this place on vessels from New York. I am intrusted with additional labors. The Supervising, the Assistant, and all the Local Special Agents in the Agency have to make their deposits with me under a recent circular of the Commissioner of the Customs.

I to-day received me first Treasury Adjustment of collection accounts under Treasury Regulations, being for the quarter ending June 30th. 1863. No difference. I hope my disbursement accounts under Treasury Regulations will turn out as good. The weather has been very warm to-day. Mr. H.H. Helper[1] left here last Sunday was a week for Wilmington. He said that he intended to establish himself there.

Mr. Norcum is still lingering and as I think a little more feeble than usual. I fear that he will not last much longer.

Tell Mr. Pigott that his friend David W. Whitehurst died night before last. He died of apoplexy and had not been sick for any length of time. He was in town last week and looked as hearty as I ever saw him look. I hope that Mr. Pigott has recovered ere this.

Vessels drawing 17 feet of water can go to Morehead Depot. They can carry to the wharf all that they bring over the bar, which ranges from from 14 to 17 feet. Morehead is bound to leave this place as far behind nearly as New York has Harlem. Beaufort is a right good fish market and Summer resort and that is about all.

Your brother,
John A. Hedrick

[1] Hardie Hogan Helper (1822-1899), brother of Hinton Rowan Helper, was an abolitionist who worked with the American Colonization Society. After the war he was a newspaper editor and a moderate Republican leader in North Carolina. *Dictionary of North Carolina Biography*, s.v. "Helper, Hardie Hogan."

Duke
Beaufort, N.C.
April 18th. 1865,

Dear Brother:

I yesterday received your letter of the 10th. inst. containing the news that Mr. Pigott was slowly recovering. I sent the letter to his sister, who has been very much alarmed about him. It was reported yesterday that President Lincoln and Secretary Stanton's son had been assassinated in the theatre in Washington.[1] The report was brought by a schooner from Fortress Monroe and it is hoped to be untrue.

The fall of Richmond and Petersburgh and the capture of Lee's Army[2] have not been mentioned in my previous letters because I thought that the events were known to you before they were to me. It was rumored here yesterday that Johnson had surrendered to Sherman but I could not find any foundation for the rumor.

In the paper of the 11th. inst. I find a Proclamation from the President blockading certain southern ports to the introduction of foreign goods, on which the duties have not been paid. I would infer from this that the intention is to open these ports under coasting regulations. The weather is very pleasant and I am well.

Your brother
John A. Hedrick.

[1] Secretary of War Stanton and his wife had been invited to go with the Lincolns to Ford's Theater on April 14 but declined. The president and Mrs. Lincoln were accompanied by Clara Harris, daughter of Sen. Ira Harris of New York, and her fiancé, Maj. Henry R. Rathbone. John Wilkes Booth, after shooting Lincoln, stabbed Rathbone in the arm. Rathbone's wound was serious but not fatal. On the same night, Secretary of State William H. Seward's son, Frederick, was gravely injured by Booth's fellow conspirator Lewis Powell (also known as Lewis Payne). Powell attacked Frederick during an unsuccessful attempt to assassinate Secretary Seward in the Seward home. David Herbert Donald, *Lincoln* (New York: Simon and Schuster, 1995), 594, 597; Van Deusen, *William Henry Seward*, 413-415.

[2] Robert E. Lee surrendered the Army of Northern Virginia on April 9, 1865, at Appomattox Court House, Va. Richmond and Petersburg had fallen on April 3. Long, *Day by Day*, 665, 670.

———————

Duke
Beaufort, N.C.
April 26, 1865,

Dear Brother:

I have had no letter from you later than the 10th. but Chronicles to the 16th. inst. have been received.

The news here is rather confused. It was reported yesterday that Johnson had resigned and that Breckenridge had taken charge of the Rebel Army, and had refused to surrender. Hostilities are expected to be resumed to-day. Genl. Grant arrived here last Sunday and proceed to the front.

Political harangues have commenced in this State again. Yesterday a meeting was held in front of Front Street House and speeches were made by Senators Arendell and Carter,[1] and Messrs. Warren,[2] Satterthwait[3] and Ritch. All ex-Rebels except Ritch. Of the ex-Rebels I think better of Sattherwhait though I have very little confidence in any of them. He was Chairman of the Governor's council until he and Vance fell out. Carter has be a Rebel Colonel and was wounded in the seven days battle. Rumor says and I think it correct that he was Judge Advocate at Kinston in March/64 and condemned 50 of the N.C. Union Vols to death. One thing is certain, that there was a mighty growling among the N.C. soldiers when they heard that he was going to speak. The meeting was called nominally out of respect for the memory of Mr. Lincoln.

These Rebs are trying very hard <u>now</u> to get the State back into the Union, and by the aid of Genl. Grant & Sherman I guess they will succeed. They have applied through Genl. Palmer at Newbern to Genl. Sherman to allow them to call the Legislature together but their request has not yet been granted, and my desire is that it will not be. The very men, Dr. Arendell among others, who voted the State out of the Union are now going about and making Union speeches, and passing eulogiums on Mr. Lincoln. They now think that he was one of the greatest men that we ever had. I did not go to their infernal meeting, because I thought that I had no business there.

They sent word that they wished me to act as Secretary, and I sent message back that I did not think that they did.

A salute was fired at sun rise at the Fort this morning but I did not know what it was for.

I received yesterday Estimates of expenses of Heaton's office for this month. The total amount required is a little over $3100 $^{00}/_{100}$ The weather is beautiful.

All well as usual.

> Write often,
> John A. Hedrick.

---

[1] David Miller Carter (1830-1879) had been lieutenant colonel of the Fourth North Carolina State Troops. He was wounded at Seven Pines, Va., on May 31, 1862, which led to his resignation the following December. He subsequently served as a military court judge and state senator during the war. Carter was also a member of a group secretly sent to Richmond to induce Confederate officials to negotiate for peace. *Dictionary of North Carolina Biography*, s.v. "Carter, David Miller."

[2] Edward Jenner Warren (1824-1876) was a lawyer and old-line Whig. As a delegate to the secession convention, he supported North Carolina's withdrawal from the Union. He also represented Beaufort County in the state senate during the war. *Dictionary of North Carolina Biography*; s.v. "Warren, Edward Jenner."

[3] Fenner B. Satterthwaite was a delegate to the secession convention and the 1861-1862 and 1865-1866 constitutional conventions. He served as president of the Council of State from 1863 to 1864. Cheney, *North Carolina Government*, 179, 386, 825, 832.

> *Duke*
> Beaufort, N.C.
> April 28th. 1865,

Dear Brother:

We received the news of the surrender of Johnson yesterday.[1] I have not heard the particulars but I believe the terms were similar to those required from Lee.

The Rebs are returning to this place quite thick. Yesterday about seventy came down on the train. They all belong in this place. I guess they have their rights except hanging.

The weather is still fine.

Mrs. Norcum has a boy baby.

> Write often
> Your brother
> John A. Hedrick.

---

[1] Gen. Joseph E. Johnston surrendered the Army of Tennessee on April 26, 1865, at the Bennett farmhouse in Durham. The army mustered out in Greensboro. Barrett, *Civil War in North Carolina*, 388.

Duke
Beaufort, N.C.
May 1st. 1865,

Dear Brother:

Your letter of the 19th. ult. was received day before yesterday, and Chronicles to the 21st.

We have New York papers to the 27th. ult. The evening editions contain a dispatch from the Secretary of War announcing the capture of Booth.[1]

The surrender of Johnson to Sherman has been known to you sometime. It is reported that Sherman has been relieved of his command and sent to Savannah.[2] I cannot see what could have induced Sherman to have offered such terms of surrender as those contained in his articles of agreement with Johnson. Had they been received and accepted at Washington City, I should have considered the four last years of war a total loss to the country.[3]

The weather is still fine.

We had fresh peas for dinner yesterday. All are well.

Your brother
John A. Hedrick.

---

[1] John Wilkes Booth died, either of a self-inflicted wound or from a bullet fired by a Union soldier, on April 26, 1865, at the Garrett Farm near Port Royal, Va. Sifakis, *Who Was Who in the Civil War*, 62.

[2] In a letter dated May 2, 1865, Sherman notified Grant that he was relinquishing command of troops in North Carolina and South Carolina because of the successful completion of the campaign in those states. Sherman left Raleigh on April 28 on a journey that included stops at Goldsboro, Savannah, Morehead City, and Beaufort harbor, before his arrival at Fort Monroe, Va., on May 8. *OR*, ser. 1, 47, pt. 3:337, 345-346, 371-372, 387-388, 411-412, 434.

[3] Unlike Grant, who had avoided political issues in the terms offered to Lee at Appomattox, Sherman addressed sweeping civil and military questions in the treaty presented to Joseph E. Johnston at Durham on April 17 and 18. Sherman offered amnesty to Confederate soldiers and civilians, with political and property rights guaranteed; permission for troops to keep their arms to deposit in state arsenals; and the promise that current Southern state legislatures would be considered legitimate state governments once members took a loyalty oath. Officials in Washington, still angered and shocked by the recent assassination of President Lincoln, quickly killed the generous treaty. Michael Fellman, *Citizen Sherman: A Life of William Tecumseh Sherman* (New York: Random House, 1995), 238-240, 245.

Duke
Beaufort, N.C.
May 3rd. 1865,

Dear Brother:

I wrote you the 1st. inst. but as the steamer is going in the morning I thought that I would write again.

Nothing of importance has happened during the last three days.

There are some very poor, emaciated negro refugees in town now. Some are so weak that they can scarcely work their jaws to eat.

All well
John A. Hedrick.

———————————

[*John A. Hedrick to Mary Ellen Hedrick*]

Duke
Beaufort, N.C.
May 7th. 1865,

Dear Sister:

Bennie arrived here last Thursday morning the 4th. inst. and left for Raleigh Friday evening. I went with him as far as Newbern, and saw him leave on the Saturday morning train.

There has not been much change in his appearance except that you have fattened him up considerably since I was in Washington City. I fear that you feed him too well. Next thing you know you will have him so corpulent that he can't walk, and then he will be in a pretty fix.

The Rebs belonging in this town have pretty much all returned. At first they seemed to be somewhat insolent but now they have cooled down.

The weather is quite pleasant. I have a very bad cold which I contracted the other night at Newbern, but am otherwise well. Mrs. Norcum is as well as might be expected

Your brother,
John A. Hedrick.

Bibliography

MANUSCRIPT COLLECTIONS

Adjutant General's Papers. State Archives, Division of Archives and History, Raleigh.

Chase, Salmon P. Papers. Manuscript Division, Library of Congress, Washington, D.C. Microfilm, Pennsylvania State University Library, State College.

Cleveland, Edmund H. Diary. Southern Historical Collection, University of North Carolina Library, Chapel Hill.

Credle, Mary F. Papers. Southern Historical Collection, University of North Carolina Library, Chapel Hill.

Hedrick, Benjamin Sherwood. Papers. Southern Historical Collection, University of North Carolina Library, Chapel Hill.

Hedrick, Benjamin Sherwood. Papers. Special Collections Department, Duke University Library, Durham.

Lincoln, Abraham. Papers. Manuscript Division, Library of Congress, Washington, D.C. Microfilm, D. H. Hill Library, North Carolina State University, Raleigh.

Martine, Alfred H. Papers. Southern Historical Collection, University of North Carolina Library, Chapel Hill.

Myers House Papers. Brown Library, Washington, N.C.

Pigott, Levi Woodbury. Papers. Private Collections. State Archives, Division of Archives and History, Raleigh.

Stickley, Julia Ward. Papers. Private Collections. State Archives, Division of Archives and History, Raleigh.

Thirty-fifth Regiment, United States Colored Troops. Descriptive Book. Microfilm, State Archives, Division of Archives and History, Raleigh.

PUBLIC DOCUMENTS

Compiled Service Records of Volunteer Union Soldiers Who Served in Organizations From the State of North Carolina. Record Group 94. National Archives, Washington, D.C. Microfilm, State Archives, Division of Archives and History, Raleigh.

Eighth Census of the United States, 1860. Multiple Counties, Population and Slave Schedules. National Archives, Washington, D.C. Microfilm, Genealogical Services, State Library of North Carolina, Raleigh.

Journal of the House of Representatives of the General Assembly of the State of North Carolina at its Session of 1891. Raleigh: Edwards and Broughton, 1891.

Marriage Bonds. Carteret County, North Carolina. State Archives, Division of Archives and History, Raleigh.

Minutes of the Carteret County Court of Pleas and Quarter Sessions, February 1861 and February 1862. State Archives, Division of Archives and History, Raleigh.

Ninth Census of the United States, 1870. Multiple Counties, Population Schedules. National Archives, Washington, D.C. Microfilm, Genealogical Services, State Library of North Carolina, Raleigh.

Public Laws of the State of North Carolina passed by the General Assembly at its Second Extra Session, 1861. Raleigh: John Spelman, 1861.

Rowan County Estates Records. State Archives, Division of Archives and History, Raleigh.

Seventh Census of the United States, 1850. Multiple Counties, Population Schedules. National Archives, Washington, D.C. Microfilm, Genealogical Services, State Library of North Carolina, Raleigh.

Sixth Census of the United States, 1840. Multiple counties, Population Schedules. National Archives, Washington, D.C. Microfilm, Genealogical Services, State Library of North Carolina, Raleigh.

Tenth Census of the United States, 1880. Rowan County, N.C., Population Schedule. National Archives, Washington, D.C. Microfilm, Genealogical Services, State Library of North Carolina, Raleigh.

Twelfth Census of the United States, 1900. Rowan County, N.C., Population Schedule. National Archives, Washington, D.C. Microfilm, Genealogical Services, State Library of North Carolina, Raleigh.

CONTEMPORARY NEWSPAPERS AND PERIODICALS

Beaufort Journal, 1857.

Beaufort Look Out, 1910.

Carolina Watchman (Salisbury), 1907.

Charleston Mercury, 1861-1862.

Halcyon and Beaufort Intelligencer, 1854.

Hillsborough Recorder, 1852.

New Bern Progress, 1862-1863.

New Era (Washington, N.C.), 1862.

News and Observer (Raleigh), 1890.

New York Herald, 1862-1864.

New York Times, 1861-1865.

New York Tribune, 1862.

North Carolina Times (New Bern), 1864.

Old North State (Beaufort), 1865.

Patriot and Times (Greensboro), 1868.

Scientific American, 1861.

PUBLISHED PRIMARY SOURCES

Barden, John R., ed. *Letters to the Home Circle: The North Carolina Service of Pvt. Henry A. Clapp, Company F, Forty-fourth Massachusetts Volunteer Militia, 1862-1863.* Raleigh: Division of Archives and History, Department of Cultural Resources, 1998.

Butler, Benjamin F. *Private and Official Correspondence of Gen. Benjamin F. Butler During the Period of the Civil War.* 5 vols. Norwood, Mass.: Plimpton Press, 1917.

Duncan, Russell, ed. *Blue-Eyed Child of Fortune: The Civil War Letters of Colonel Robert Gould Shaw.* Athens: University of Georgia Press, 1992.

Hamilton, J. G. de Roulhac, ed. *The Correspondence of Jonathan Worth.* Vol. 1. Raleigh: Edwards and Broughton, 1909.

Harris, William C., ed. *In the Country of the Enemy: The Civil War Reports of a Massachusetts Corporal.* Gainsville: University Press of Florida, 1999.

Hayes, John, ed. *Samuel Francis Du Pont: A Selection from His Civil War Letters.* 3 vols. Ithaca, N.Y.: Cornell University Press, 1969.

Johnson, Frontis W., and Joe A. Mobley, eds. *The Papers of Zebulon Baird Vance.* 2 vols. to date. Raleigh: Department of Archives and History, 1963-.

Niven, John, ed. *The Salmon P. Chase Papers.* 5 vols. Kent, Ohio: Kent State University Press, 1993-1998.

Official Records of the Union and Confederate Navies in the War of the Rebellion. 30 vols. Washington, D.C.: Government Printing Office, 1894-1922.

Schneller, Robert J., Jr., ed. *Under the Blue Pennant, or Notes of a Naval Officer.* New York: John Wiley and Sons, 1999.

Singleton, William Henry. *Recollections of My Slavery Days.* Edited by Katherine Mellen Charron and David S. Cecelski. Raleigh: Division of Archives and History, Department of Cultural Resources, 1999.

The War of the Rebellion: A Compilation of the Official Records of the Union and Confederate Armies. 128 vols. Washington, D.C.: Government Printing Office, 1880-1901.

SECONDARY SOURCES

Ames, William E. *A History of the National Intelligencer.* Chapel Hill: University of North Carolina Press, 1972.

Appleton's Annual Cyclopedia and Register of Important Events. Vol. 1. New York: Appleton, 1861.

Appleton's Cyclopedia of American Biography. 7 vols. New York: D. Appleton, 1887-1901.

Ash, Stephen V. *When the Yankees Came: Conflict and Chaos in the Occupied South, 1861-1865.* Chapel Hill: University of North Carolina Press, 1995.

Auman, William T. "Bryan Tyson: Southern Unionist and American Patriot." *North Carolina Historical Review* 62 (July 1985): 257-292.

Bailey, Hugh C. *Hinton Rowan Helper: Abolitionist-Racist.* University: University of Alabama Press, 1965.

Barbour, Ruth. "Exploits of Emeline." In *North Carolina's Coastal Carteret County During the Civil War.* Edited by Jean Bruyere Kell. N.p.: Jean Bruyere Kell, 1999.

Barrett, John G. *The Civil War in North Carolina.* Chapel Hill: University of North Carolina Press, 1963.

Bassett, John Spencer. *Anti-Slavery Leaders of North Carolina.* 1898. Reprint, Spartanburg, S.C.: Reprint Company, 1971.

Battle, Kemp P. *History of the University of North Carolina.* Vol. 1. Raleigh: Edwards and Broughton, 1907.

Bernstein, Iver. *The New York City Draft Riots: Their Significance for American Society and Politics in the Age of the Civil War.* New York: Oxford University Press, 1990.

Biographical Directory of the United States Congress, 1774-1989, Bicentennial Edition. Washington, D.C.: U.S. Government Printing Office, 1989.

Biographical Encyclopedia of Kentucky of the Dead and Living Men of the Nineteenth Century. Cincinnati: J. M. Armstrong, 1878.

Boatner, Mark M., III. *The Civil War Dictionary.* Rev. ed. New York: Vintage, 1988.

Brown, Alexander Crosby. *Juniper Waterway: A History of the Albemarle and Chesapeake Canal.* Charlottesville: University Press of Virginia for the Mariners' Museum, Newport News, Va., and the Norfolk County Historical Society, Chesapeake, Va., 1981.

Brown, Norman D. "A Union Election in Civil War North Carolina." *North Carolina Historical Review* 43 (autumn 1966): 381-400.

———. *Edward Stanly: Whiggery's Tarheel 'Conqueror.'* University: University of Alabama Press, 1974.

Browning, Judkin Jay. " 'Little Souled Mercenaries'? The Buffaloes of Eastern North Carolina during the Civil War." *North Carolina Historical Review* 77 (July 2000): 337-363.

Browning, Robert M., Jr. *From Cape Charles to Cape Fear: The North Atlantic Blockading Squadron during the Civil War.* Tuscaloosa: University of Alabama Press, 1993.

Burlingame, John K. *History of the Fifth Regiment of Rhode Island Heavy Artillery, During the Three Years and a Half of Service in North Carolina.* Providence: Snow and Farnham, 1892.

Carman, Harry J., and Reinhard H. Luthin. *Lincoln and the Patronage.* New York: Columbia University Press, 1964.

Carter, Arthur B. *The Tarnished Cavalier: Major General Earl Van Dorn, C.S.A.* Knoxville: University of Tennessee Press, 1999.

Catawba County Cemeteries. Vol. 7. Hickory, N.C.: Catawba County Genealogical Society, 1991.

Cedar Grove Cemetery. New Bern, N.C.: Historical Records Survey of North Carolina, 1939.

Cemetery Records of Carteret County, North Carolina. Carteret Historical Research Association, n.d.

Cheney, John L., ed. *North Carolina Government: 1585-1974, A Narrative and Statistical History.* Raleigh: North Carolina Department of the Secretary of State, 1975.

Civil War Naval Chronology, 1861-1865. Washington, D.C.: Navy Department, 1961.

Clark, Walter, ed. *Histories of the Several Regiments and Battalions from North Carolina in the Great War, 1861-1865.* Vol. 3. Goldsboro: Nash Brothers, 1901.

Collins, Donald E. "War Crimes or Justice? General George Pickett and the Mass Execution of Deserters in Civil War Kinston, North Carolina." In *The Art of Command in the Civil War.* Edited by Steven E. Woodworth. Lincoln: University of Nebraska Press, 1998.

Coulter, E. Merton. *The Confederate States of America, 1861-1865.* Vol. 7 of *A History of the South.* Edited by Wendell Holmes Stephenson and E. Merton Coulter. Baton Rouge and Austin: Louisiana State University Press and the Littlefield Fund for Southern History of the University of Texas, 1950.

Cox, Monty Woodall. "Freedom During the Frémont Campaign: The Fate of One North Carolina Republican in 1856." *North Carolina Historical Review* 45 (October 1968): 357-383.

Current, Richard, ed. *Encyclopedia of the Confederacy.* 4 vols. New York: Simon and Schuster, 1993.

Cyclopedia of Eminent and Representative Men of the Carolinas of the Nineteenth Century. Vol. 2. Madison, Wis.: Brant and Fuller, 1892.

Davis, Maurice. *History of the Hammock House and Related Trivia.* Beaufort, N.C.: M. Davis, 1984.

Degler, Carl N. *The Other South: Southern Dissenters in the Nineteenth Century.* New York: Harper and Row, 1974.

Delaney, Norman C. "Charles Henry Foster and the Unionists of Eastern North Carolina." *North Carolina Historical Review* 37 (July 1960): 251-362.

Denney, Robert E. *The Civil War Years: A Day-by-Day Chronicle of the Life of a Nation.* New York: Sterling Publishing, 1992.

Donald, David Herbert. *Lincoln.* New York: Simon and Schuster, 1995.

Doughton, Virginia Pou. "The Atlantic Hotel." In *North Carolina's Coastal Carteret County During the Civil War.* Edited by Jean Bruyere Kell. N.p.: Jean Bruyere Kell, 1999.

Durrill, Wayne K. *War of Another Kind: A Southern Community in the Great Rebellion.* New York: Oxford University Press, 1990.

Dyer, Frederick H. *A Compendium of the War of the Rebellion.* 2 vols. Dayton, Ohio: Morningside Press, Broadfoot Publishing, 1994.

Elliot, Robert G. *Ironclad of the Roanoke: Gilbert Elliot's Albemarle.* Shippensburg, Penn.: White Mane Publishing Company, 1994.

Everhart, William C. *Vicksburg National Military Park, Mississippi.* National Park Service Historical Handbook Series, No. 21. Washington, D.C. 1954. Reprint, 1957.

Farnham, Thomas J., and Francis P. King. " 'The March of the Destroyer': The New Bern Yellow Fever Epidemic of 1864." *North Carolina Historical Review* 73 (October 1996): 435-483.

Faust, Patricia, ed. *Historical Times Illustrated Encyclopedia of the Civil War.* New York: Harper and Row, 1986.

Fellman, Michael. *Citizen Sherman: A Life of William Tecumseh Sherman.* New York: Random House, 1995.

Foote, Shelby. *The Civil War: A Narrative.* Vol. 2, *Fredericksburg to Meridian.* New York: Random House, 1963.

Foster, John Y. *New Jersey and the Rebellion: A History of the Services of the Troops and People of New Jersey in Aid of the Union Cause.* Newark, N.J.: Martin R. Dennis, 1868.

Freeman, Douglas Southall. *Lee's Lieutenants: A Study in Command.* Vol. 3. New York: Charles Scribner's Sons, 1944.

Garraty, John A., and Mark C. Carnes, eds. *American National Biography.* 24 vols. New York: Oxford University Press, 1999.

Grant, Daniel Lindsay, ed. *Alumni History of the University of North Carolina.* 2d ed. Durham, N.C.: Christian and King, 1924.

Hamilton, J. G. de Roulhac. "Benjamin Sherwood Hedrick." *James Sprunt Historical Publications* 10 (1910): 5-42.

Harris, William C. *William Woods Holden: Firebrand of North Carolina Politics.* Baton Rouge: Louisiana State University Press, 1987.

————. *With Charity for All: Lincoln and the Restoration of the Union.* Lexington: University Press of Kentucky, 1997.

Heitman, Francis B. *Historical Register and Dictionary of the United States Army.* 2 vols. Washington, D.C.: Government Printing Office, 1903.

Hesseltine, William B. *Lincoln and the War Governors.* New York: Alfred A. Knopf, 1948.

Hewett, Janet B., ed. *The Roster of Confederate Soldiers.* 16 vols. Wilmington, N.C.: Broadfoot Publishing, 1995-1996.

———, ed. *The Roster of Union Soldiers, 1861-1865, Rhode Island and Connecticut.* Wilmington, N.C.: Broadfoot Publishing, 1997.

———, ed. *The Roster of Union Soldiers, 1861-1865, New Jersey and Delaware.* Wilmington, N.C.: Broadfoot Publishing, 1998.

———, ed. *The Roster of Union Soldiers, 1861-1865, New York.* Wilmington, N.C.: Broadfoot Publishing, 1998.

———, ed. *The Roster of Union Soldiers, 1861-1865, ... North Carolina....* Wilmington, N.C.: Broadfoot Publishing, 1998.

Hinshaw, Clifford Reginald, Jr. "North Carolina Canals Before 1860." *North Carolina Historical Review* 25 (January 1948): 1-57.

Howell, Andrew J. *The Book of Wilmington, 1730-1930.* N.p., n.d.

Hubbell, John T., and James W. Geary, eds. *Biographical Dictionary of the Union: Northern Leaders of the Civil War.* Westport, Conn.: Greenwood Press, 1995.

Johnson, Allen, and Dumas Malone, eds. *Dictionary of American Biography.* 20 vols. New York: Charles Scribner's Sons, 1928-1936.

Jordan, Weymouth T., Jr. " 'Drinking Pulverized Snakes and Lizards': Yankees and Rebels in Battle at Gum Swamp." *North Carolina Historical Review* 71 (April 1994): 207-231.

Jordan, Weymouth T., Jr., and Gerald W. Thomas. "Massacre at Plymouth: April 20, 1864." *North Carolina Historical Review* 72 (April 1995): 125-197.

Kirkman, Vic. *The Heritage of Adam Alexander Young.* N.p., 1995.

Konkle, Burton Alva. *John Motley Morehead and the Development of North Carolina, 1876-1866.* Philadelphia: William J. Campbell, 1922.

Long, E. B. *The Civil War Day by Day: An Almanac, 1861-1865.* Garden City, N.Y.: Doubleday and Company, 1971.

Lucas, Marion B. *Sherman and the Burning of Columbia.* College Station: Texas A&M University Press, 1976.

Mallison, Fred. *The Civil War on the Outer Banks.* Jefferson, N.C.: McFarland and Company, 1997.

Marvel, William. *Burnside.* Chapel Hill: University of North Carolina Press, 1991.

Mathews, Mitford M., ed. *A Dictionary of Americanisms: On Historical Principles.* Vol. 1. Chicago: University of Chicago Press, 1951.

McPherson, James M. *Ordeal by Fire: The Civil War and Reconstruction.* New York: Alfred A. Knopf, 1982.

———. *Battle Cry of Freedom: The Civil War Era.* New York: Oxford University Press, 1988.

The Medical and Surgical History of the Civil War. Vol. 6. Wilmington, N.C.: Broadfoot Publishing, 1991.

Miller, Edward A., Jr. *Lincoln's Abolitionist General: The Biography of David Hunter.* Columbia: University of South Carolina Press, 1997.

Moore, John W., ed. *Roster of North Carolina Troops in the War Between the States.* Vol. 1. Raleigh: Ashe and Gatling, 1882.

Morris, Richard B., ed. *Encyclopedia of American History.* Rev. ed. New York: Harper and Row, 1965.

National Cyclopedia of American Biography. 37 vols. New York: J. T. White, 1892-1951.

Nevins, Allan. *The War for the Union.* Vol. 4, *The Organized War to Victory, 1864-1865.* New York: Charles Scribner's Sons, 1971.

Osborne, Charles C. *Jubal: The Life and Times of General Jubal A. Early, CSA.* Chapel Hill: Algonquin Books, 1992.

Paludan, Phillip Shaw. *The Presidency of Abraham Lincoln.* Lawrence: University of Kansas Press, 1994.

Pfanz, Donald C. *Richard S. Ewell: A Soldier's Life.* Chapel Hill: University of North Carolina Press, 1998.

Pleasants, Samuel Augustus. *Fernando Wood of New York.* New York: Columbia University Press, 1948.

Pohoresky, W. L. *Newport, North Carolina, During the Civil War: The True Story.* N.p. William L. Pohoresky, 1978.

Powell, William S. *North Carolina Gazetteer.* Chapel Hill: University of North Carolina Press, 1968.

————. *North Carolina Through Four Centuries.* Chapel Hill: University of North Carolina Press, 1989.

————, ed. *Dictionary of North Carolina Biography.* 5 vols. Chapel Hill: University of North Carolina Press, 1979-1996.

Ramage, James A. *Gray Ghost: The Life of Col. John Singleton Mosby.* Lexington: University Press of Kentucky, 1999.

Reid, Richard. "Raising the African Brigade: Early Black Recruitment in Civil War North Carolina." *North Carolina Historical Review* 70 (July 1993): 266-301.

Roberts, Robert E. *Encyclopedia of Historic Forts: The Military, Pioneer, and Trading Posts of the United States.* New York: Macmillan, 1988.

Roll of Honor. Vol. 10. 1866. Reprint, Baltimore: Genealogical Publishing, 1994.

Rowan County Cemeteries. Vol. 4. Salisbury, N.C.: Genealogical Society of Rowan County, N.C., n.d.

Sifakis, Stewart. *Who Was Who in the Civil War.* New York: Facts on File Publications, 1988.

Smith, Michael Thomas. " 'A Traitor and a Scoundrel': Benjamin S. Hedrick and the Making of a Dissenter in the Old South." *North Carolina Historical Review* 76 (July 1999): 316-336.

Spann, Edward K. *The New Metropolis: New York City, 1840-1857.* New York: Columbia University Press, 1981.

Swicegood, Frank, et al., eds. *Cemetery Records of Davidson County, N.C.* 8 vols. Lexington, N.C.: Genealogical Society of Davidson County, 1986-1989.

Thomas, Benjamin P., and Harold M. Hyman. *Stanton: The Life and Times of Lincoln's Secretary of War.* New York. Alfred A. Knopf, 1962.

Van Deusen, Glyndon G. *William Henry Seward.* New York: Oxford University Press, 1967.

Warner, Ezra J. *Generals in Gray: Lives of the Confederate Commanders.* Baton Rouge: Louisiana State University Press, 1959.

————. *Generals in Blue: Lives of the Union Commanders.* Baton Rouge: Louisiana State University Press, 1964.

Watson, Alan D. *A History of New Bern and Craven County.* New Bern, N.C.: Tryon Palace Commission, 1987.

Weeks, Stevenson L. "The Federal Occupation of Morehead City and Beaufort." In *North Carolina's Coastal Carteret County During the Civil War.* Edited by Jean Bruyere Kell. N.p.: Jean Bruyere Kell, 1999.

Who Was Who in America. Vol. 1. Chicago: A. N. Marquis, 1963.

Williams, Kenneth P. *Lincoln Finds a General: A Military Study of the Civil War.* Vol. 1. New York: Macmillan, 1950.

Wilson, Mamré Marsh. *A Researcher's Journal: Beaufort, North Carolina and the Civil War.* New Bern, N.C.: Griffin and Tilghman, 1999.

Index